Sa[...] [...]ley — 2668

Day	Folio		Account			£	s	d
16		To the Acct [...]						
14	32	To Sundrys	Sim[...]					
17	128		Me[...]					
	130		Art[...]					
19	281		Car[...]					
	282		Hor[...]			40		
	34		Palmer	/	/	100		
20	120		Gainsborough	/		150		
	121		Gausson	/		60		
	137		Palmer	/	/	40	7	3
	188		Handley	/		30		
21	52		Hiffe	/		20		
				72		3860	7	3
25	142		Waldron	/	/	100		
27	108		Moore 4160·7·3	/	/	200		
	16		Palmer 4210·7·3	/	/	50		
5	81		Ashwin	/	/	100		
6	167		Goffitt	/		50		
8	126		Towzel	/		50		
	34		Fack	/	/	40		
9	160		Palmer	/	/	100		
10	201		Do	/		27		
	93		Hare	/	/	40		
			Handley	/		30		
				72		4647	7	3
11	65		Smith	/	/	20		
13	183		Waldron	/	/	300		
14	211		Dind	/			15	5
16	192		Dyer	/		100		
20	135		Harrison	/	/	40		
	72		Stevens	/		30		
	63		Webb	/	/	30		
22	195		Palmer	/	/	10	4	7
	199		Wickstead	/	/	30		
25	172		Waldron	/	/	20		
	212		Morrison	/	/	25		
27	125		Fellows	/	/	50		
	136		Stevens	/		30		
30	191		Vasin	/	/	20		
	192		Herman	/	/	40		
			Morrison	/		60		
	176		Montesquieu	/		50		
	181		Waldron	/		40		
			Carried up	72		5543	7	3

Date	Folio		Account			£	s	d
			[...] this Acct folio	267		3923	16	
			[...] Tolet 4090·7·3			166	11	3
				/	/	30		
			Blount Aug 23 4420·7·3	/	/	250		
			4620·7·3	/	/	200		
Sep 3	34			/	/	50		
8	161			/	/	150		
10	44			/	/	50		
11	67			/	/	100		
14	211			/	/	360	10	5
23	143			/	/	1300		
30	181			/	/	150		
				/	/	30		
				72		6810	17	8
Oct 1	229		Bankside	/	/	100		
7	247		Cocke	/		20		
12	213			/	/	200		
14	119		Bernard	/	/	150		
22	186			/	/	50		
23	232			/	/	50		
25	263		Bankbill	/	/	40		
	187		Lammas	/	/	266	10	
26	125		Hickman	/		15		
			By my Acct from folio	267		7702	7	8

Debit

Date	Folio		Account			£	s	d
1736			Debt brought up			5543	7	3
Sep 30	221	To Sundrys	Trevisa	/	/	71	5	
Oct 1	140		Stevens	/	/	20		
			Palmer	/		10		
2	94		Iliff	/	/	50		
5	234		Herman	/	/	30		
	235		Waldron	/	/	10		
6	98		Thomas	/	/	200		
8	211		Farris	/	/	100		
9	104		Twells	/	/	34		
	107		Palmer	/	/	8		
12	257		Waldron	/	/	10		
13	156		Hinch	/	/	40		
15	166		Do			50		
	267		Craddock	/		100		
	270		Palmer	/		43	15	
			Haigh	/		70		
19	197		Morris	/		150		
22	141		Gabriel		/	100		
26	177					6712	7	8

The Search for Gainsborough

Adrienne Corri

To Elle
Best Wishes
Corri 85

JONATHAN CAPE
THIRTY BEDFORD SQUARE LONDON

First published 1984

Jonathan Cape Ltd, 30 Bedford Square, London WC1B 3EL

British Library Cataloguing in Publication Data
Corri, Adrienne
The search for Gainsborough
1. Gainsborough, Thomas 2. Garrick, David,
1717–1779 3. Portrait painting—
Attribution
I. Title
757′.3 ND497.G2

ISBN 0–224–02162–1

Typeset by Wyvern Typesetting Ltd, Bristol
Printed in Great Britain by
St Edmundsbury Press, Bury St Edmunds, Suffolk

To the Royal Academy of Arts

Thomas Gainsborough to John Henderson:

Bath, 27th June, 1773

Never mind the fools who talk of imitation and copying; all is imitation, and if you quit that natural likeness to Garrick which your mother bestowed on you, you'll be flung. Ask Garrick else.

Why, Sir, what makes the difference, between man and man, is real performance, and not genius or conception. There are a thousand Garricks, a thousand Giardinis, and Fischers, and Abels. Why only one Garrick with Garrick's eyes, voice, &c.? One Giardini with Giardini's fingers, &c.? But one Fischer with Fischer's dexterity, quickness, &c.? Or more than one Abel with Abel's feeling upon the instrument? All the rest of the world are merely hearers and see'rs.

T.G.

1977

Sometimes it is difficult to distinguish the difference between creating an event or the event creating you. You are never in charge of your own life as much as you like to think. Perhaps others are. I am not. Events have a tendency to pick me up and shake me as a dog would a bone.

I keep a sporadic diary. Not to jot down memorable moments but simply to see where I have been and to cope with mundane matters like the gas bill or the income tax.

Looking at my notes of the last six years and trying to unscramble them, I cannot decide what it was that made me pursue, to the exclusion of all else, the identification of a picture from a shabby provincial theatre. There was no sense apparent in my single-minded quest, against all odds, for the justification of my opinions, no promise that the outcome would be successful. I cannot explain my actions in ordinary terms except to compare them with the illogicality of falling hopelessly in love and clinging tenaciously to the thought that one day that love would be returned.

Perhaps it all began when I was a child in Edinburgh. I went to a strange school where one teacher taught us, along with religious knowledge, Egyptian hieroglyphics and Chinese. I think she hoped we would become missionaries or archaeologists, or both. School, not unnaturally, puzzled me. Or the key might lie in a Victorian poem by Walter Savage Landor we were made to learn:

> I strove with none, for none was worth my strife.
> Nature I loved and, next to Nature, Art.

My attention must have wandered there, because 'Art' became a person like Alf, Bert or Fred. 'Art' was as real as a friend from early memories, not outside me but a cosy companion. That fine balance in me that made me love the Honourable Mrs Graham in the National Gallery in Edinburgh and dislike as fervently my mother's three-piece suite of uncut moquette in pink and grey. (I used to pull the threads in hate – it wasn't me, please – it was 'Art'.)

The ugliness that surrounded me as a child puzzled and confused me. I was a bad pupil, at a school that would have made Miss Brodie feel very much at home. Nothing they taught made much sense there and I played truant as often as possible. This wasn't easy in Edinburgh as it rains most of the time, so I found refuge in the many antique shops and libraries. I gained most of my education in these havens, and it was a very good one, too. It taught me to see, that objects could be beautiful, and words could reach me where staring at a blackboard and confusing past participles could not.

One day, to avoid being soaked and the subsequent explanations, I wandered into the Edinburgh National Gallery and there I found order in a world I had to make no effort to get to know. This world put into colour and form everything I could not express. The people on the canvases breathed an air I already knew; not all the same air, or even quite the same worlds, yet each picture opened up a miracle of sorts.

The first time you see a picture is always the best; you never look at it in quite the same way again. The energy the artist has transferred to the canvas rebounds, and for a moment you become him, you exchange your eyes for his and there is a never-to-be-repeated union, an understanding you cannot recapture. After that you look *into* the picture; try as you will, the first surprise is gone and you look with judgement. You will find pleasure always, if it is an artist with whom you have rapport, but you never give yourself as much as that first time, nor does the picture reveal more. Pictures you love become old friends, but it is that first moment of mutual captivity that counts. It is an emotional impact, one in which reason, as in all loves, plays little part.

To find you must also give. A piece of music or a picture needs effort before you will find a reward. If you are not capable of that effort you will find only second- or third-hand tastes, and probably be a lot more comfortable. I would have been a great deal better off if I had never discovered that there was more in life than my mother's ornaments and brocade curtains. A hunger was born on that day of truancy that can never really be satisfied, an unrest that will always be there, but the moments of satisfaction are beyond any price and incomparable.

Who can say what 'Art' is? I can for myself but not for another. I know what I like and why I like it; that I agreed with the taste of others mattered not at all, nor had I any wish to pit my opinion against anyone else. I was remarkably liberal in allowing others their likes and dislikes (as long as I didn't have to live with them) until the middle of my life when old 'Art' intruded again.

On the whole, he had never really gone away. All the men in my life had been chosen with his approval. I knew I was sunk when I found myself seeing them in the style of some painter I loved. My children's father, Patrick: Gainsborough, High Style, late Bath, London (the Hon. Mrs Graham striking again). My ex-husband: Picasso, Blue period. Lawrence, Tiepolo, Ingres, Michelangelo – I may never have been able to own any of their pictures, but I have had a few good models for them in and out of my life.

One thing about falling in love with good-looking people is that even when they are being disagreeable they are quite pleasant to look at. So, if I have frequently been a bloody fool, it wasn't me, please – it was 'Art'.

My longest, most recent encounter with 'Art' started in the summer of 1977. At the beginning of the year I had been very ill from a pneumonic patch, contracted during a play when, in order to comply with the age-old tradition, 'The Show Must Go On', I had staggered on to the stage night after night with a roaring temperature. By the time I emerged from the months of illness that followed, things looked pretty bleak.

Out of sight is out of mind in the theatre, and a gap of such length means you have almost to begin again from scratch. Once, when I had worked for Laurence Olivier, I heard a fan gush at him, 'It must be so wonderful to have arrived!' To which he replied, 'You never arrive.' Afterwards he said that the one thing in life he wanted to do at that moment was to film *Macbeth*, and no one would finance it. All the great work he had done counted for nothing. He was in his prime and the perfect age to have been a Macbeth for all time, yet he was 'box office poison' (his own words), for although his films had eventually made money they had not brought the fast returns distributors demanded; the future was cheated of that experience and is poorer for it. So, if I was in a 'trough', who was I to complain? The only thing to do was to ride it out.

It was a real trough, the year 1977, in all ways. Personally, professionally and emotionally. There is low and *low*. I thought I had seen most of them, but this was the worst of all: a negative low. At least something had been going on in the others; this one didn't even have incident.

So, in the middle of the year, with very little to nothing in sight, I found myself in a tour of an old Somerset Maugham pot-boiler called *The Sacred Flame*. It had a compensating factor. I was working again with my old friend, Jean Anderson. The play itself was a very creaky piece, once scandalous, now hallowed by time into that doubtful thing called a 'revival' – such an appropriate word. Not even the kiss of life would have helped this one, but rent must be paid and actors and managements are ever hopeful.

Our management was an ex-actor called Bill Kenwright, a nice man, whose attitude to the theatre is that of the gambler that he is: if you put on enough plays one of them is bound to win. He is a great enthusiast and can talk you into anything. Once you have signed the contract it is too late. It was to be a limited tour and then, God willing, into town.

My diary noted tersely the pleasures and the horrors of the ensuing weeks.

June 26th: We open in Lincoln. Bill has splashed out on the clothes.

The set is not all it should be. Bill must have had it in stock. It should have a French window, instead the hero has to make his last-Act entrance through a sash one, bent double! Not quite the effect Somerset Maugham intended, I think. Bill promises he will get us one for the next date, Ashton-Under-Lyme.

Lincoln is a lovely place, the cathedral an incredible piece of sculpture, all angles, beautifully lit at night. My son, Patrick, came to stay for a week from university. I had taken a flat and it was good to be able to spend some time with him. We explored every inch of the cathedral, guided by a little verger who nipped about with incredible speed, looking at his watch all the time like the White Rabbit in *Alice*. There is a Wren Library, tucked into the middle of the building, with very early books, examples of Caxton's best work. I noticed a lot of vellum-bound ones with 'Prayers' and 'Devotions' written on their spines, and the librarian told me they were part of Dean Honeywood's library and she hadn't catalogued them yet. Dean Honeywood was described by Samuel Pepys as 'the dullest man in England'. I took one of the books down out of curiosity, as the title lettering seemed seventeenth-century but the bindings looked older. The first one I opened was a prima facie *Decamerone* by Boccaccio, the next Aretino, and so on. Dean Honeywood had been walking about the cloisters, reading one of the most elegant collections of pornography in the country. We reckoned they must have come from the Medici Library when it was dispersed. The librarian shut the library and we spent the rest of the day translating them. Poor Pepys, he would have loved them.

The timbers in the roof are huge – oaks like American redwoods – and give an idea of what the medieval forests must have been like.

The play is going surprisingly well. The audience cry in the weepy bits and the gents love the heroine's (Alexandra Bastedo) red dress that plunges to the navel and threatens to come off. No laughs in the wrong places so far.

July 11th: Ashton-Under-Lyme. We still don't have a French window, but Bill turned up unexpectedly and gave us all a party!

Next week Oxford, so I can commute. That means I can see a little of my daughter, Sarah, and a little will be quite enough. She is behaving like all Chekhov's heroines in one. I can't stand her and she loathes me, and lurks in the flat downstairs in a permanent bad mood – it comes up through the floor like rising damp. All my friends seem to be having problems with their teenage daughters. Mothers and daughters should not live together.

The trouble with touring is I spend too much money. Oxford

is filled with wonderful bookshops – fatal. I arrive at the theatre each night filled with guilt, clutching a new 'find'. Jean and I are adding our 'buys' on the tour to the set dressing, so Bill has gained a pair of Nottingham lace curtains (to cover the offending sash window), two rather good watercolours, various pieces of china and a pretty fire screen.

July 22nd: Southsea. The hotel is terrible. I rather like it.

Faded grandeur, at its peak during the war, probably. Elderly men with handle-bar moustaches come into the bar at night and swap jokes and chat up the barmaid. The décor is rose pink and maroon with Regency stripes. I have a large, comfortable, shabby room with a sea view. Most of the lifts are erratic, but I get my breakfast whenever I want, in my room, and that is all I need on tour!

'Sian Phillips is here,' they say. It seems unlikely, but I leave a note for her. When I come in there is a reply. She doesn't have to leave until eleven next morning. Shall we have coffee?

About a year ago, Sian had asked me to give Peter O'Toole, her husband, some help and tips on Roman history (another of my loves acquired in the libraries and bookshops of Edinburgh) for his part of Tiberius in Gore Vidal's *Caligula*. I duly arrived in my role of historical adviser to find Peter whirling around the house in a dressing gown, playing opera tapes and not in any mood to learn about ancient Rome. The house is a lovely mixture of old and new, singular taste, marvellous exotic objects acquired on their travels. 'What is this? I bet you don't know!' As a matter of fact, I did. It is a gondola prow set upright in a piece of dark polished stone – lovely. Peter was quite put out, but after all my family come from Venice.

Sian's mother is coming in later and she will make some lunch. Meanwhile Peter *must* have a history lesson. He couldn't be less interested; all he wants to do is have a good gossip. I have to insist, so he turns on the tape recorder and I start on Suetonius and Tacitus. It became perfectly obvious that what he really wants is enough information to cope with Gore Vidal.

The best I can do for Peter is to try to give him some reality on which to base his character. Augustus' words about Tiberius help, 'Poor Rome, to be masticated in those ponderous jaws!' This gave Peter a clue for the voice, slow and indistinct, like Churchill's. He has records of the war speeches so we put them on. Very good idea. It even makes the dreadful lines sound a little better.

In the end, we managed to build up quite a good picture of Tiberius with some truth, unlike the script. We have rewritten some of the more absurd lines, but they may make the others sound even worse. At any rate, Peter now knows a little about the man, and the rest is up to the director and the camera.

I didn't think the film should be made at all.

Sian was in the cavern of a foyer sitting, placid and chic, in good jeans and the right Missoni scarf, beautifully knotted. I asked her how Peter was; she looked at me and then laughed. 'Oh dear, you would be the last to know!' I hadn't been reading the papers. She and Peter have separated. She is down here to play Boadicea for ITV. The split-up started some time ago. Whatever the reasons, all separations seem to me such a defeat for both sides. I asked if it had been friendly. 'Oh dear, no!' Sian's soft Welsh accent can make the simplest sentence take on new dimensions. Peter is so upset at the moment that he won't let her into their house in Hampstead: 'I have no clothes. All those Jean Muirs rotting in trunks.'

I thought of all the years, the good and bad patches. 'Was it worth it?' 'Oh yes.' Short pause. 'Oh yes, nearly all worth it.' I can't help thinking of them both as they were. Hampstead was very much Sian, her taste, her style. It is hard to think of them apart, of our group in the theatre they had managed to stay together longest of all. It is the end of a passing-out parade.

August 8th: This week it is the Alexandra, Birmingham.

I remember a rather nice portrait of David Garrick there. The last owner, Derek Salberg, showed it to me. I hope it is still in the theatre; it was in his office, I think. I saw it fifteen years ago, but I still have a picture of it in my head. Only a good painting stays with you like that. It was attributed to Gainsborough. If it is still there I shall look at it properly. I told Derek to have it valued and he was going to ask Sotheby's.

Everyone groans at the thought of Birmingham. It is an actor's nightmare; you are a displaced person in a wilderness of bad hotels, indifferent restaurants and concrete ring roads. All you can hope is that the week will pass quickly. Jean and I have decided to stay at the most expensive hotel to console ourselves. At least it is near the theatre and you can't get lost. The heart of Birmingham was torn out in an orgy of civic planning and it has never recovered. You can't cross any of the main roads except by underpass, and you are never sure where you will emerge. As it rains there rather a lot, the underpasses fill with water. Every aspiring architect should be made to live there for at least a year to learn what not to do.

The Alexandra is a huge theatre. Its heyday is over, passed with the Music Hall; it is friendly, with a good feeling and tradition in its walls, although very dilapidated. I looked for the painting before the first night. The new manager didn't seem to know where to find it – he says it was in the bar (which is called the Garrick) but was moved during redecoration. It is such a big theatre, it could be anywhere.

August 9th: I found the picture in a back corridor leading from the bar to the street.

It is in a mess, very dirty, yet it has got style. Michael Bullock, the new manager, has given me permission to clean it. If I don't it will soon be damaged beyond repair and in such a state that it will be thrown out. Who knows, it may be an early study for the Gainsborough/Garrick portrait destroyed in Stratford during the war, or a contemporary copy. If it is, he *should* be leaning on a plinth. At the moment, it is anybody's guess; only the eyes are really clear. They have the look of Gainsborough. An artist always paints a bit of himself into every picture. This is particularly true of portraits. All Hogarth's sitters have that square little man's literal looks, while with a Gainsborough there is, I can only describe it as a caressing, teasing quality in the way the subject looks at you. The eyes of a flirt, of a man who knows a certain kind of world very well. It is impossible to write about paintings, they are there to be seen, and yet I can always tell a Gainsborough by the eyes. The eyes of this picture, even through the years of smoke and industrial grime, have the right look. God knows what the rest of it is like.

Garrick is fixed firmly to the wall and I shall have to clean him in situ. I have found a rickety chair and even then it is a bit high up for me, so the years of dirt roll down my arms as I work.

The first thing I use when I clean a painting is baby shampoo and the purest cotton wool; here, I am afraid, the dirt is so thick that I will never make an impression. Fortunately, no parts of the picture are lifting or peeling. The great danger is that whatever you are cleaning with may get *under* the paint and lift it off the canvas, so it is essential to dry every patch you clean as you go along. The patches, at first, should be quite small, getting larger each successive time until you are cleaning big areas evenly. *Never* use chemicals, detergents or, as I saw one professional cleaner do, acetone!

August 10th: The picture is slowly emerging.

I have started to remove some of the 'improvements'. You can always tell manufactured paint, it is softer. I tested one corner and the early varnish is as tough as linoleum. I reckon there are at least three coats of it under the later work, which means it should be quite safe for the original picture.

The line from the right shoulder to the cuff is beautiful. The hand holding the hat is a lovely piece of work. It sounds silly, but yesterday when I saw what was there for the first time, I found myself shaking with excitement. It was like finding buried treasure.

August 11th: Something lovely happened today.

The boy who helps in the bar has taken to leaving me a pile of clean rags to mop up the dirt that is rolling off the canvas. The cleaning is going very slowly, as I reckon no one has touched the picture for over fifty years and before that there seems to have been a great deal of mid-Victorian 'restoration'. There is a beauty spot on the cheek which is quite wrong for a man at that date; the coat seems to have been over-painted and the wig is odd. I have decided to remove the paint from the right hand and sleeve to begin with.

This afternoon I was up on my chair when I heard a little

murmur behind me. I had just cleared the hand and sleeve and it was looking marvellous. I turned round and found some of the front-of-house staff were watching me, for how long I don't know as they hadn't made a sound. They seemed as pleased and as interested in the picture as I am; they practically applauded. It was very encouraging. The cast is complaining about my arriving on the stage reeking of paint solvent, and my hands are not as hygienic-looking as they should be for a nurse. Jean has promised to tell me if my face is dirty. Last night I apparently had a streak of oil on my nose for the whole of the first Act.

I shall have to continue with the cleaning when we get to Wolverhampton. I can commute as it is not far away, but I do want to see the whole picture at least partially cleaned before we go south with the play.

By the end of the week the Victorian improvements, which included a dark coat, a heavy orange and red waistcoat and a later-style wig, as well as a beauty spot on the cheek, have completely gone and I think he looks great.

The canvas is about three and a half feet in width and about four in height, the standard size for a three-quarter figure portrait. Now he stands revealed in a smart buff coat, a white satin waistcoat with gold embroidery and a sword at his side in a red hanger. He is much younger than I expected and has a rather high, ruddy complexion. Garrick not in make-up, which is unusual, or as a character from a play, even more unusual. He seems to have been painted as himself for once, and in the style of a gentleman of the period. Although there is a theatrical quality simply in the bravura of the pose, he is definitely more a man of the town than an actor. The figure is elongated as it is a three-quarter portrait, which means that it is not the whole figure but stops at the knees. If it were carried out to a full canvas, Garrick would be about nine feet tall. This supports the idea that it could be Gainsborough, as he had a tendency to make his people taller (what actor would want to be thought short?). Garrick was a small man, and yet 'neatly made'; he never seems to have given the impression of being short on the stage. His stature came from inside and he made the audiences believe in it, too.

August 13th: An air of conspiracy seems to have settled over the theatre. The picture has been taken from the wall I found it on, and now it is in the manager Michael Bullock's office under lock and key.

Every time I mention it, Michael puts his finger to his lips and looks around to see if anyone can overhear us. It is all like a bad spy movie. At last I realise that he and the board are terrified that some long-lost relative of the man who first owned it will pop up and claim the portrait, if it is of any value, even though I have pointed out that it has been part of the fixtures and fittings of the theatre for years. It seems that it was left there in 1910 by an actor-manager called Lester Collingwood, an early owner of the Alexandra. I believe it was only valued at £20 at the last sale of the theatre in 1970. It may not be worth that much more now – I could well be wrong, and it is not a style immediately identifiable with Gainsborough, but there is something haunting about it that seems to be him and no one else. I just think it is a marvellous picture; all the theatre management and its board ask is, 'How much is it worth?'

One of the staff from the art department of the Barber Institute came in today. He studied the picture for about an hour and then said, 'Hoppner!' It is nothing like his work. Hoppner was born in 1758, Garrick in 1717, and as this is clearly a *young* Garrick it wasn't even an educated guess. He retreated when I pointed this out, saying that his period was really Pre-Raphaelite. Still, he should have known better.

August 15th: Wolverhampton Grand Theatre, another immense, crumbling Victorian pile, very decrepit.

The art gallery here has some splendid eighteenth- and nineteenth-century pictures including Gainsborough, Ramsay and Raeburn, and a very unusual Richard Wilson, a view of Niagara Falls. This picture was found by the curator – it had been patching up the museum coal cupboard! It is quite large and I suppose some local workman felt 'waste not, want not'.

Also some explorer pictures of the Far East. Not inappropriate, as the only restaurants open after the show are Chinese or Indian.

The journey between Birmingham and Wolverhampton may

not seem much on a map, but the planners have made it a small hell. I became so tangled in the euphemistically named ring road one evening that I nearly missed the show. I found myself in the pouring rain, windscreen wipers jammed, under a large sign saying: NORTH AND SOUTH (it omitted to say of *where*). But David Garrick was worth it. Every day he looked better with my cleaning. I wanted to clear enough of the dirt to have him photographed. The manager promised to have it done for me, so that I could give galleries in London some idea of his quality.

August 22nd: I said goodbye to David Garrick reluctantly and left for our next date in Peterborough.

The hunt was now on for the picture's provenance. I started to collect everything I could about Garrick and Gainsborough. Although I had a good surface knowledge of both their lives, it was not enough to consider myself an authority on either. All my previous reading had been from letters, diaries and biographies of the times, and the pure pleasure of such acquaintances; it meant I had yawning gaps to fill on the practical side. As I believe that there is nothing you can't learn if you put your mind to it, I set about filling those gaps.

It seems that the main modern authorities on Gainsborough are, in order of seniority: Sir Ellis Waterhouse; Sir Oliver Millar, Master of the Queen's Pictures; John Hayes, National Portrait Gallery; the Tate; Mary Woodall, who was at Birmingham Art Gallery; and I will also try to get Sir Anthony Blunt to look at the photographs when the theatre sends them to me. I admire his scholarship and he writes so well. I would value his opinion. He is quite formidable, by all accounts, and inclined to be pretty sharp, but I think it would be worth the risk.

To make sure I know what I am talking about, I have decided to read all their books on Gainsborough *and* their source material – that seems a good way to begin. I had better make sure my subscription is paid up at the London Library. This is not as silly as it may sound. I have a short time to learn what they have had a lifetime to absorb. At the moment what I know is 'good in parts', but it is not enough to tackle them on their own ground, although I would match my eye against any of them. I also have the advantage of not being of their world, which means

I come to the whole thing fresh.

The thought of Sir Ellis Waterhouse is daunting. His credits are so long and so grand that the prospect of meeting him on his own territory is petrifying. I shall not look at any of these experts' academic honours until the search is over; I will lose all courage if I become too awestruck.

August 29th: There is one date on the tour which is a mystery. No one knows where it will be.

Bill tends to be disorganised and we just hope it isn't too far away. It is the week before Brighton, and Bill is quite likely to send us to Dundee, inflicting a marathon journey on us. It is so much of a London audience in Brighton, and we would all be exhausted. We are praying, and someone has organised a sweepstake – Dundee is the favourite!

Now we know – it is Whitley Bay! Alex, organised and hopeful, armed with her Egon Ronay guide, says there is a four-star hotel. She must be mad – we didn't even know there was a theatre.

Our worst fears were realised. There is no theatre in the town, it is a converted cinema. How does Bill find them?

The four-star hotel was at a crossroads. Jean and I never even gave it a chance. After they had refused to serve us tea at three o'clock, we ditched poor Alex and went in search of somewhere else. The first glimpse of the theatre confirmed our forebodings. Across all our posters was a sticker saying: LIVE ON STAGE! The last company to play there was a Gang Show – lots of nasty little boy scouts. The dressing rooms were dreadful, painted pea green and looking as if the scouts had rioted there, or worse. Jean and I were so depressed that we tried to get a breath of sea air, but even that was out. Not even a hurricane could have shifted the smell of fish and chips; it was like a solid wall along the promenade. The other hotels we passed looked pretty terrible, and I tried to cheer Jean up by saying we would take two rooms at the first hotel to give us a glass of champagne. The first two behaved as if we were out of our minds, but the third said solemnly that they were afraid they only had a bottle of Krug on ice and would that do? They had two customers at once. It turned out to be an excellent little place and looked after us beautifully for the rest of the week. Egon Ronay must do better. The theatre cleaned our dressing rooms up a little, but not enough to prevent me catching a very vicious flea. Now I know what it means to be 'live on stage'!

Around Whitley Bay is naval country. All the masts for the fleet of Nelson's day are supposed to have come from here, and one house has the trees of its park laid out in the formation of the battle line of Trafalgar. It was the home of Collingwood, one of Nelson's commanders, so perhaps I can find out if the Birmingham one has anything to do with him.

I didn't find any clues to Lester Collingwood, but I did learn a few irrelevant bits of information about the Navy.

Junk shopping and sightseeing are part of the compensations of touring. Whitley Bay gave Jean and me a chance to do some more 'collecting' and to go to Alnwick Castle, which has a spectacular display of Sèvres, and a wonderful, seductive Lely in clinging cigar-coloured silk and nothing else. Very sexy lady; one of his best for my money. Two or three pretty awful Gainsboroughs; very late and very bored. My David Garrick is far better.

Jean and I both like porcelain and will go to great lengths to find new pieces. I had a bit of luck in the local market. I saw an unusual green bowl – I don't know what drew me to it – lovely colour, interesting glaze and a silver lustre rim. It turned out to be a Jenny Lind memorial bowl. Jean has a collection of theatre figures and memorabilia, and covets it greatly. It will be her seventieth birthday soon – I shall give it to her then.

I have enjoyed this tour. It is a very good way to see the country in the company of people you like. Acting isn't such a bad job sometimes.

Bill has shoved in another couple of dates which shuttle us up north again, and then fast down south. We are doing well, but apparently another of his tours is not. Their company manager arrives to take some of *our* money to pay *his* company every Saturday. We shall never see that French window.

September 5th: Bath. The drive from the north was a killer and I arrived aching with tension. Jean and I are treating ourselves to the Royal Crescent Hotel, so it will be a comfortable week.

I found the King's Bath was open when I arrived, filled with Druids (at least that is what they called themselves), so I went in and soaked myself in the boiling, rather murky waters for an hour and every ache accumulated on the drive disappeared like a miracle. It was lovely swimming around in the steaming, bubbling water. The Bath is open to the sky and a light rain was falling. My Druids threw in a shoulder massage for good measure. The upshot was that I was so relaxed I nearly fell asleep on stage.

It was a lovely week on the whole. Bath was a perfect place to research Gainsborough's later working life, as he had lived here from 1759 to 1774. I was lucky enough to see his studio in the house in the Royal Circus. The room has been cut in half to accommodate a bathroom, but it is sufficiently intact to give a good idea of what it was like originally. There is a pub next to the theatre with a bust of Garrick as its sign, called the Garrick's Head. It is the only known replica of a portrait bust done of him during his life, the original having been lost, and excellent for me as it is very like the Birmingham picture; rather a lumpy, round face, slightly bulbous nose. I shall come back to take some pictures of it after the tour.

September 17th: My friend Coral Browne has arrived in town.

An Australian actress of great beauty and a salty tongue of lethal wit, she is admired by half the theatre and feared (without cause) by the rest. She recently married Vincent Price and together they make a formidable couple. Wit of Coral's order would have been greatly admired fifty years ago, but today, when everyone wishes to be loved, it is not at all understood. She once described one of her leading men (an actor of tremendous worth but impenetrable stolidity) as 'ten stone of condemned veal'; this description was so apt that people found it hard to think of him as anything else ever after. Vincent is an art expert, Courtauld Institute-trained, belying his horror-film image. He became an actor by accident, when Helen Hayes needed an Albert for her Queen Victoria, and has remained in the profession in an amused way ever since. He won't be with Coral this trip, which is a pity, as I would have liked his opinion on the Garrick.

Coral is staying with the director, John Schlesinger. They are discussing a project based on an incident in her life when she was kind to Guy Burgess in Russia, during a tour with the Old Vic. Alan Bennett has written a play about it. Coral will play herself. Although the incident took place over twenty years ago, such is the enduring quality of her remarkable looks that she is still perfect casting. It would be extremely difficult to find anyone else with such panache; they don't make leading ladies of her ilk any more. John is giving a party for her. I look forward to it. He gives a good party.

Now I was back in London it was possible to give all my attention to the picture and to work out the steps needed to discover if it really was an early Gainsborough of David Garrick. The signs were not favourable. None of the books I had read on the tour mentioned the two men knowing each other before the 1760s, and the picture is of a young Garrick, barely thirty judging from the look of him. One thing I could do was to go ahead on the practical side and find out where he could be properly cleaned and restored while I continued to work on the provenance and history.

September 20th: The Alexandra Theatre board insists on taking counsel's opinion to establish its ownership of the picture before I make a move.

It is not necessary and it seems to be taking forever. It is the full cloak-and-dagger bit, and is wasting a lot of time. I have tried to explain to them that it is not an accepted Gainsborough until it has been approved by the proper experts. Until then, it is just a nice, unknown picture.

I am determined that the picture, if it is a Gainsborough, shall not leave this country. An early identification, one way or the other, will help.

They have had photographs taken, in colour, of my final cleaning. Not too bad, a bit grey, but they give a good idea of him. There is one homely touch: he is standing on two red ashtrays – not very dignified. I shall have to find out who would be the best to complete the restoration.

The National Gallery seemed as good a place as any to start. I telephoned and was put straight through to the head of the cleaning department, a Mr Arthur Lucas. He sounded wary but not discouraging and I arranged to take the photographs along so that he could give me further advice. I made an appointment to meet him on October 5th.

By the time the tour ended I had ploughed my way through all the 'definitive' versions by modern writers, and the main early sources which they all quoted.

A puzzling aspect about everything I had read on Gainsborough was that there seemed to be so little fact. A great deal of conjecture, nothing solid. So much emphasis is placed on his being a 'countryman', yet so much belied this idea of him. One story tells how he had a sheep in his studio, much to his wife's annoyance. No countryman I have ever met would do such a thing; sheep, on the whole, are bad-tempered, stupid beasts, not very clean and quite destructive. When Constable was asked by the Royal Academy to write a 'Life', he eventually had to decline the commission as he, only a few years after Gainsborough's death, could find out so little about him. 'It was as if her greatest son had never lived,' he wrote of Suffolk. Constable wrote very well, his autobiography is delightful, he admired Gainsborough, and yet, because of lack of facts (he could not even find his birth registration), he did not write the proposed book. There had to be some reason why Gainsborough's life was such a mystery. All the biographies used the same sources, all end in a jumble of hearsay and opinion, insubstantial and uninformative. The real Thomas Gainsborough has given history the slip. The first years in London seem to be pure guesswork on the part of every author of Gainsborough's life.

The earlier books are sparse: one by an Ipswich bookbinder called Fulcher, published in 1856, another by William Whitley in 1915. There is also a nasty little pamphlet written by a contemporary and sometime friend of Gainsborough's called Philip Thicknesse. His book was rushed out the year of Gainsborough's death, mainly to tell everyone that it was to Philip Thicknesse that he owed his career and to insult Gainsborough's wife and Gainsborough himself for ingratitude to his patron. I somehow don't believe a word of it. Thicknesse seems to have been a nasty bit of work and it shows in his writing, but his word has been taken as gospel. William Jackson, the musician, another friend, writes quite jolly little anecdotes hinting at evenings spent drinking and womanising. This does have a ring of truth. A later friend, the Reverend Henry Bate-Dudley, appears anxious to whitewash. There are letters in the British Library, some scattered papers, and that is all. The book by Sir Walter Armstrong written at the turn of the century is regarded as outdated, but it contains some useful anecdotes.

A lot of Gainsborough's letters to his male friends were destroyed as 'too licentious'; the ones at the British Library are censored by Victorian historians and have bits literally cut out of them, but those that remain don't need much guesswork. They are very ballsy; definitely a man's man.

The museum world, backstage, was not entirely new ground. I had often asked (and received) help from its members, but now I was very anxious not to put a foot wrong as the picture was so important to me. To make sure that I started correctly, I wrote to Dr Roy Strong, an old friend, at the Victoria and Albert Museum. He confirmed that John Hayes would be the best person to start with, being the most recent Gainsborough pundit. John Hayes had succeeded Roy at the National Portrait Gallery, but Roy offered to look at the picture for me and asked me to send him photographs as he thought it sounded interesting.

September 21st: John Schlesinger's party is splendid. Very much Coral's guest list.

I remember her once sending one to me. It was full of comments, 'Don't care if *he* can't come!' and so on. I could have blackmailed her for years.

This list included Harold Pinter, with Antonia Fraser standing over him like a guardsman – she is beautiful but they make a funny pair. At one point Harold wants to check a date (we are talking about John Evelyn). Antonia promptly supplies it. 'She remembers everything,' he says. 'She is my filing cabinet.'

Albert Finney and Diana Quick; he has got very fat, pudge all round the waist. She is very pretty. Men are lucky, getting fat and plain doesn't seem to spoil their chances! Francesca Annis is looking ravishing. John needs to raise £4,000,000 for his next picture. We reckon if we could sell Diana and Francesca to rich

Arabs, it would be in the bank. Alec Guinness is there, Charles Gray and so on. A good cast. It breaks up very late.

September 25th: Our last week, Richmond, and the tour of the Flame *is over.*

There were a couple of offers to take it into town, but some of the cast have other jobs and it would mean replacing them and rehearsing all over again, altogether too costly for the management. It is very sad, we have all got on so well. The end of the play coincides with Jean's seventieth birthday, so we can have our farewell party and a celebration for her at the same time. The end of a play is always sad, but we are all pretty tired and it is nice to be home and to stay in the same place and to lead a normal life for a time.

I like actors, but really only the ones who don't talk exclusively about acting – these are rare, so they don't figure largely amongst my friends.

The narcissistic quality present in most actors doesn't make for sparkling conversations, unless one is talking about them. Old Wilfred Lawson (Doolittle in the first filmed *Pygmalion*) once caught sight of himself in the mirror at his local pub and said, 'Oh my God, I've looked at myself twice in the mirror – only bad actors do that!'

Wilfred was responsible for a terrible episode in my life when I was at the Old Vic. In *Peer Gynt*, to please Wilfred I had glued an emerald (with great difficulty) into my navel for Anitra's Dance. He was delighted. 'Now,' he said, 'I shall do something for you.' That put the fear of God into me – he was inclined to get through a large quantity of Guinness every night, so there was no telling what it might be. He walked grandly on to the stage and, to Leo McKern's question 'Who are you?' replied, 'I am a Mutton Boulder!' The Button Moulder makes about ten separate entrances, announcing himself each time – it was a nerve-wracking evening.

Most of my friends tend to be writers or artists and, among them, I am lucky enough to know a couple of the best theatre designers in England (or perhaps the world): David Walker and Carl Toms. When in doubt about costume, I run to them for advice.

Carl Toms is elegant and vague, with the kind of unstudied taste that is inclined to make anyone else look brash. He was Oliver Messel's assistant and trained for his theatre career with him. He collects awards for his work all over the world, in an absent-minded manner. The director who secures his services counts himself very fortunate.

David Walker is my other authority. The two men, apart from their talent, could not be a greater contrast. David is as neat as a Victorian doll – as a child he was a pupil at the Royal Ballet school and has the precise movements of a dancer. He can make opera singers look like goddesses (no mean feat), and he knows more about eighteenth-century costume than anyone I have ever met, being able to date a cuff or a lace cap in a picture practically to the day.

Stanley Kubrick failed to keep either Carl or David in his employ for his great eighteenth-century epic *Barry Lyndon*. They found his working methods too tiresome. When they both declined his offers and vast salaries he was bewildered. 'Life is too short to waste on people like Stanley,' said David snappishly, having done three months' work on designs for the *Napoleon* which never transpired. Carl left *Barry Lyndon* after three months, too. He grew tired of explaining to Stanley why a Victorian candlestick could not be used in a Georgian setting, for instance. Stanley is inclined to grind away in the manner of the mills of God, and although he has the sense to employ the best talents, he is also pernickety to a degree when they give him the advice he is paying for so highly.

I decided to ask them both for their opinions as soon as possible. I also went to the costume department of the Victoria and Albert Museum to check on the coat and wig myself. In arguing the case for the picture, I had to be quite sure of all my available facts and the date of the clothes was one bit of important evidence for the experts when I eventually faced them.

I always go to the V & A to look at costumes when I am in a period play. Fashions change from week to week, no matter what the century, and it is possible to take the dresses out there and put them on a stand to study them in detail. There is something so valuable in actually being able to handle them and see exactly how they were made and worn. The museum has vast wardrobes, three tiers high in huge rooms, filled not only with the clothes themselves but everything that goes with them: shoes, hats, underwear, dated to the smallest button.

October 5th: Today I went to the National Gallery to meet Arthur Lucas.

He turned out to be a dapper, small man with a beard and a faintly theatrical air, almost as if he dresses the part of an artist. His sense of humour is evident. He hasn't much time for humbug or for fools.

I grew to like him, but that first meeting was a strain. I was venturing on to such unfamiliar territory and into such a new world technically. Although I knew what I was talking about in theory, it was the first time I had to put it to the test in any exposed way. I had done battle for other pictures successfully in the past – a Lely in a hotel in Manchester, a Ramsay in Scotland – but never such an important or difficult subject as the present picture or, if I was correct, such a potentially exciting find.

I took the photographs from Birmingham. Arthur Lucas came down to the foyer at the back of the gallery (the new part) to meet me. He seemed very guarded, as if he thoroughly anticipated meeting some sort of lunatic, and he certainly didn't seem to expect much of the painting. However, he looked at the photographs and his interest altered perceptibly. He peered at me over the top of his spectacles and suggested that we had better go up to the cleaning rooms to see the photographs in a better light.

The cleaning department is daunting. Lucas was working on the ravishing portrait of Madame de Pompadour by Drouais, recently purchased by the gallery for around £450,000. All around, leaning against the walls or on easels, were other wonderful pictures usually only seen at a respectful distance – Van Eyck, Raphael, Titian, you name it. Lucas put me through a mild test. When we were looking at the Drouais he said suddenly, 'What do you think of her?' At least I have learned by now that there is not much you *can* say that doesn't sound foolish or pretentious, so I retreated into muttering, 'Very nice, beautiful silk …', etc. 'What's wrong with her?' he asked. Panic set in. It seemed to be a perfect painting, nothing wrong with it at all, but I realised there must be some catch or he wouldn't have asked the question. Consequently, I looked wildly for some flaw – there seemed to be one minor inconsistency: Pompadour is seated at an embroidery frame; somehow the arm *under* the frame did not quite seem to match the plump little arm poised *above* the silk holding the needle. It was beautifully painted, but there just seemed to be some indefinable difference, so I said that it did not seem quite right to me, although I couldn't say why.

'Clever girl. She was dead, it isn't her arm.'

I breathed again. After getting a couple of other pictures (a John Singleton Copley and a Zoffany) right, he seemed to be satisfied as to my judgement and, more important, *how* I looked at a picture and *what* I looked for in it. Anyway, thank God he didn't ask me any more awkward questions. It was like facing an exam, but at least I seemed to have passed.

At last he looked at my photographs again. I began to think I had a hell of a nerve to trouble him with a doubtful, provincial, would-be Gainsborough. Still, even surrounded by the real authenticated McCoy, David Garrick looked good to me, in spite of my incomplete cleaning and the bad colour of the photographs.

'What do you think I should do now?'

'Well, he needs cleaning and restoring,' said Lucas.

'Where should I take him?'

Lucas looked surprised. 'I'll do it, of course.'

'Where?'

'Here.'

'When?'

'Week after next will be fine.'

And that was that. I left the gallery in a happy daze. Soon my David Garrick would be in the same company as Madame de Pompadour and the odd Titian and Rubens. It seemed more fitting for him than a back corridor in Birmingham.

Lucas has advised me to bone up on every painter I can find around that date who might have painted Garrick. I followed up his suggestion on research by trying to find all the examples I could of artists to whom the picture might also be attributed. The best place to start this search was the Courtauld Institute's Witt Library, where they have collected together photographs of

pinned on the outcome, but it is all a bit silly. I am afraid I have given them dizzy visions of untold fortunes. I have tried to explain that it is probably only a first attempt at a grand portrait and may fetch nothing like the amount they envisage, but they will not listen. It is the fault of the auction rooms and the press that beautiful things have lost their intrinsic value and become commodities.

I hope, secretly, that the Tate may be interested – then one could see Gainsborough's progression from early to high style in the same gallery and get a more accurate idea of the dating of his pictures by comparing his development. The truth is, I am in love again. No not love, passion.

The 'experts' must be able to come to a definite conclusion soon, even if they don't agree with me or the attribution on the frame. There were a lot of competent artists about at that time, but none I know of with quite this quality. I am sure it is an early immature work. Some bits are superb and some uncertain, just as they would be if the artist had not painted many large portraits. In many ways, it would have helped if Garrick had been in make-up, then we could have dated it by the role he was playing. He has the 'nothing' face of the true actor, one that can be turned into anything he chooses. Alec Guinness is like that, and no two photographs of Olivier look alike. I must ask Olivier to come and see the picture when it is cleaned – he knows so much about Garrick, I am sure he will like it.

The theatre doesn't seem to be able to tell me anything more about the first owner, Lester Collingwood, only a few bits of doubtful gossip about his private life which are no help at all. He doesn't seem like a connoisseur of art, but a rather boozy entrepreneur. He died in a car crash, which must have been hard to accomplish in 1911 with so few other vehicles on the road. There are still people around who remember him, but there seems to be no family remaining. The theatre was sold after his death, with the painting as part of the fixtures and fittings. He could have bought it anywhere.

October 25th: I was at the National Gallery before it opened, I was so nervous.

I wanted to know what Arthur Lucas thought of the picture

when he saw it in its raw state. The crate must have been made by the theatre carpenter; it was just a little too small, so the top and side of the frame had been hacked away to get it in. That will have to be restored. To secure the top, some hefty nails had been slammed into the lid, one of them just touching the picture itself; a little longer and it would have been through the face. I felt sick. All the rubbish about Securicor, and then to pack it in this way, no cover or padding. I can't believe the idiocy.

The frame is an early one. Arthur Lucas thinks that the picture was rebacked somewhere around the beginning of the nineteenth century, when it was common to iron the new canvas on and, sadly, the brushwork has been slightly flattened.

The canvas is correct, mid-eighteenth-century. The paint is also correct. Lucas congratulated me on the care I had taken. I had got down to the early varnish. I felt very flattered; it had simply been guesswork when I started to take off the Victorian 'improvements'. I grow cold when I think of it.

October 28th: I have been asked to play a nice part in the new Pink Panther.

A very smart gangster's wife, good scenes, though none with Peter Sellers which is a shame, but my 'husband' is played by Robert Webber, an actor whom I have admired in masses of films. Looking forward to it. I have been told I can go to Jean Muir for my clothes – I have to look expensive – hooray!

October 30th: David Walker is coming round this evening. He is in the middle of designing for Covent Garden.

He hadn't seen the photographs of Garrick so far. An awful blow. He didn't think they were very good or that it could be Garrick and certainly not Gainsborough. The wig and coat he dated around 1740, not later than 1744 at the outside as the wig would have been different and the cut of the cuff changed, and the man in the picture was clearly fashionable. He suggested I join the Society of Genealogists to research Lester Collingwood. I ring the manager to see if he knows why it is supposed to be Davy. 'Of course it is,' he replies. 'We named the bar after him.' That is not going to help much with galleries.

Back in my court.

I have to leave suddenly for Paris – no time to get clothes, they will buy them for me there.

November 1st: Paris. The whole company in a vast, Japanese-built hotel, miles from the centre. It is raining; apparently it has been raining for days.

The crews, English and French, are desperate. Robert Webber has a terrible cold; no, that is wrong, he is a one-man plague. I know I will get the bloody thing, he's breathing on everyone, balefully. Blake Edwards seems fine, attractive, lots of charm – lucky Julie Andrews! We meet in the bar. The technicians are pleased to see me and they have lined up so many drinks for me that he must think he has engaged an alcoholic. I keep slipping them to the wardrobe guy who is wearing the longest false eyelashes I have ever seen – must ask him where he gets them.

The wardrobe department has bought me some very pretty clothes, sight unseen; they fit perfectly. They're good about that sort of thing in France. Blake Edwards approves the wardrobe, but he has a worried look on his face – the weather forecast is not good. He stays for about half an hour then is called away. A phone call from Gstaad – Julie Andrews, presumably.

Jimmy Liggatt and Chalky White, our casting director and unit manager, insist we go to dinner; they have found a good little place around the corner. It turns out to be the bistro for the local night ladies. The wardrobe guy joins us – he is now in full drag, beautifully made up, more eyelashes. He asks me if I approve. I hear myself quoting Baudelaire, 'Vous êtes très beau, vous êtes très belle, vous êtes ma vie et ma santé.' Some of that drink must have got through; my French always improves immensely after a couple of vodkas.

I am on early call so I go home, leaving Chalky and Jimmy in pretty capable hands. The hotel is a nightmare. The windows don't open and the breakfast comes up on a nasty little lift which you have to set on a timing system. Very plush room. I get the window open at last and break my hairbrush in the process – still, at least I can breathe.

Out to the location at seven-thirty. I share a car with Robert

Webber. His cold is even worse and he has lost his voice. He looks like a miserable moose. We can't even go through our lines. Thank God we have separate caravans on the location.

The location is a swamp. They have put down duck boards so that we can walk to the set, which is supposed to be my house. My stand-in speaks no English. Good for me, it makes me speak French and I have remembered more than I thought.

Blake Edwards arrives. He doesn't spare himself and sits under a large umbrella in the freezing cold, waiting for the rain to stop. He is like King Canute, *willing* it to stop – it doesn't. Robert Webber puts his head round my door. He finds my caravan is larger and more comfortable than his *and* his heating doesn't work. I have to ask him in. He doesn't get on with the others (my stand-in and a couple of French actors who have come in from the deluge) – he only speaks English and is resentful if he is not able to join in. After an hour I feel that his germs have taken hold on me.

Blake calls us to rehearse. We do a long scene we can't possibly shoot in this weather. Blake thinks it could be played indoors. He also decides I should look more tweedy and wear a lot of jewellery. The wardrobe lady escapes to Paris to buy some. I envy her. It goes on raining.

After a week of identical days, without any warning, Blake Edwards boarded his private jet and went to Gstaad, cancelling the Paris location. This was sad because it meant the French unit was out of work. By this time I was in the grip of the lethal cold and just very glad to get home. I had never even got to the centre of Paris to see the Beaubourg, or any friends. We had a party on the last evening and said goodbye for the present. The scenes have been rescheduled for the spring. I don't think I shall live to see it. Thanks to Webber, I think I might die before Christmas.

Back in London, Arthur Lucas phones – he has a surprise for me. His first cleaning has revealed scars on the right hand. 'Was Garrick a duellist?' I can't remember any mention of a duel; it is conceivable that they might have been from a stage fight. The cuts are very clear and he seems to be displaying them rather proudly. I feel depressed at my own ignorance. I still have a lot to learn.

November 10th: Arthur Lucas has got the old varnish completely off, and all the later Victorian work.

Good and bad. The good news first; much fresher and more lively. The bad is that there has been more damage caused in that awful corridor than I realised, tears in the corner where a beer crate seems to have gone through it, and other small holes in various parts of the canvas. No damage, however, to the figure, and the background is very sketchy and unfinished, more like a theatre backdrop than a real landscape. The colours have come up beautifully, warm and glowing. The buff of the coat and the white satin of the waistcoat; lively dark eyes looking even more flirtatious, high colouring on the face – all this exceeds my original expectations.

The greenish-blue used in the waistcoat looks exactly like that of the white in the aprons of the portraits of Gainsborough's little girls. Arthur Lucas and I go to the main gallery to compare, and it is identical. The light, flicking brushwork, which had still been partly hidden by the varnish, seems to be the same, too. My heart rises with hope; it must be very early, but it *must* be right.

The scars on the hand are very clear, painted round the curve of the fingers. They are a puzzle to me. If Garrick did fight a duel it must be mentioned somewhere, and that will give us the date of the picture.

The heavy stretcher is warped and has to be replaced and the picture rebacked again, so for part of next year he will be under wraps and I won't be able to look at him. We both examined the stretcher closely; no clues on it as to artist or date. Arthur has got sick of my being formal, so now we are on first-name terms. To celebrate Garrick's resurrection we trundled out to a very good wine bar, where they serve champagne by the glass, and drank a toast to him. I don't think I shall ever forget the sight of him in the sunlight today.

November 25th: Went to the British Museum Reading Room.

In an attempt to find out more about a possible duel, I decided to go through the news sheets and periodicals of the day, starting in 1742, the year of Garrick's début in London. My timing is bad and most of them are unavailable for the dates I need, having been sent away to be microfilmed. One or two are there and the *Gentleman's Magazine* (essential reading for social news in the eighteenth century), but I could find nothing in that. I got sidetracked when, to my delight, I discovered that the *Morning Post* I was reading had belonged to the musician, Dr Burney. My early reading on Garrick had come from the pages of the famous diary of his daughter, Fanny Burney, or Madame d'Arblay as she later became. I had fallen in love with the eighteenth century through her pages. Dr Johnson, Garrick, Boswell are so vividly portrayed by her.

From 1742 onwards Garrick is very well documented, his performances lovingly recorded by critics and theatre-goers of the day. In *Tom Jones*, Fielding, also a theatre manager, describes his Hamlet in great detail. No mention of a duel as yet. Indeed, it would have had to have been hushed up. Garrick could have been in trouble had it been known, actors still being rogues and vagabonds.

November 30th: Carola Oman's book, published in 1958, pretty well as definitive as you can get on Garrick. She has the story of a duel, and gives her sources.

Thank God! Lovely short cut. Look up Percy Fitzgerald's *Life of Garrick*; he has a lot of gossipy, green room stories and quotes a critic, William Cooke (Macklin's biographer), who mentions a duel between Garrick and his first actor-manager, Henry Giffard. The circumstances seem a bit vague, but Cooke speaks of it pretty confidently, saying that 'none but their seconds knew at the time and very few ever since'. It seems to have been fought at the end of the first London season in 1742, just after Garrick's great success as Richard III. Garrick had been fooling around on the stage and Giffard, angry to have his performance spoiled, had challenged him. Garrick had been wounded in the sword hand and arm, and this was the first and only painting I had seen with the sword marks. Both he and Giffard were officers' sons, therefore allowed to carry swords, and Garrick was very anxious, especially in later life, to stress that his background was a 'gentleman's'; the painting of the scars shows an amiable bit of vanity. For them to be so obvious meant that the painting must be even earlier than I had originally thought. I still could not find a record of the two men knowing each other at this time. Gainsborough was ten years younger than Garrick, and it seemed unlikely that the rising young star of the English stage would have much in common with a gauche young country apprentice.

Of all the books I have read so far, I am most intrigued by that of Sir Ellis Waterhouse. Curiously cagey, unconvinced in many ways as to the datings, especially of the earlier works; full of 'ifs' and 'buts' and 'perhaps'. Qualifications all the way if he has no definite documentation to back up the evidence; a very careful book. I get the impression he doesn't like Gainsborough's character at all.

Mary Woodall's *Letters* is quite funny; very naive, she doesn't seem to know what the bawdy bits mean and is very innocent about them. John Hayes is simply an all-out Gainsborough enthusiast; anything, and everything, seems to be all right by him. He doesn't question much.

There still seems to be more of Gainsborough to be discovered. He says in letters that he began working 'as a child', for instance; if so, where is the evidence of that work? Or any other work in the London years from 1740 to 1749? I cannot understand why his picture was accepted by the Foundling Hospital in 1748, along with all the well-known artists of his day, if he was not 'discovered' until 1752, as Philip Thicknesse maintains. Nor can I understand why he was given the chance to paint Admiral Vernon, MP for Ipswich and hero of Portobello unless, as my son commented, Vernon was a very poor Admiral, which of course he was not.

Sorting through all the reading I had done on tour, and the work I had managed to do in London, a pattern began to emerge. Garrick and Gainsborough both came from Huguenot families – both had connections with Ipswich (Garrick is said to have made his début there under the assumed name of Lydall, the stage name of the actress married to Henry Giffard).

Both were supposed to have connections with Hubert Gravelot, the French engraver and artist, and Francis Hayman. Gainsborough's connections could only be substantiated on stylistic grounds, but Garrick corresponded with them both socially and through business matters. Hayman was employed by Henry Giffard on the redecoration and the scenery of Goodman's Fields, the theatre where Garrick made his official début and had his great success as Richard III. Giffard's wife played Lady Anne, and London was greatly shocked and excited by the novel way Garrick played the seduction scene, very realistically, using the coffin almost as a bed.

Gainsborough's conversation pieces certainly showed Hayman's influence, and some of his drawings are very close to Gravelot, but nothing concrete was produced by any of the writers to show that either man had taught the boy. Indeed, all the books steadfastly stick to the idea that he was untaught, a natural talent, although the mature technique of his early landscape style, which in turn differs from both Hayman's work and Gravelot's, complicates matters even further and would seem to contradict this. The Huguenot link was important, as the French who settled here tended to be clannish and to help each other, no matter how long the families had been in England.

The stories of Gainsborough's early years were idyllic – too much so to be believable. A loving, doting mother, a ne'er-do-well father, a country 'character', bankrupt in 1733 and never discharged officially of his debts. An apprenticeship had to be paid for – Gainsborough's father could never have managed it. From the time he is supposed to have left Ipswich in 1739 until his return in 1748, nothing definite is known of Gainsborough's life other than his marriage in 1746 to the mysterious young Scotswoman, Margaret Burr, and the acceptance of a view of the Charterhouse by the governors of Captain Coram's Foundling Hospital in 1748.

Other early contacts with Garrick could have been made through the publication of the Hanmer Shakespeares. Sir Thomas Hanmer was a Suffolk man, and Garrick had taken a close interest in the plates. Hubert Gravelot, with whom Gainsborough is supposed to have studied, was a great friend of David Garrick; this seemed a very slender chance, though he never mentions Gainsborough in a long and thorough correspondence with Garrick, even when Gainsborough has become famous. Nor does Francis Hayman, although both men engraved the Shakespeares. Neither of them appears to have been ungenerous, but there is no evidence at all, so far, to support the theory that Gainsborough was ever a student of either of them. Hayman was not a great painter by any means, but he was a popular man and an admirer of talent in others. The most charming works left are conversation pieces thought to have influenced Gainsborough's work in the same field.

Another possible avenue for research arose in the person of Henry Russell, later the fourth Duke of Bedford. Russell (and his wife Diana Spencer) appears to have been one of the greatest, and unsung, patrons that England ever possessed. Every artist at some time or other fell under his patronage: Arne, Linley, Sheridan, Canaletto, and many others, including Garrick, who took the lease of Drury Lane Theatre in 1746 and lived in Southampton Street, Covent Garden, part of the Bedford Estate.

The Bedfords were patrons of both Garrick and Gainsborough, although the social distinctions seem evident. Gainsborough was treated as a highly regarded employee, the fourth Duke even advising him to keep his prices down. Garrick was more of a friend. He spent part of his honeymoon at Woburn when he married the dancer 'La Violette', another protégé of the Bedfords, who contributed handsomely to her dowry.

At the end of exhaustive reading, the chronology I came up with for both men was as follows:

GARRICK

1739–40: Summer Season – Garrick's supposed début at Ipswich in Henry Giffard's company as Mr Lydall. First play produced by Fielding in London.

1741–42: Garrick's début and triumph as Richard III. Duel with Giffard rumoured (Summer Season 1742). In February 1742 Hanmer Shakespeares begun – G. supervising plates – Irish visit – Gravelot, Hayman.

GAINSBOROUGH

1739–40: Leaves Ipswich for London (month unknown).

1740–41: Thought to have been a student of Hubert Gravelot or Francis Hayman. Not known with whom he lodged.

1743–44: Small unidentified drawings signed and dated 1743–44 'Thomas Gainsborough, fecit'.

GARRICK – *contd.*
1744–45: Hanmer Shakespeares published. Gravelot returns to France. Garrick visits E. Anglia, stays with William Wyndham.
1745–46: Summer in Dublin; London, Drury Lane, Winter Season.
1746–47: Garrick and Lacey go into management at Drury Lane – Duke of Bedford backs him.

GAINSBOROUGH – *contd.*
1744–45: Gainsborough said to have set up a studio in Holborn (no evidence). Dog 'Bumper' painted for Hill family, date on back of relined canvas 1745.
1745–46: Marries Margaret Burr, Mayfair Chapel, July 15th (Dr Keith's clandestine marriage chapel).
1747–48: Returns to Sudbury after failure in London. Death of his father 1748.

There would have seemed to be relatively little chance of them meeting, and certainly not on an equal level. It was all very unsatisfactory and difficult to reconcile with the portrait from the Alexandra Theatre.

The comparisons and disparities of the two men's lives were interesting and puzzling – Garrick's as open as Gainsborough's was closed – and yet somehow I had to make them meet.

I began to see that if I could achieve this, I might reveal the secret of a great deal more, but to do so I would need to find new sources and, as most of them seemed to have been used, not to say over-used, I was at a loss as to where to turn. I did have a set of people in common to both men to research, and I could only hope that I would, in this way, find out something that had been overlooked, using the picture as a starting point, a focus, perhaps a catalyst – a charming, silent witness to unlock the past.

December 7th: John Copley rang me today from Covent Garden.

Joan Sutherland is in town with her husband Richard Bonynge to do some performances of *Maria Stuarda*. She is wearing her own dresses and doesn't want to put on black velvet for the last Act.

John wants to enlist my help to persuade her (and Ricky, by the sound of it). Don't know what I can do. A bit of luck; looked through my Victorian song sheets to find Joan a small, silly present for the first night, and came across a lovely copy of Mary Stuart's Prayer, complete with a soulful picture of Mary, *in black velvet*! That should do it. I shall give it to Ricky, who likes old music covers – I remember seeing some in their house.

It is lovely to hear opera in the morning. Joan in good voice and apparently good form. Ricky bad-tempered and pretty rude from the pit. However, gets his come-uppance. After stopping Joan yet another time in front of everyone and making her go back, *he* made a mistake. Joan had just got on to her knees for the plea to Elizabeth. Mary Stuart vanished and left in her place a very comical Australian with shades of Mae West. 'Well, dears,' (to everyone) 'it seems *we* were wrong again.' Everybody laughed and the tension was defused. Ricky was like a lamb for the rest of the rehearsal.

She liked the song sheet and she agreed to the black velvet. I played along with John and said things like 'but nobody would dream of *not* wearing black, it always looks so good', plus a lot of historical rubbish about Mary being in mourning; so black it is.

Leaving the theatre later in my battered Morris, I saw Joan standing on the street corner trying to hail a taxi! They hadn't even got a car to take her to her fitting, so I gave her a lift. It was nice to be able to talk to her without lots of people around. My Morris is hardly the best car to transport the greatest prima donna in the world, nor the most comfortable considering how much of Joan there is, clutching at shopping bags in mountains of mink.

We talked about our children; her boy seems to be doing very well. He has gone into the hotel and catering business. We are gossiping so much that I nearly drive the wrong way around Trafalgar Square. EMI would die if they could see one of their most valuable properties at risk in my car, with my driving.

When we arrived at Hartnell's the doorman ignored us until he realised who was in the car. Then he overdid it and jammed the car's door handle and Joan couldn't get out. Joan started to laugh and became unable to move at all. We held up the traffic for at least ten minutes. The door eventually gave way and she sailed into the place, still laughing. If the Garden had provided a car (which they should have done) there would have been more dignity about her arrival, but less fun. No other country treats artists quite so badly as this one. Joan fills the Opera House – surely they could show their appreciation by making a bit of a fuss of her.

In the context of the now ever-present Garrick/Gainsborough search, Covent Garden and its surroundings had a new significance. Edward Shepherd, the architect, had built much of it for the fourth Duke of Bedford. He had also worked on the Goodman's Fields Theatre; another name to add to my possible links.

December 12th: An American writer, George Baxt, is here because a play of his is going to be done by Sian Phillips – Spine Chiller. *He is very excited and very nervous and very wearing.*

George was lovely years ago when I did a series with Edmund Purdom. It was called *Sword of Freedom* and one of the more polite titles we had for it was 'Sword of Boredom'. It was set in the Renaissance, with socialist overtones (the writers were all fugitives from the McCarthy witch-hunt), and I was the comedy relief, a sort of Florentine Lucille Ball. George used to sit in a room near the shooting stage with a book entitled *A Hundred Best Plots* and rehash them so they could take place in Italy, sixteenth century. We had some excellent writers, including Ring Lardner Jr, who was later to write *Mash*. George has since had a great success with some very good detective novels, where the detective was a gay, coloured cop. It was all very avant-garde a few years ago, but there is not much that can be written now on those lines that can be news. I haven't read the play but I have a bad feeling about it, I don't know why.

I like George, but he becomes more like a Brooklyn Bette Davis every time I see him.

Suddenly the Pink Panther struck again. One day's filming in a church in Clapham! Clouseau's funeral. Nothing to do except sit in a pew in black and watch Herbert Lom be brilliant. Now I have the photographs of Davy; he goes everywhere with me. Blake Edwards, and anyone who would listen, got the Gainsborough Lecture. I think Blake eyes me a little warily now. He says the church looks just like France! At least it is dry. We are to do the scenes we didn't shoot next year. I have lost my script; will have to get another.

The Christmas of 1977 was, in many ways, a turning point for me. I entered a new phase in which I realised my life no longer centred on the family, nor even on my profession of the last thirty (God help me!) years. A Thurber image impinged itself with renewed meaning on my life – it was the cartoon of the husband and wife, with the caption, 'You're disenchanted, I'm disenchanted, we're *all* disenchanted.'

December 22nd: Bloody Christmas and I feel like Scrooge!

All the tinsel and forced jollity. I used to love it when the children were little. I know it is my fault; I think I want those days back again too much. I am beginning to feel terribly distanced from them both. I am making the mistake of trying to keep them 'children', at an age where they interested me most because fresh minds are always fascinating. I make a stab at what is expected of me, in other words to be like everyone else's mother, but it isn't working. My heart sinks at the thought of the charade of Christmas, *and* their respective new boy and girl friends. The plain truth is, we would all be happier with friends of our own choice, but instead we re-enact the ghost of Christmas Past.

I am like an athlete training for a fight – I loathe turkeys!

Patrick and Sarah partly humour me and we do a ritual of getting the Christmas tree, last-minute shopping at Hatchards, and tea at Fortnum's. Presents to their grandparents in Ireland via Floris – and suddenly I love Christmas again as much as I ever did! Perhaps it is the run-up to it that makes me feel sour.

My son and daughter, not unnaturally, wanted to spend New Year with their friends, and I was left to clear up the debris of the 'holiday'. As I took the Christmas tree down, with its attendant mess of pine needles, I swore it would NEVER HAPPEN AGAIN!

George Baxt insists I spend New Year with him. I can't think of any way to say no without hurting him, so we go to Provans in Fulham. At least Wayne Sleep is there – he's all right. I last saw him at the dancer, Sally Ashby's, wedding where we danced a pas de trois in the Crush Bar of the Opera House with Sergeant Martin. He says there were some very funny photographs taken, none of them in focus I should think (and hope). I must make a New Year resolution *not* to remember my ballet training when I get sloshed – two glasses and I become the Thurber lady kicking her height. I wouldn't mind feeling like that tonight, but, sober and gritty, I say goodbye to 1977.

Why must the holiday last so long? I just want to get back to Garrick and Gainsborough.

1978

As soon as Arthur Lucas had made the picture presentable, I tried to interest some of the curators of the leading galleries in seeing it. The lack of response was deafening, as was the scepticism in the National Gallery itself from the others in the restoring department. They were kind, but they treated me as a kind of oddity, a whim of Arthur's, on the same level of amusement value as when Arthur had once decided, by way of relaxation, to build a boat in the cleaning rooms. I didn't mind being patronised and humoured, or the mild jokes at my expense, but their attitude did make me worry about the fate of other pictures and how much was lost or not recognised.

I realised that the necessity to date it so much earlier than any other known portrait was the root cause of their indifference, for it really had no right to exist. The elation I had felt started to evaporate. I knew I would have to fight tooth and nail to get them to see it with my eyes. The picture of Garrick did not fit into any acceptable niche and questioned the experts' scholarship. I had to equal theirs, and even surpass it, before I could convince them.

My main task in 1978, therefore, was to turn myself into an expert in the field of eighteenth-century art and artists, a genealogist (in order to find Collingwood), and a historian on what seemed to be an already far too well-documented century. There were moments when I wished I had left David Garrick on the walls of the Alexandra Theatre, but the search was on and there was no turning back.

January 3rd: The year has been very slow in starting. I can make no progress in the Lester Collingwood enquiries. I can't even find a death certificate for him.

I had written to Sir Hugh Casson, who was an old friend. He had done the sets for a disastrous musical by John Osborne in 1958 (in which I had the doubtful distinction of changing into a man, one of the few legitimate laughs in the piece). He is a lovely man and no matter how busy he may be, he always has time to help. He has infinite patience, which is probably why he is such a good president of the Royal Academy. He alsc advised me to write to John Hayes at the National Portrait Gallery re my picture. I had been rash and telephoned. The response had not been encouraging, to say the least. I was very dashed – I had hoped John Hayes would come and look at the picture but although it was only next door, he seemed reluctant to do so.

Garrick's bicentenary was coming up, and I had thought that a nice new portrait of him would be a fine way for it to be celebrated in a major gallery, whether it was by Gainsborough or not.

In his later years, as the most successful actor of his time, he was able to dictate his 'image' to artists. In the Gainsborough in the National Portrait Gallery his double chin is carefully shaded, his nose more aquiline, his eyebrows carefully shaped. He was one of the first to use the trick of plucking the hair between the brows to accentuate the eyes – we use this method to this day. He was a tremendous snob and his later portrait is that of the actor as a 'gentleman', an image he was anxious to project to counter the seamy reputation of the theatre of his time. The picture I had found had none of these affectations. He was young and didn't need them.

I like the beginning of things, and those two young men had become so very real to me. There was a vitality on that canvas that *had* to be recognised. I felt a sort of duty to it, and to them; not the famous Garrick and Gainsborough, but to the ones challenging the future. I was in love with the moment of the picture. Arthur said to me one day, 'Don't you wish he was alive?' Sadly, I didn't; he was probably like so many actors I know. Oliver Goldsmith's epitaph tended to confirm this view, ending:

> On stage he was natural, simple, affecting;
> 'Twas only that when he was off he was acting.

Bless him – a typical actor. That moment caught on the canvas in 1742 was quite enough for me.

Nineteen seventy-eight, apart from the picture, did not show much sign of improving on 1977. I caught a dreadful bout of a malignant flu bug, accelerated by trying to help Nicholas Parsons' wife find a dress for her appearance on *This Is Your Life – Nicholas Parsons!* As everything has to be kept secret from the unfortunate subject (the programme is scrapped if he finds out), it was difficult to make up excuses to Nicholas as to why his wife and I had to go shopping *every* day.

We went to Jean Muir first, but her clothes were too understated and we needed something for Denise that made her feel more spectacular. We went day after day to every shop in town. I wanted to kill her – in one shop they gave me champagne because I looked so exhausted. Finally, I shoved her into a beautiful Zandra Rhodes (our fourth visit to the same shop) and that was that.

During the frantic dress shopping I had met Peter Hall in a restaurant. He was immediately stuck with the instant Gainsborough Lecture, which he took very well. The National has Somerset Maugham's collection of theatre pictures, and among them are several of Garrick. Peter was interested, saying if I needed any help I could go and refer to the Maugham ones at any time. There is a portrait of Garrick by Van Loo which looks quite different from mine. It is dated *c.* 1742. He looks much older in it and I very much doubt its attribution. It has been used as an unfavourable comparison against mine by one of the National Portrait lot, a John Kerslake, a friend of Arthur Lucas. He doesn't think mine is of Garrick either.

The programme was a success; Denise looked great. We told Nicholas the cost of the dress later (it was in the hundreds). If we had told him before he might have died and there would have been no programme.

January 5th: George Baxt's play Spine Chiller *opened and was fairly disastrous.*

It is the most dreadful thing I know to go to a friend's first night and see it fail. Sian was wonderful and looked marvellous, but she was fighting a losing battle. You can never judge what a play is like until it is before an audience. This play must have been fun to rehearse, but the joke just didn't come off. If it is your own first night that is a mess, you can at least do something about it. The John Osborne musical was about the biggest flop ever known to the West End stage, yet being in the thick of it had a kind of exhilaration for me – for the audience too, who practically threw the seats at us. I booed at them, which gave me a bit of satisfaction but scarcely raised the tone of the evening. The theatre is a mess of hazards, and I mean mess.

January 11th: Dashed in to see Hugh Casson at his house in Kensington.

I saw Hugh for only long enough to show him the Alexandra photographs. He was kind and encouraging but advised me to get new ones as soon as I could. He seemed to think the picture a nice one and gave me a little heart. He has promised all the help I need by way of introductions, etc., when I get a little further on with my research.

January 12th: Today when I went to the cleaning rooms I had a wonderful surprise. Garrick was in the main, larger room hanging beside Madame de Pompadour.

The contrast between the dirty, neglected picture I had found and worked on last year and the way he looks now was so great that it nearly made me cry. The freshness and vivacity nearly leap off the canvas, almost as if Garrick is anxious to be seen at his youngest and best. It seems a very mature work, and this does worry me. It is far better than many that are at present dated well into the 1750s; either their dating is wrong or mine is. Arthur Lucas thinks it is by Gainsborough, and he has cleaned most of his other work now hanging in the main gallery downstairs, including the famous *Morning Walk*. He thinks I will never convince the 'experts'; I will, and I must, even if I die in the attempt. This picture must be recognised.

January 26th: Arthur is going to start the rebacking soon so the picture will be out of sight for some time.

I go in every day I can to look at him. Even unvarnished I still love what I see. There is so much to do on the research side I scarcely know where to begin. It really is very difficult.

My days and my diary began to be filled with meetings with curators and visits to places for the research. Using Covent Garden and the Bedford patronage as a starting point, I wrote for permission to look at the Bedford Archives. They are wonderfully complete and were a good way to begin what was to become a way of life. Until the picture is rebacked and properly photographed, I have to content myself with exploring every avenue to find its background.

Marie Draper, the Bedford archivist, was more than helpful. She was keen and interested and sent me anything she could find that might be of use to me.

February – most of the month: The Bedford Archives have not yielded too much except some receipts and some names connected with Goodman's Fields, which was on Bedford land.

The fourth Duke seemed passionately interested in the theatre, even paying for scenery directly, and for a lawsuit when Garrick and other actors were not paid. Gainsborough's portrait of him makes him look like an amiable bulldog. He made Covent Garden into an arts centre. Houses were rented to artists, actors and musicians at peppercorn rents, and because of this you can find out where studios were and who lived where and for how long. Canaletto had a house on the estate. The Garrick/Bedford connection is well documented. I cannot, as yet, find out exactly where the Gainsborough/Bedford one begins.

I sent letters to libraries and museums and started to compile a collection of every photograph I could find of Garrick at all ages. A couple of them struck me as being very similar in the face to my picture: one was of Garrick in his garden, leaning on the balustrade of a little summer house, looking up at his wife. She is enchanting, very smart and not at all in the English style of dress for the time; very European and chic. He plays an adoring husband and wears a coat of buff, much the same colour as in my portrait and the later Gainsborough in the National Portrait Gallery. It was obviously part of his image throughout his life.

Olivier, when he was young, always wore dark suits to set off his rather gipsy complexion. Buff must have been Garrick's favourite colour for himself. The garden picture is by Zoffany, who painted Garrick many times, so he knew his face well. Although there must be twenty years between the one I am working on and this picture, it is the same man, I would swear it.

The other picture was Hogarth's dramatic one of Garrick as Richard III. The face was exactly (to me at least) like the face of my man in make-up, even to the angle. I cannot understand why there has been any doubt that it is Garrick.

March 1st: I rang Roy Strong to ask if he could let me see some of the theatre collection which is sitting in boxes waiting to go to the, as yet unborn, museum in Covent Garden.

The Enthoven Collection has been waiting for a permanent home for years. It *would* be the moment I need it that they decide to pack it up. Once in those boxes God knows when it will be seen again. I must find out as much as I can about those early years.

Roy says he will come and look at Garrick when he can. I am given permission to try to find what I can in a wilderness of tea chests. There are some useful things about the first performances in London and the début in Ipswich. It seems to have been the centre for a lot of cultural activity. In the summer it was much healthier to leave London, and very prestigious for the local squires to bring a little of London to their friends. The country ladies in Sheridan's plays, or those of Congreve and Wycherley, talk of a London known only by these summer diversions, or the scandal sheets brought by more worldly friends. Actors came to Ipswich every year. There is not much written about Henry Giffard's company. He is described as an 'Irish actor-manager', a sort of eighteenth-century Bill Kenwright, I suppose. Nothing much else seems to be known about him other than the information Carola Oman's book had given me. I wish I had met her, but she died last year. Roy was related to her through his wife, Julia Trevelyan Oman, the designer. Roy is at present sorting out her estate. I can't get much more from the boxes available to me. Next stop, Ipswich and Gainsborough's House.

April 4th: Have to go to Sudbury to see the Gainsborough's House Museum.

Sudbury was a bit of a waste of time. I arrived a little early and the young curator and his wife were rather put out. He says he doesn't know much about the eighteenth century or Gainsborough come to that, and hadn't had much interest in him until he got this job. He did Modern Art, and the gallery downstairs is filled with rather nasty, trendy stuff, nothing to do with the house or Gainsborough. Funnily enough, I don't feel the house has much to do with him anyway. The nicest thing there is a work desk, supposed to be his, but all the things seem to have been collected after his supposed time there.

It is a very pretty house, on the main street, but curiously it doesn't have much atmosphere. They asked me to stay to lunch and we whisked out and got an extra chop and some wine. They have two small children, and at least it seems to be a nice home, but everything was in a bit of a muddle.

I can't quite explain my feelings about the house. It is just not right. There is a portrait of Sir Thomas Vere, which is in a very tight style, the closest I have seen to my Garrick. The waistcoat and the embroidery are almost the same pattern. The catalogue is full of rubbish, judging from what I have been able to find out about Gainsborough in this short time. Supposition given the assurance of fact. I don't know who wrote it. I wish I could be half as assertive with so little foundation.

April 6th: Today the rebacking process will begin and I will see the picture for the last time for a few weeks.

I went to the National Gallery side door, the tall one beside the steps. I always got rather a kick out of going in that door – it made me feel very official. Usually it was opened by a security guard, but this day was different. One of the female secretaries opened the private door in floods of tears. Inside it was worse. Everyone was in tears, even strong guards!

It took me a long time before I could get an explanation, but finally I was told. Someone had slashed the Poussin *Moses and the Children of Israel Worshipping the Golden Calf*. It is one of the gallery's great treasures, one of the world's greatest pictures, or rather, was. They had closed the main galleries and the police were in charge. The only people not weeping were the science department. They were beside themselves with delight, sweeping up the tiny bits of paint which lay on the ground, and conserving them carefully. Now they would know exactly what pigments Poussin used in his paints. It's an ill wind ... !

The picture wasn't there. Nothing remained of it except a fringe of canvas around the edges. The rest lay on the ground in shreds or hunks, already curling at the edges; it was the most expensive jigsaw in the world. After the police had finished taking photographs, the bits were placed carefully on large trays and taken to the restoration department. Arthur was to be the one to put the jigsaw together again. It was the most dreadful sight; so stupid. In one moment a maniac had reduced an exquisite piece of philosophy, beauty and geometry to chaos. The keepers in the gallery were utterly shattered. They care deeply about the pictures. The man had gone to the tea room and taken a knife back with him. And they search women's handbags! It wasn't the knife that did the real harm. After the initial attack, the man had been pulled away by other visitors to the gallery and the guards, but he managed to get free and in seconds had torn the rest of the picture out with his bare hands. This had done the worst damage. Just as it happens with any cloth, the canvas had been pulled out of shape, long threads snarled so that even the areas not affected by the direct cuts had been disturbed and distorted. To put it together again, the canvas will have to be made wet enough to allow the weave to shrink into something like its original shape, and only then can they attempt to restore it – if they can. Arthur's usual cheer was gone; he looked very, very tired and rather ill. I neglected David Garrick. The whole of the gallery seemed to pay their last respects to the corpse. Arthur couldn't speak. I took my last look at Davy and, in deep gloom, we left the National and went round the corner to a very good and sympathetic Australian wine bar. Arthur perked up again after a glass of champagne. 'I can't work any more today,' he said, tackling his second glass much more cheerfully. Some of the National Portrait people joined us; the news had got round and we tried to work out what political convictions could have caused the attack. Was he anti-Semitic? Had he got anything against calves? The calf was, after all, a representation of

Mammon. Was he against the rich? Two hours later none of us cared much about the motive. I poured Arthur on to his train and went home. I had looked at my own picture for the last time for four months.

April 10th: Sudden telegram to go out to France to finish my bit in the Pink Panther.

I had forgotten all about it and I have cropped my hair! It is quite different from the last time we filmed. Thank God I was wearing a hat, though not a large one – please don't let Blake Edwards notice.

They are very behind schedule, the filming in Japan went on for ever. My one decent scene with Robert Webber no longer exists, so all I have is a scene in a graveyard at Clouseau's funeral. I lost the script ages ago and never asked for another – let's hope the scene is not a long one. I notice a wonderful bit of chauvinism in the Charles de Gaulle airport, a notice saying, 'Si vous avez un cardiaque mécanique, informez la Douane'. This I take to mean a pacemaker, so I go and check; I am quite right, but the notice is only in French. 'What,' I ask, 'about the English, Italians, Germans, Japanese, etc., who may not speak French?' (Apparently the metal detector doors stop such machines.) 'That is their look-out,' say the Customs, falling about at their own joke. I must warn the film company; Peter Sellers has a pacemaker.

We are all staying in yet another monstrous modern hotel in Nice, the top floor of which is a beauty parlour, sauna, the lot. The place is like a very grand bordello, *poules de luxe* everywhere in fabulous dresses; noisy at night, to say the least. I don't do anything until the last day, so I have a very happy week wandering about making friends with the locals, including a lovely old Italian who owns a bistro and knew my father, and who brought out his best wine for me; and a lovely organ-grinder with a little monkey who is *enceinte* and who wears a little smock! The working day I spent in a cemetery in the hills.

Robert Webber is without the cold but no better tempered; Peter, dressed as a priest and being far too jokey, blessing nuns and that sort of thing. Lynne, his wife, seems to think he is wonderful and repeats all his jokes. She was my vampire daughter in a Hammer film years ago. I always knew she would go far. We get to the scene. Webber has no more idea about it than I have, although we both vaguely remember that I am supposed to be blackmailing him. 'You begin,' he snarls out of the corner of his mouth, and I am on my own, so we both 'wing it'. Blake can't remember it either; one take, print and wrap. My part is over. I needn't have worried about the hair.

Sue Lloyd is on the film too, and we have planned to go out to celebrate. She was my ex-husband's girl friend for a short spell before we had made up our minds to get married. 'I was in between you and you,' she explains. She is curious to know how I coped with Dan and his tantrums. Once, after a row with her, he locked himself in a wardrobe and refused to come out. That wouldn't have been so bad but she couldn't get at her clothes and had to go to work in a nightdress and jeans – sounds like the life that I once led. When she came back he was still in the wardrobe.

We have a good evening; the crew is very tired, Jimmy Liggatt in a state of hysterical giggles. They have to finish a scene begun in Japan, and Blake has asked him to find twenty matching Japanese!

The plane back next day is filled with French mayors visiting their twinned towns in England. They insist I join them, and I leave the plane filled to the gills with caviare and champagne.

The need to earn my living kept intruding, and I was hauled away from Garrick and Gainsborough by accumulations of bills.

April 18th–May 19th: Agreed to play the part of Mistress Overdone in the BBC's version of Measure For Measure.

It was a quiet nightmare. As it was a project partly financed with American money and intended to be used (to bore unfortunate young Americans to death) as the 'definitive Shakespeare', the whole thing took place with a superimposed cultural 'hallowing'. Earnest young Americans were putting the actors' opinions about their parts and the play on tape, and a professor, who was writing some sort of accompanying book, was in attendance all the time. Also he was to be consulted as to the meaning of words and pronunciation. The result was a strait-jacket on performers and play alike. Kate Nelligan was the lead as the novice-nun, Isabella, and had sufficient intensity and sincerity to carry it off in spite of the atmosphere. I had that splendid actor, Frank Middlemass, playing my Pompey; as most of my scenes were with him it was some relief, but not enough for either of us. Frank has a splendid sense of humour and this was the last thing we were called upon to exercise, even though our parts were the low comedy bits of the play. I tangled with the professor only once. There is a bit of double talk before Overdone's first entrance as the owner of the bordello, and it confused the young actor saying it no end, so he asked for assistance. It was a tricky play on words containing phrases about 'thrice-cut French velvet'. The professor went on at great length about Elizabethan fashions until I could stand it no longer, and anyway it was only making the actor more puzzled. The references were to having had the pox three times, the 'French' disease at that time in England and the 'English' disease in France – dissertations on slashed sleeves were getting us nowhere. I butted in with this explanation and the young man accepted it happily – at least it helped him say the line but I don't think it appeared in the American textbook. The play was pretty awful, sanitised beyond all help. So depressing to think of this lifeless thing being held up as the best of British acting and drama.

The English theatre at its best is a theatre of personalities. There are no two ways about it, a leading role is best when it is played as a lead. A king cannot creep on to a stage telling you that he is just one of the boys really and quite ordinary. If he is, what is he doing on that stage? Garrick's Richard III was such a great king that the bailiffs tried to seize his crown backstage, thinking it was real. Financial difficulties were, even then, part of an actor's life.

April 24th: I went down to Woburn to see if I could find anything to show an earlier link with Mr G., but not much luck.

It was a bad day. The present Marchioness of Tavistock, née Henrietta Tiarks, was being posed beside some car she was advertising. I had met her a few times when she was a deb, but she looked so fed up and gritty that I didn't interrupt the photographic session to remind her of our acquaintance. It must be a ghastly place to live, a sort of stately Butlin's. There is even a suite that guests can stay in (paying a large sum for the honour) and have dinner with the Tavistocks thrown in. Awful; no privacy and very hard work, too. The building must cost a fortune to keep up, an enormous staff and open all the year round.

I was given every bit of help I needed, and had one bit of luck in an old inventory (superb library); the landscapes, which are generally thought to have been painted for Woburn, did not arrive there until the early part of the nineteenth century, and came from the London House, and one of the portraits of the Duke could be earlier as it was seen in Dublin just after he was Lord Lieutenant in 1756–57. Given that, and the dates of the landscapes, he must have known Gainsborough earlier than the Bath period, yet until then there is no real evidence of patronage on his part, or of any connection. One of the many puzzles starting to emerge – why should he choose an unknown country painter to do landscapes and a portrait? He can have hardly gone to Suffolk for his sittings, so they must have been in London when, according to every book, Gainsborough was only just being 'discovered' by that nasty Philip Thicknesse in Ipswich.

As I left they were still trying to photograph the car which had decided to break down. If they don't finish soon (it has been four hours) it seems very likely that the Marchioness will join it!

May 18th: I went to the Rowlandson exhibition at the Royal Academy with Carl Toms.

He is one of the few people I can go to a show with and not get irritable. David Walker is the other – there the list ends. Carl wanders about like a lovely elegant greyhound, we get drawn to the same pictures and don't talk. I hate people who feel obliged to say something. The last time we were at the Academy together was the 'Light Fantastic', and I bullied him into becoming a 'friend', which means a sort of member of the 'best value' club in town. You can go to all the exhibitions for a mere £10 and take a friend at no extra charge. When we went to the 'Light Fantastic' exhibition it was the last day, and Carl was fascinated by the holographs. There were some sets by Ralph Koltai using the lighting techniques, but it was all very smoky and smelt, well, as far as I was concerned, herbal. It was only when we fell over the bodies littering the ground that we realised every hophead in

London was there, getting high. The Academy could have been busted. The Rowlandson is a more sedate affair.

Afterwards, tea at Fortnum's. I rushed out without thinking today and threw on all the wrong colours. Carl flinches but does not comment. He makes me feel like a great clumsy carthorse. I am in all the wrong shades of red and pink – he avoids looking at them like the plague. He is in toning greys.

The year of 1978 did not improve: Ursie, my children's grandmother on their father's side, whom (for reasons that have no place here) they had only known for three years, became very ill. Part of my diary for the next few weeks is taken up with this, and her subsequent death.

Due to complicated family feuds, my children's father, Patrick, dislikes his stepfather, Stephen. As he is an invalid, Stephen must go everywhere with his manservant, Gerard.

Ursie is to be flown over to the Nuffield Clinic for treatment. Stephen can stay with me.

May 26th: The weather is stifling, hot and heavy.

Ursie seemed to respond a little to treatment, but it was only for a few days. She died on Sunday, June 4th.

The funeral is to be near Chester, on the tenth. My son is coming down from Newcastle, even though he is in the middle of exams; Sarah is being a tower of strength – she looks so like Ursie when she was young. At the last moment their father, Patrick, has asked me if I would like to go down to Chester and stay with the family before the funeral. I would not. Perhaps I should for the children's sakes, but the less I see of them the better.

The funeral was macabre. Patrick was at the gate of the church with poor Josephine, his wife, whom I hadn't seen since the days she was a Rank starlet. We went into the right-hand side of the pews, behind Ursie's immediate family: her sister and Patrick and Josephine, with Serena who had been so kind to Pat in Yorkshire. Serena was very upset – she and Ursie were cousins and had their coming-out ball together. She is the only one of the bunch who seems human. I think Ursie was always rather the glamorous one of the family to her.

Why is there always something so risible about funerals? This one was quite particular in that respect. The left-hand side of the church held the current lot; the old Duke, bad-tempered, as all get out, with a game leg. The younger ones rather blank, quite good looking, shorter than Pat or Sarah and darker in colouring. That family face, on both sides of the aisle, male and female. Sibby, Ursie's cousin, in a hat. She looked very odd (she is Master of the Gloucestershire Hunt), but then so did all the hats – more race meeting than funeral. I may be biased, but Sarah and Pat looked the best of the lot, Sarah with that marvellous hair down to her waist, Pat in his C & A suit – money is *not* everything. It all went to the vicar's head, having so many duchesses in his congregation; he didn't miss one of Ursie's names or titles. I could almost hear her saying, 'Oh come on, get on with it!'

The coffin looked so small. The choir was hysterically funny; middle-aged ladies in mortar boards.

Serena broke down completely at the end and I suddenly saw my son's arm go round her protectively. Then the coffin was taken up the aisle, followed by Stephen with Gerard snuffling, pushing the wheelchair. Mary Grosvenor, Ursie's sister, looking like Gertrude Stein in a hacking jacket, went next, then Patrick, and then a pause, for Pat and Sarah, the first and only time – and probably the last – that the rest of the family has ever acknowledged them.

The graveside was farcical, too. Another grandson leaned on the tombstone weeping loudly and mopping his face with a large and rather dirty handkerchief. Everyone tried to pretend he wasn't there. He was very like the Walrus in *Alice* – Ursie had provided the oysters in his life and now the source had been cut off.

Then we went back to Nancy Westminster's; only Stephen, the children and myself. The others split in several directions. Serena was going to drive straight back to Richmond, she was too upset to see anyone. We had a fairly grisly tea with Nancy W. being hearty; at one point she came up from what appeared to be under the tea table with a large cigar clenched between her teeth. 'Nothing, I always say,' she said, 'like a good cigar!' I thought Sarah might burst trying not to laugh.

Ursie's sister lives in the Dower House at Eaton, so Nancy has to make do with a large kind of Victorian gatehouse in red brick, but to console her for the ugliness of the exterior she does have about eight of the most beautiful Stubbs I have ever seen. They also have a Gainsborough seascape, a dead painting in a way; one can see why he didn't paint many! Also numerous dreadful reproductions of *The Blue Boy*. The Stubbs, one gets the impression, are by way of being horse pictures first, great works second, because equal value is given to other, perfectly awful horse pictures. There is a picture of Bendor, the children's great-grandfather, at the top of the stairs. I don't know who painted it, but he did not like the old boy. It is a coarse, vulgar, choleric face. He is wearing hunting pink – there is something rather repellent about it. He had a long affair with Coco Chanel; Ursie told me a lot about him and Winston Churchill, who used to make pounces at Ursie when he got drunk, and he and Bendor used to recite 'Let there be no moaning at the bar' together. The yacht in Noel Coward's *Private Lives* was her father's, but there was also another one which Ursie used to take around Corsica and the Italian coast when she wanted to escape from him. I asked her why he had sold Gainsborough's great masterpiece, *The Blue Boy*. 'Oh, to get some extra pocket money, I think.' And here was I fighting for an unknown Gainsborough portrait that didn't even belong to me.

The weather was beautiful. On the way back we drove past the new house the present lot has built. The park is lovely, but Sarah and I gave an involuntary shriek when this dreadful thing hove into view. Behind very beautiful wrought iron gates is – a squat Hilton! Even the trees in front are horrible, yellow, privet umbrellas. The Georgian stables are lovely and the tower of the Victorian house Ursie knew stands there like a fugitive from the Houses of Parliament. Such a funny clutch of buildings. There is an equestrian of the first Duke, Hugh Lupus, hawking I think; it looks as if he is waving his hat – very odd. A statue of Arkle in front of the stables.

Later Stephen said, 'Nancy is so clever, she has made that little house look so pretty.' Anywhere would look pretty with those Stubbs.

My son, Pat, said next day, 'Mum, why should people who sell *The Blue Boy* have plaster replicas of it stuck all over the place?' Well might he ask.

I asked Stephen about Mary Grosvenor. It would have been impossible to guess that she and Ursie were sisters, she certainly doesn't look very feminine as Ursie did. He suddenly looked rather vague. 'Poor Mary – glands, you know.'

June 13th: I have joined the Society of Genealogists.

It is in South Kensington, a glorious muddle of information and confusion, reference books on every county, some in longhand from zealous local historians. It takes a bit of finding your way around. There is a certain amount of one-upmanship from the staff, but mostly help. I am a fool, but I seem to have a kind of 'shelf luck', in so far as I have found a few bits of information on Gainsborough by instinct, nothing else.

My frustrations over Lester Collingwood continued. I began to think he was a figment of the theatre's imagination. So far, I was learning the ropes at the Society of Genealogists but getting nowhere. I could not even find a background for him in the theatre world; it was as if he had never existed until he had bought the Alexandra in 1902. Various suggestions were made by other researchers, amongst them the proposition that he had come back to England from America or Australia – possible, but no help to me for the picture.

Mr A. J. Camp, the expert on wills, thinks I am an idiot and shows it. I am determined to prove him wrong. I cannot tie up the Collingwood family in any way with the man who was at Birmingham. He may have been illegitimate, which would account for him not being on the family tree. I wish they would include these branches, they were so often fully accepted by the family; it makes things so confusing. Much easier and more sensible when the bar sinister is used – at least you know where you stand then.

June 16th: My son, Patrick, telephoned today.

He has got his degree, a First with Honours! He was so excited and surprised he couldn't speak. I was very worried that the gap he had taken from college when Ursie died might have held him back with his work, but obviously not.

June 19th: I have just heard that John Wedgwood is selling the Wedgwood portrait by Stubbs.

I met John years ago when I made a film with Peter Finch written by Wolf Mankowitz called *Make Me An Offer*. It was an excellent script, well directed and I was allowed to break an awful lot of Wedgwood. I came into conflict with Barbara Woodhouse and her Great Dane, Juno, a very amiable bitch, quiet to the point of inertia. She was my dog in the film and was in every scene with me. Consequently, Peter and I spent a lot of time with bits of meat flying past our noses as Mrs Woodhouse tried to keep an interested look on Juno's face. It made the scenes very difficult, especially as the meat-throwing was accompanied by encouraging whooping noises. Mrs Woodhouse thought we were unreasonable when we asked the director to restrain her. I got to know most of the Wedgwood family then, and have known them ever since.

None of the family wants the picture to be sold. John doesn't need the money. What will he spend it on? Another walking-tour in the Himalayas? I rang up and tried to make him change his mind – no good.

He won't tell me what his reserve is, bloody fool. I could find out easily from the auction house. I tried to convince him that it was much wiser to keep it, but all he would say is, 'I don't think so.' Like all the rich he has a terror of losing money. He seems to think that if he waits a revolution of some kind will break out and he, John Wedgwood, will be a pauper. Painted on an oval plaque made by Josiah himself, it is a unique work and is sure to leave the country; but John is utterly committed to public auction.

A public auction is so daft – when they are taking 10 per cent from the seller and 10 per cent from the buyer, how can the auction rooms be disinterested? It is a lunatic practice and bumps up the real price of everything by 20 per cent. The English museums just cannot compete. It will go to America in the end, I am sure – I really could kill him.

June 23rd: The Stubbs made £300,000 at auction, to be sold a week later for around £450,000.

John informed me that he intended to go on a tour of Pakistan and Afghanistan. When I pointed out that it could be a little dangerous and that I doubted if it would be possible, he replied, 'It is a package holiday', as if wars and revolutions stopped for them. He was quite put out when the tour was cancelled.

June 24th–July 27th: Jimmy Clellan Jones, head of drama at the BBC, has just phoned to ask me if I would like to be in a rather grand television version of Kean *by Jean Paul Sartre.*

I have never been happier than when playing Mary Amberley in Aldous Huxley's *Eyeless in Gaza* for Jimmy, he is a dream of a director, patient and kind and, wonder of wonders, likes actors. You feel he is with you, not against you. I am not mad about the part, the kind I am always getting stuck with; boring English lady, style and epigrams, but I don't care. The cast promises to be splendid – Robert Stephens as the Prince of Wales, Frank Middlemass again, Barry Ingham, Sara Kestelman, and Cheri Lunghi is the girl.

Tony Hopkins is to play Kean himself. I have only seen him in films up to now, and I remember Alan Badel on the stage, with Felicity Kendal as the girl being so funny. Maxine Audley played my part then, and even she had a job to make it register. There is only one small snag. Patrick gets his degree during rehearsals and I must be there. Jimmy has promised to let me have that one day off. It will be a great treat to work with him again.

It does no good to anticipate anything. Tony Hopkins seems brooding and bad-tempered, Jimmy a bit edgy because of this, but otherwise his cheerful self, doing his best to make us all feel happy and create a good atmosphere. Robert is in good form. Sara Kestelman seems nice, a sexy intellectual, no make-up, tight slit skirts (very good legs) and freckles (I suspect she will drive Robert wild).

The read-through seemed fine – a bit low-key; costumes will be splendid. Hopkins did not talk to anyone. Interesting eyes, very blue and intense. He is a sort of cut-price Richard Burton.

Rehearsals are dreadful. I suspect Hopkins realises he is wrong for the part. It needs size and bravura, and under the looks there seems to be a very small man roaring to get out.

Barry Ingham is lovely. He is very funny; he is playing the part of the Swedish Ambassador, Sara's husband, with the most outrageous yet accurate accent I have ever heard. Income tax nearly ruined him once and he spends most of his free time plotting to outwit it. He is manic about it; he has a small desk with him and very complicated calculators, and he lunches a lot with his accountant – carrying on his own personal vendetta. He also wears a bleeper so that his agent can contact him at any time.

Cheri Lunghi is quiet and very, very good. All her scenes are with Hopkins, so she will need patience.

Today Jimmy made some sort of suggestion – he is, after all, the director – and there was a muffled explosion from Hopkins and he swept out. We were all stunned, Jimmy quite white. Telephone calls were made all over the place to no avail. Hopkins did not return. Barry retreated to his computer, me to my research, Frank to *The Times* crossword, and we waited. There is not much that we can do in this play without the leading man. At five, a very depressed Jimmy let us go and said he would get the stage manager to let us know when (if) we were next needed. Next day, all seemed fine. Hopkins there, and not a word about the day before. Directly after lunch he had gone again. This time we all went up to the canteen and drank far too much BBC wine labelled 'Sans File'. Dreadful hangovers next day. The doorman looked at us and roared with laughter. We were all wearing dark glasses.

Hopkins stayed the whole of the next day, and the one after; we couldn't think what had gone wrong. Two days without incident, and just when we felt safe he was gone again. The following day I was due to go to Newcastle for Pat's graduation. Jimmy said I couldn't go and that made *me* angry and threaten to walk out! As if poor Jimmy needed it. He lost his temper, too, and it nearly became serious, when a young man who hadn't uttered much (and we all thought was a bit of a pain because he had been running around after Hopkins) said, 'I was on my own when I got my degree, and it was the worst day of my life.' His name was Julian Fellowes, and he shamed Jimmy into allowing me my promised day off.

We worked late next day. No sign of Anthony Hopkins, and no news; and Jimmy didn't let me go until late and I nearly missed the train to Newcastle. There was that great lump of a son waiting for me, looking so pleased with himself.

Next day we had a silly lunch with champagne. I overdid it, I wanted a celebration for us both; even Newcastle seemed quite attractive. Then back to London and the Acton Hilton.

That day was Jimmy's birthday; Hopkins seemed to feel obliged to leave again, even though we had organised a small birthday party. We have become almost blasé about it – still, it made the party fairly gloomy. I had brought a good sharp knife to cut the cake and suggested that Jimmy keep it for some other similar occasion (and actor). We get on so well apart from this one, very big, fly. This time it was Jimmy who offered to resign. It seems Hopkins doesn't want to work with him. We reminded Jimmy that we are there because *we do*, and if he goes, so do we. In the end an uneasy truce is the result. It means that Hopkins goes his own way at the expense of everyone else, especially poor Cheri Lunghi, who is marvellous with him.

The last days of *Kean* are in Bury St Edmunds in the Regency Theatre. It is meant to be Drury Lane, and we have the immense treat of watching Hopkins play the scene of Othello for three sweltering days. He looks very odd in a replica of Kean's original costume and a freak-out hairdo. He has a tag around his neck. I asked Barry what he thought was written on it. 'If found please return immediately to Los Angeles,' he replied. He really is very funny. I heard him say during rehearsals, when Frank admired a sweater he was wearing, 'I knitted it during the walkouts.' He is giving up the theatre after this and emigrating, he says, and he means it.

At one point, I notice tears running down Cheri's face during the scene. She has never complained.

There is little time left to do anyone else's scenes. Some of the best moments have to go. The atmosphere is glacial whenever Hopkins is around; even he has noticed it and tries (too late) to be ingratiating. No one except Fellowes can bear to speak to him. His wife is with him, a shadowy lady who seems entirely given over to pampering the great actor.

There is a party afterwards. Even the crew has joined in sympathy. One thing Hopkins has done is to unite the entire unit and cast. The next day Jimmy drove me back to London; he is resigning as head of drama. Apparently, I had said something that triggered off all that he had been feeling about the Beeb when we had our row about Newcastle. I said he had lost his humanity (what a lousy crack), but he is sick of all the administration and feels that a few more years would make what I had said true. He is such a good director; it was killing him, all the red tape of the Corporation. He is going back to do a film – I am glad. He isn't going to look at *Kean* for a month or two; he says he doesn't know how he will cut it together.

None of us will forget Anthony Hopkins.

August 1st: With the picture under wraps, there is very little to do except research and take the photographs and the evidence I am building up to as many of the recognised authorities as possible for their opinion.

Now I have nearly every early picture of Garrick in my folder, and I can't see how they are so adamant about it not being him. There seems to be a wish to prove it wrong in every way. I am miserable about it. I had thought they would be pleased to have a nice new portrait of Garrick for the bicentenary, but the general reaction seems to be of bad temper that it exists at all. The theatre board behaves as if I am dragging my feet, and is not very helpful. Some relatives of Collingwood's came into the Alexandra last week, and the manager never told me or took an address. I could not believe it, it might have saved me so much time. All part of the fear that someone might lay claim to the picture. I nearly cried when he told me. They apparently live in Portugal. He said he couldn't remember their name. I try to tell him how hard it is to get anyone to accept that a seedy (for that's how he sounds) actor-manager could have had a Gainsborough of Garrick. I don't blame people for being sceptical, I would be myself. It is only the quality of the picture itself that makes me persist, and in spite of the fact they say it is not Gainsborough, they cannot come up with another attribution. I go into the National to see Arthur regularly, and he is on a sort of hydraulic crane in front of the Poussin. It is taking up all his time, and Garrick is still face downwards being unglued from the other canvas, so I can't even look at him to cheer myself up.

I have done one bit of work that has at least satisfied David

Walker that it *is* Garrick. I was looking at the photographs one evening and tried a tracing of the Richard III make-up from the Hogarth and it fitted perfectly. There is even a lovely touch of actor's vanity in the way he puts the beard over his double chin to hide it.

The Hogarth portrait is at the same angle as my picture, and as it is a young Garrick as well, *c.* 1745, it is good for the age factor too.

Poor Julian Fellowes, I feel I have been rather hard on him. I think he genuinely admired Hopkins in a dog-like, devoted way, and God knows the man needs friends. Julian is much younger than I thought him at first. He was born looking middle-aged, so perhaps that is some excuse. He is a good historian, too, so that is another plus. He turned up on the doorstep the other day without warning (something I generally hate); he had just had some very bad news concerning his mother's health and needed to talk to someone. I was rather touched that he had come round to me, although sometimes it is easier to talk more freely to a virtual stranger when you are very upset, like conversations with people on trains. I gave him tea and then asked, 'Why me?' 'Because although you were beastly to me, I didn't think you altogether loathed me.' Poor Julian. What a way to choose one's friends. He is a dreadful snob, so much so that it is almost disarming. He looked at the invitations on the desk and said enviously, 'Why do you get asked to go to so many places; no one ever asks me.' 'Because I don't go to them,' I replied. I loathe parties and my memory is so bad for names and faces that they are a nightmare to me, as are first nights – I always end up upsetting someone. Julian, on the other hand, loves them and remembers everyone, so we have made a bargain: he can take me to the next 'smart' do, if he will tell me the name of anyone heading towards me.

There is a portrait of a Colonel Bullock (high Bath period), and Julian knows one of the Bullock family and has promised to ask him to lunch. I would very much like to see the picture, as the hand holding the hat is very like my Garrick. The Bullock picture is in Marlborough House.

Julian arranged the lunch, which he cooked himself. Two rather nice deb girls, Osmond Bullock, Julian and me. It was rather like bachelor rooms in a university. Osmond is also interested in genealogy and says he will gladly help there. As I don't know what should be where, and am lousy on titles, etc., it will probably cut many corners if I can get them to help me. Osmond is an actor, too, I fear they are both more Home Counties than rogues and vagabonds. Julian cannot understand why there should be a gap, and although he is a very good actor, never feels accepted. It is hard to explain. The theatre is like a family – either you belong or you don't. You may not like all the relatives, but you recognise the link. Hopkins, much though I dislike him, is one of the family – Julian and Osmond will always be outsiders no matter how hard or how well they work. It is 'in the blood' and there is no getting away from it. Sadly, you cannot join or even be related by blood, which is why there are exceptions even in acting families.

I know I am a throw-back; there was no immediate theatre around me, and yet it is where I found 'home' as a child. The first time I ever stepped through the pass door and left the red velvet front-of-house for the smell and dirt of backstage, I knew which side of the curtain I preferred. It was a rehearsal of *Giselle* and the company manager had let me in to watch. I was about ten and dodging school as usual. After seeing those visions in Taglioni tulle, I crossed that fatal space of the pass door and my life was never the same again. The first thing that hit me was the smell of size and then the tattiness of the sets, the grubby shoes, the torn net, the sweat rolling down these ethereal creatures' faces – that all this could create the illusion I had just seen was a miracle. I wanted to be part of it, and from that moment nothing else would do. I recognised it; I had found where I belonged.

If the theatre is an illusion, it also has its legends and David Garrick is one of the greatest and most enduring. He is the father of modern theatre; he lifted a debased art from the gutter. He revived Shakespeare and, in doing so, made him popular not only in England but in Europe. He brought a new status to actors. Royalty received him, and when he died he was buried in Westminster Abbey not as an actor but as a poet ('Hearts of Oak' was one of his compositions). Acting had managed to get in by the back door, so to speak. His friend Samuel Johnson wrote, 'I am disappointed by that stroke of death that has eclipsed the gaiety of nations and impoverished the public stock of harmless pleasure.'

An ancestress of mine, Marie Riccoboni, translated all his works into French and they exchanged very flirty letters; he called her his 'sweet, witty barbarian', and her letters are full of shrieks and cries, half in English, half in French. A lot of 'Mon Dieu!' or 'Help! Help! Murder!' etc. – gossipy and charming, as if she were talking to him. One letter from him begins, 'My Dear, and Very Dear Riccoboni.' I did try to keep the name which had plagued me at school (so many Miss Brodie pronunciations), but it was not allowed and so Corri it had to be. He ends, 'I love You Ever and Ever, D. Garrick.' There are times when I feel this old flirtation is still going on at my expense.

When I first went to Italy and to my father's family house in Venice, I looked to see if anything remained of Marie's letters or writing. The house had been inherited by an aunt who sold souvenirs to tourists. Pretty revolting objects, glass animals and ashtrays, faintly reminiscent of open-heart surgery. It was a thriving business and for years she had packed these things into boxes firmly and safely with old papers from the attics. There was just enough left to see what had gone. Letters from Hume, Voltaire, Rousseau and, of course, the manuscripts of the novels. I sat there, amongst the scraps that remained. It wasn't worth saying anything: what was Voltaire to my Aunt Lola? Italians have little sense of the past on the whole. My father had never bothered to tell me about his family's early theatre history, nor my mother about her connections with the Corris (the musicians) until I was already part of the theatre. My Garrick painting is tied up with all this. If I can prove it is him I shall feel in some way that I have paid a debt; I shall have given something back for all that I have been given.

August 9th: David Garrick is out from under the rebacking process.

He looks a bit dull without his varnish, even so it is good to see him again. Arthur is going away and will continue the restoration when he gets back. Meanwhile, I think Garrick looks presentable enough to ask Roy Strong to give me his opinion.

September 13th: Roy was worried by the picture; he couldn't place him at all, but he does see that there are quite a few things about him which make him a possible first attempt by Gainsborough.

He thinks it is a puzzle picture, like a Holbein he is looking into at the moment. Roy is sure his picture is authentic but he doesn't think he will ever find the definitive proof. When a director of a museum admits to this kind of difficulty, what hope do I have? I feel very depressed. He can come up with no suggestions as to who else can have painted my David Garrick; he says he will rack his brains and get back to me if he can find anything positive, for or against.

I have arranged for the picture to go to Cooper's, the photographers, in early October. The tiny holes will all have been repaired by then, and Arthur will have varnished him. He's looking very good (the picture, not Arthur, who is his usual cheerful self again). I am sorry he is retiring, but I don't think he will be too unhappy. He brings a kind of life to the department. When he goes it will become much more Civil Service. There is an enormous Rubens in at the moment, taking up half the big cleaning room, a lovely, lush picture; but they are all very grand about it. 'Not all his own hand.' Well, perhaps not but it is huge and the figures are certainly Rubens, very lively and warm; beautiful composition. I don't see how anyone can expect those very large ones to be 'all his own hand', any more than the ceilings. It would have been impossible for him to have painted every inch. They are all such picture snobs. This one is from the Queen's collection. Anything after the fifteenth century is modern to the National Gallery.

Roy Strong advises John Hayes again. I would prefer to show Hayes pictures of Davy cleaned and revarnished; but that may not be possible for a month or more, so I shall take Roy's advice and send the early photographs. I feel I am wasting time. I would like to have something definite to send to Birmingham.

September 19th: To the National Portrait Gallery to look at Admiral Vernon.

Gainsborough's first 'grand' portrait is supposed to be of Admiral Vernon, MP for Ipswich in 1752. I couldn't find it in the NPG, where it is meant to be. Eventually, it was located in a cramped little office, half behind a filing cabinet. I had to climb up on a desk to see him properly. He is pretty dirty and neglected, much more loosely painted than Garrick, still with a great deal of similarity in style; the hand and sword seem almost identical. It is a shame to see him in such a state. So much for poor Gainsborough's first portrait. It is really quite awful how much there is backstage in museums that the public never sees. I don't understand why there can't be more interchange between them all so that provincial ones with small collections could benefit by having loans. Must get Arthur in to look at him.

September 25th: I knew sending John Hayes the old photographs had been a mistake.

Polite thanks, but no, definitely not by Gainsborough, although the date could be mid-1740s or thereabouts. I felt desperate for the theatre's sake; I had told them about Arthur Lucas' opinion and dreaded dashing their hopes. Still, there was no other positive identification, and the letter promised they would do their best to give me one.

It will be interesting to see what attribution they come up with; they say it should be easy. The Cooper's photographs will be ready this week and I will send those to Hayes. I will not show this refusal to the theatre until I can give them a re-attribution as a consolation prize. I feel terrible about raising their hopes, and yet I still think the picture is right, and so does Arthur.

I wish he would not regale me with stories about people spending their entire lives trying to prove pictures in vain. I do not intend to let that happen here, damn it! It is not even my picture, and yet I do love it.

September 28th: Tried to show Arthur the Admiral; strangely he is gone!

For cleaning and restoration, they say, and about time too. Funny it should happen so soon after my letter to John Hayes, which pointed out the similarity between Vernon and Garrick.

Arthur thinks it is not entirely coincidental.

The internecine warfare between the various museums is becoming more and more apparent to me. The National Portrait Gallery won't use the cleaning facilities at the National Gallery, even though it is next door, and uses a private firm which is, of course, more expensive. Perhaps that is why I can't even get John Hayes to come and look at the picture. I believe Michael Levey has seen it and said Zoffany. Dear God! Not only the date wrong, but nothing like Zoffany's style – my respect for these eminent gentlemen dwindles even more.

Looked at the Mentmore Fragonard. Why the hell was it left to a commercial dealer, David Carritt, to identify it, selling it at three times the price to the National? Is it, perhaps, because a lot of the best brains in the art world are on the commercial side, or is it that Carritt was prepared to take the risk? Even as a Van Loo, it was a good buy at the sale price; it would have done the museum no harm to buy first and research after, as Carritt did.

It is no use pleading budgets; they never buy until a picture has become inflated in price by dealers – *that* is what cripples the museums. Lack of taste and lack of courage are the main problems. I know many pictures in all the major galleries that are just simply not what they claim them to be. The Tate Constables are a very obvious example, and there are so many more. It is not just England; I got so angry about a so-called Luini in the Met. in New York that I asked for its provenance. They did all they could to get rid of me, including keeping me hanging around for two hours. When they saw I wasn't going to be put off, they confessed they knew it was wrong but it had been presented by the Kennedys and so they had to hang it. But it *does* do harm, in that the public is often presented with indifferent works and told they are masterpieces. They are, consequently, bored by them but don't know why, and the really good works are tarred with the same brush.

It is exactly because of the attitude I am faced with on the Garrick that such expensive mistakes are made, and so many appeals launched to 'save' pictures that should never have been in danger in the first place.

Then again, perhaps overpaying and overspending boosts the idea of the value of the purchase, on the basis that if £500,000 is spent on a picture it must be good, whereas getting it at £100,000 two weeks earlier is not news or prestige for the gallery who buys.

September 29th: John Kerslake (of the NPG) FEELS the picture is not of Garrick – official.

I knew already he didn't *think* so, but are feelings allowable as evidence? They don't take much notice of my few facts so far. If I had gone to them only with *feelings* about the picture, I don't think I would have stood any chance; as it is, it seems I don't have one as far as Dr Hayes is concerned. Still, he hasn't seen the picture and it is better than even the Cooper's photographs show, good though they are. Perhaps I can get him to change his mind.

October 4th: Letter from the assistant keeper of the NPG, Malcolm Rogers, (obviously Hayes is getting tired of my nagging).

Same thing: not Garrick, not Gainsborough. No alternative, however, but a 'competent professional hand'. This is all sight unseen of the picture itself.

October 10th: Late last night I got round to The Times. *First chance that day.*

I was utterly enraged by a letter from David Somerset trying to vindicate the selling of the Warwick Canalettos on the grounds that a 'private man' should be able to sell his own property. I tried to sleep but I was seething with rage at the hypocrisy of the letter, which did not point out the profit margin David Somerset might make as part of the gallery that instigated the sale. This temper kept me awake until the early morning, when I had to get up to send a letter to *The Times*:

> Mr David Somerset's letter (Oct. 10th) would be more persuasive and palatable were he not an art dealer with a profitable interest in Lord Brooke's possessions. His criticism of Mr Hugh Leggatt is in poor taste. Mr Leggatt is attempting to change a situation in which excessive taxation necessitates

> the sale of works of art which many families would prefer to retain, not only for themselves but for the nation. Lord Brooke is not a private person. If he wishes to be regarded as one he should renounce his title along with his inherited responsibilities. You cannot have your coronet and eat it.

My letter was duly published; you can always trust the editor to take and print a bad joke, but I did want to make a serious point. Sometimes that is the way to do it.

October 12th: I have made an appointment to see Elizabeth Einberg at the Tate. She says she doesn't need to see the painting at present and that the photographs of the new cleaning will do.

I am disappointed, but the photos *are* good and she can at least get some idea from them. She is supposed to know her stuff, and every opinion helps.

My meeting with Einberg was extraordinary. She is a large, hearty lady, hockey captain in approach, quite amiable but treated me as though I were a backward child. She met me in the little hallway at the Tate (I was not asked into the offices), and, to give her her due, she studied the photographs for a long time (fifteen minutes) with great care, then she made her pronouncement.

'Yes,' she said, 'it *is* eighteenth-century.' I wasn't quite sure I had heard her correctly. 'I know that, Miss Einberg,' I said. 'I have traced its background, and Lucas tells me the paint and canvas are correct.' (I did not add that any bloody fool could see it was the proper date.) 'But is it Gainsborough?' 'Ah,' she said, 'that is another question.'

She then proposed that we should go to the main gallery and look at the other Gainsboroughs (which seemed fair enough) before she said anything else. On the way, however, she stopped in front of a rather dreary little Hayman portrait. 'There,' she said. 'Don't you think?' I wasn't sure what she meant. I think she saw my confusion, so she prompted me gently. 'The white satin – don't you think?' I realised that she was suggesting Hayman because my Garrick is wearing a white satin waistcoat, and the lady's dress of the Hayman is a similar white satin. 'No, I don't,' I said, not as charmingly as I should have, but the comparison annoyed me. She gave me a pitying look. 'We mustn't underestimate Hayman,' she said gently, and led me on to the larger room. Here, her love and enthusiasm for the larger pictures gave me a bit of heart. She stopped in front of *La Baccelli* and said, 'Isn't she lovely?'

'The Garrick has a similar theatrical quality,' I said hopefully (another pitying look), 'although, of course, it isn't the same high style.' She shook her head kindly and smiled. *La Baccelli*, with all that splendid rouge, had much the same expression on her face – very, very satisfied with herself. Miss Einberg seemed as sure in her judgement, although unspoken as yet, on my poor Garrick as Baccelli was in her beauty and her dress and the silly tambourine with its blue ribbons, and her rich lover who was paying Gainsborough to paint her.

The rest of the meeting was a waste of time. We looked at another Hayman, the Vauxhall Gardens one, and we agreed with each other in our liking for the unfinished Hogarths, but Garrick had not passed the test, although she agreed to think about him and write to me with her final opinion. I could not get her to come and see the picture. A few days later she sent me a long, careful letter suggesting Verelst, whom I know very little about, so I wrote thanking her for her trouble and set about looking for as many examples of his work as I could find.

Einberg did give me one valuable bit of advice. 'Try to find out as much as you can about the Collingwood family, the people they knew, and if any of their friends owned a Gainsborough.' She didn't seem to think there was much hope, because the dates were too early during the Garrick–Giffard partnership, and in comparison with the later Suffolk portraits, the Garrick was far too accomplished and too mature. In other words, another turn-down, but quite kind and well meaning.

October 15th: Arthur has been able to have the picture photographed by infra-red.

Something strange has shown up. A small shield painted on the plinth at the top, under the ledge; very faint, it seemed to have been wiped off and then painted over. There appear to be some letters further down and a Roman 'I' in a circle; they are faint but there. The infra-reds are dark and perhaps we can get a better result with new prints. We went back and looked at the area where the letters have shown up. They can be seen by the eye if the canvas is tipped so that light rakes across it. I don't want to hope too soon, but they seem to be a 'T' and a 'G'. They are indentation marks, as if scored into the base coat. Arthur says he has not seen any like it, as far as he can remember, on any other pictures. He is going to try to get the X-ray unit in and the scanner to see if we are right. He told me to go and look at other early Gainsboroughs to see if there were similar markings.

This advice resulted in my behaving quite madly at a few museums, and fearful that they would throw me out. The light has to be raked across the pictures to see if there is anything there. As you can't touch pictures in the galleries, the alternative is to squint at them sideways and hope for the best. I found indentation marks, as far as I could see, on one in Kenwood and one at the Tate. Perhaps I *am* going mad.

After Arthur Lucas had told me about the odd letters on the infra-red photographs, I had another surprise from the photographer at Cooper's. He was in the process of turning the negatives into full-size colour transparencies for me, as Agnew's had said they would like to see them before deciding whether the picture was worth a personal visit. After the transparencies were made I could see their point. They brought up the full quality of the original in a much better way than the prints which, no matter how fine, tended towards stiffness. They also acted as a kind of X-ray, showing the brushwork and where a tree had been overpainted behind the head.

The photographer noticed them first, 'What are these letters, Miss Corri?' We put them on the light box – no question, a 'T' and a 'G', very similar to those on his early drawings. Down in the left-hand corner, far clearer than in the infra-red, were the same 'T' and 'G'.

The celebrated shield was much clearer too, but the 'T' and 'G' were definite and traceable, no figment of my overheated imagination. What more do I have to produce? Gainsborough alive? But it does seem a bit like trivia compared to the canvas itself; still, I must build up all the evidence I can. Now Arthur is retiring I shall have to find another home for the picture.

October 16th: Another letter (the fourth) from John Hayes.

As soon as the pictures had come through from Cooper's, I sent them to Dr Hayes to try to correct the bad impression the old ones had made. It did me no good at all, nor did the comparison with the Hogarth, which had managed to convince my friend David Walker that at least it was Garrick. Hayes said that 'seeing the actual picture would not really help at this stage'. The picture had absolutely nothing to do with Gainsborough, nor did he even think it had a Hudson influence, which I had suggested. He hoped I would be patient and said that they would compare it with other relevant photographs while they went into this.

I had written to Sir Oliver Millar and sent him the photographs, and now I got an appointment to see him. I was delighted that I also had the infra-reds to back up my case a little more.

October 26th: Today I went to see Sir Oliver Millar.

He really is wonderful casting for the Keeper of the Queen's Pictures; just the right amount of grey in his hair, lean and distinguished. I was let in at the side door of St James's Palace. Sir Oliver greeted me in his office. My bulging folder was dumped on his very tidy desk, and he examined the contents. Behind him (as with most of these gentlemen) were rows of books, including his own: *Gainsborough*, by Oliver Millar. It is very unnerving. I try not to look.

He was quite nice about the picture, not overly so. We discussed the possibility of Gainsborough being capable of painting as well as this in 1742. He seemed to doubt it very much, but did say he would come to see the picture. I explained that, good though the new photographs are, the picture was rather better. He looked at my attempts to get the 'T' and 'G' clearly, and did not seem to think them too bad. He agreed the 'T' was most clear, but said he had no knowledge of any other 'signatures'. He said he would come in and look at it, but I knew he was not convinced. He did not absolutely dismiss it, which at least offers some hope. I left rather more grandly than I had arrived, down the front staircase, with Sir Oliver waving good-bye at the top. All that white marble and red carpet; it made me wonder if it was obligatory for palaces. It must get very boring;

red is not an easy colour to live with. At any rate, I don't have to rule his opinion out just yet. 'Maybe' or 'don't know' is his vote. Not enough. Let's hope he can be won over by the picture itself.

I had been pestering Sir Hugh Casson with phone calls whenever I got miserable and started to lose heart. He had seen the early photographs and had been encouraging. Now I felt I had to start getting opinions from outside this country, so I pushed his patience even further.

October 30th: Hugh goes to America.

I have had the nerve to ask him to take the new photographs of the picture with him to show to the man at the Mellon Collection in Washington, Malcolm Cormack. Fine thing when I ask the President of the Royal Academy to add my chores to his very busy schedule. The measure of Hugh's kindness is that he took them without a murmur and will do everything he can to help.

To cheer myself up and find distraction from Thomas Gainsborough, I did what I always do when feeling low; I went on a tour of the galleries. Pictures act on me in the same way Scotch or drugs do on other people – they give me a lift. A diet of one or two beauties a week and I can keep balanced in the face of almost any adversity. A new Lely exhibition had just opened which could have been planned with me in mind. It was at the annexe of the National Portrait Gallery in Carlton House Terrace, arranged by Sir Oliver Millar. Lovely, sensual and decorative; not a really great artist, I suppose, if one is to look at him against Van Dyck or Rubens, but then I don't. I take him for what he is and he rarely lets me down. Very interesting drawings, too; all the people who waited outside the King's Chambers in Whitehall, a panoramic record of those hopeful petitioners as good as candid photographs – better, because of the comment in them from Lely. Those people and their hopes still lived, and the speculations you could weave around them were endless.

The rest, apart from a couple of formal pictures, were beautifully chosen and displayed. My favourite was Louise de Kéroualle holding her long dark hair up like a veil, dressed in a gun-metal coloured silk. Lovely catalogue by Sir Oliver Millar. I rang him next day and he picked up the phone himself, snarling.

Usually I go through his secretary; today he was in a filthy mood because some fool had given the exhibition a bad review. He calmed down a bit and we talked about it. How sad to do something so well and have some idiot make silly remarks – every bit as bad as theatre critics, perhaps worse. I saw the review later, it was asinine. He seemed pleased I had enjoyed the exhibition so much. He still hasn't seen Garrick.

November 4th: Trying the Approach Direct did NOT work on Sir Kenneth Clark.

He did not even want to bother to see the picture and said I should take John Hayes' word. Very bad-tempered on the phone. Don't consider that a turn-down, more a brush-off. The Cut Direct!

November 9th: John Ingamells, Director of the Wallace Collection, wrote to me.

He couldn't have been nicer but no, nothing to do with Gainsborough; he had offered to put me in touch with someone in The Hague who would be able to help as regards Verelst. He made a few remarks in the Einberg line, and showed me and Garrick the door:

> Dear Miss Corri,
> I now think the Verelst idea a bad one, and think there is no point in consulting The Hague. I have one other line of enquiry in operation and will let you know if anything transpires.
> I am very grateful for the photographs and return the Hogarths herewith.
> Yours sincerely,
> John Ingamells

He did say one thing I wondered at. I pointed out to him that Philip Thicknesse says that in 1752 he had seen 'several stiff, badly painted portraits' in Gainsborough's studio in Ipswich, 'including Admiral Vernon'. When I asked if the Garrick might have been one of them, as it would seem just the kind of a picture a young artist might paint to attract other commissions, he replied with great certainty, 'Oh no. They were all destroyed.' On my asking how he was so sure, he blithely said, 'They must have been or we would know about them.' I felt utterly defeated by that kind of logic.

Apropos the other line of enquiry, nothing can have transpired as I never heard another word from John Ingamells.

November 12th: For my birthday tomorrow, I have invested in John Hayes' latest book on Gainsborough's drawings.

Twice as much text as pictures, two heavy volumes. I fail to see the value of being told, when looking at a drawing of a tree, that I am looking at the drawing of a tree; even less, when looking at the drawing of a goat, to be told it is a sheep! Those damned patronising letters have made me vicious.

The dating in John Hayes' book is confusing. He puts a great many sketches in the 'sixties and 'eighties, whereas I should have thought it difficult to be quite so specific. A lot of them did not see the light of day until after Gainsborough's death, and would seem to me to be the results of a lifetime of observation kept for reference; hardly the product of later years when he was so damned busy in London. I must ask Hayes, if I ever get to meet him, how he arrives at his conclusions; even stylistically it is hard to fathom. There is a charming drawing of a sleeping child, which I would be inclined to place around the time of the drawing of the cat (signed). The sleeping child would be compatible with the pictures of his daughters, yet Hayes puts it in the 'eighties. The signature on some cat studies is like his early one (and his writing did mature). Hayes dates them mid to late 'sixties – why? They are both very domestic. My own opinion is that they are both around 1754–57, when his children were growing up.

There is that awful word, opinion. Most of the stuff I have read, and that goes for everyone except cagey Waterhouse, is opinion. I am stupid enough to hanker for facts. Yet it is only *my opinion*, up to now, on Garrick – everyone else has turned it down. Then again, it is only *their opinions* and, of course, qualifications. There must be some way of being closer than guesswork. If there is, I am going to have to find it.

Very cheeringly, the few signatures shown *do* resemble the ones scratched at the bottom of the Garrick, just initials, 'T' and 'G'; that gives me some hope. If only Gainsborough had signed his work, none of this would have been necessary. There are times when I feel pretty vicious towards him, too, for this oversight.

My attempts to bring up the lettering more clearly went on. I did a drawing of what I thought the symbols on the shield seemed to be and took them to the College of Arms. I had simply traced what was there: three small objects which could have been many-pointed stars or suns, a bar diagonally across in the upper right-hand portion and two in the lower left-hand side, one of which had a head and a tail and the other could have been a portcullis. My heraldry is non-existent, so they meant nothing to me, but they did to Mr Dennys, at the College of Arms:

Dear Miss Corri,

Following your telephone call yesterday, I am glad to know that we may have gone at least part of the way towards solving the mystery of the arms on the portrait.

You said that these appear to have a plain bend (i.e. the broad diagonal band from top left to lower right, as one views it), with three stars above it and a castle and seahorse below it. Clearly the stars, castle and seahorse are the objects used by Garrick in later life, although he appears to have dropped the bend at some time. This design, as depicted on the portrait, was not given for any family of Garrick (in any spelling) by Rietstap. Possibly a French family of the name used those arms – with or without authority – and Garrick believed he was descended from them; or it seems just possible that the arms were used by some other French family, from whom Garrick was descended in the *female* line, and that he believed himself entitled to adopt their arms.

As I explained in my previous letter, Garrick's grandfather in 1687 specifically disclaimed any pretence to arms and gentility. This could be because he was really not entitled to arms, or else perhaps he knew that with his flight from France and the loss of any papers etc., he would be unable to prove the fact to the satisfaction of the Heralds.

I very much doubt if the records here would give any

further help, beyond confirming that in later life Garrick did use a seal with stars, a tower and a seahorse included on it. In fact the design of this seal is typical of European heraldic practice, and no-one viewing it would suppose it was English in origin; whereas the shield described by you as appearing on the portrait – while it would be most unusual in English

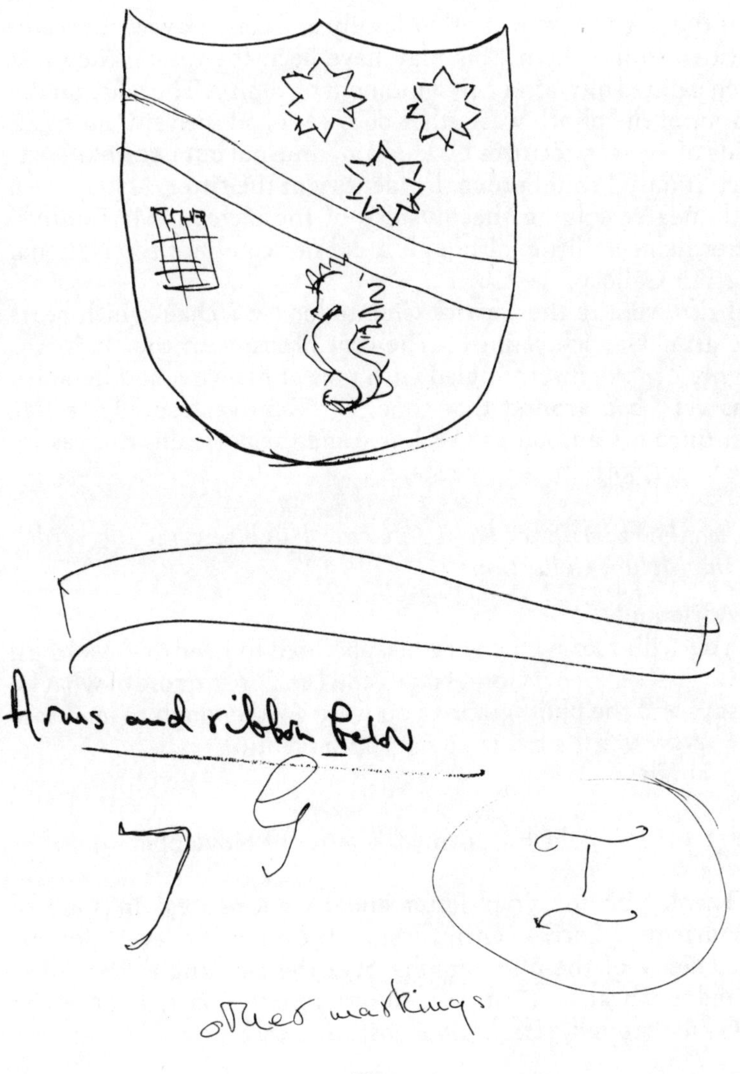

heraldry – is perhaps more like standard English heraldic practice.

Do let me know if you need further advice.

Yours sincerely,
Rodney Dennys

Somerset Herald of Arms

If the arms were of another family and Garrick was not really entitled to use them, this may have been the reason they had been painted out, after a first moment of vanity. The place on the corner of the plinth was rather odd, yet I had seen similar small coats of arms in pictures by Hudson, unusual but not unknown. I felt if only I could prove the identity of the sitter, I would be a little nearer solving the mystery of the picture. Mr Dennys' letter helped a little, although it did not convince the National Portrait Gallery.

I also went to the Garrick Club to look at a chair which bears the arms Garrick claimed. The coat of arms on the chair was highly ornate, intermingled with that of his wife, and heraldry was very bad around that time, Mr Dennys assured me. He identified my animal as a seahorse and the portcullis as a castle; the upper portion as three stars.

November 21st: Back from America, Hugh sent me the verdict of the Mellon Collection.

Adrienne!

You will, I know, be very disappointed to hear that Malcolm Cormack supports John Hayes and I enclose a quote of what he says and the photographs you were good enough to lend me.

Whoever it's by, it's a *very* nice painting!

Hugh

Extract from Malcolm Cormack's letter of November 1978:

Thank you for your letter and its enclosures. In spite of Adrienne Corri's enthusiasm, I cannot believe, on the evidence of the photographs, that the painting at the Alexandra Theatre, Birmingham, represents Garrick or is by Gainsborough. The man's costume, including his bag wig, seems to suggest a date from around 1760, when Garrick's appearance was well known from the portraits of him by Zoffany. Neither can I fit the painting into any known aspect of Gainsborough's career. I would have thought John Hayes was well qualified to judge on both these aspects of the painting.

Presumably the picture still belongs to the City of Birmingham who could hand it over to the Art Gallery for restoration and critical comment.

The reply was much the same tone as Hayes, but Cormack got the dates way out. I am *not* disappointed, only cross.

Hugh, characteristically, was delighted that I was not deterred, and wrote back in his usual cheerful, encouraging fashion:

Adrienne!
Thanks for your indomitable note. Of *course* don't despair or give up. Do you want me to twist John Hayes' arm again ... or how about David Carritt? Or Geoffrey Agnew?
Let me know if and when.
Hugh

After the letters had shown up on the photographs, and as the new pictures were so much better than the ones from the Alexandra, I at last had courage enough to tackle Sir Ellis Waterhouse. I was hopeful that he might be persuaded to come to see the picture itself. His first reply could not have been more concise or daunting:

November 23rd, 1978

Dear Miss Corri,
I am afraid Gainsborough seems to me altogether impossible at any time in his career. If the portrait is mid-40s, which is likely, and if of Garrick, which seems to me very unlikely, Gainsborough is not likely to have encountered him. The sitter looks much too tall for Garrick, as well as unlike him in face. I don't think Verelst a bad suggestion but there were too many people at that time using the same efficient drapery painter to feel at all certain.
Yours sincerely,
Ellis Waterhouse

I started to try to build my case for him. I asked him when had he ever seen a short Gainsborough? I think that rather amused him, but he was as firm as ever in his other refusals. He had not seen the hidden 'signatures', and he disagreed with the suggestion that had been made by an eminent picture dealer, that it might be Ramsay, as I did. He paid me the compliment of answering my points and not treating me entirely as a fool. I hope he does not now regret this civilised approach. On our third exchange he still refused to accept my argument, but remained a man who might be convinced (straws in the wind department on my part?):

December 4th, 1978

Dear Miss Corri,
I am afraid I remain quite unconvinced and the resemblance in the drawing seems to me quite fortuitous – there are also a great many years between the drawing and the Hayman print. I don't believe, I am afraid, in the markings on the base paint. If you want to, you can read almost any 'signatures' in this way and I believe such markings to be accidents. Ramsay seems to me equally unacceptable as an attribution.
Yours sincerely,
Ellis Waterhouse

November 24th: There is a private view at the Royal Academy of the gold from Peru.

It will be less crowded than an ordinary day; also I feel so fed up by my lack of progress that it might cheer me up.

The gold did not do as I had hoped. The objects were not as I had expected from reading Bernal Diaz – in fact, I liked the clay pots rather better.

You could see why the Indians were so amazed at the Spaniards' obsession with the metal. To them it was just the nearest and easiest thing to work. By the look of it they probably would have been just as happy with tin. They must have thought the Conquistadors quite mad. There was a picture of them trying to pour some down a Spaniard's throat – the logic was plain, and the absurdity; after all, if it couldn't be eaten what good was it to them?

I was on the side of the Indians; the nicest things were little toys. I did get a bonus, however. There was a wine and cheese do in another gallery afterwards, and among the pictures hung there for the occasion was Gainsborough's last self-portrait. I had never seen it before, except in reproduction. It is very sketchy, marvellously loose and economical, and in the corner on the painted oval was a 'T'. It is scratched quite clearly with the end of his brush, I should think; it couldn't be more plain. It is not like the one on the Garrick, more florid, this late signature; nevertheless, it is *there*. It was a bit like getting a direct message; I couldn't believe my luck. If it is on others, perhaps I can get them to accept the ones on Garrick. I came away from Burlington House profoundly grateful to those Indians.

November 28th: New infra-reds have brought the shield up a little clearer.

If only the damned identification department at the National Portrait Gallery would agree that it is Garrick, I could concentrate on other things and not have to spend so much money.

The National Gallery have the most sophisticated scanner in Europe; if it were working we could see the letters instantly, but because the department want an even better one, it sits in a state of disrepair.

When I first started out to convince the knowledgeable in the galleries and museums, I had only the Alexandra Theatre's pictures to show them. As time went on, I added to these with the infra-red photographs, comparative pictures of Garrick, photographs of all the earliest dated works, details of drawings, copies of the illustrations from the Hanmer Shakespeare (to prove that young Gainsborough could have worked on them), and to show that he might have met Garrick at that time; they were begun in 1742. My comparative tracing of the Richard III make-up, the transparencies from Cooper's, the X-rays. All this made an unwieldy lot to stagger around with and was pretty daunting for those on whom it was unleashed. It also impeded my exits at the end of interviews, taking quite some time to gather together as I tended to spread everything all over whatever office I was in, in my efforts to get an agreement.

The work on the picture also had another effect on my personal life. The inevitable result of bringing up a family on your own, without any additional support, is that you seem constantly to be running to stay in the same place. State aid was negligible years ago, and paternity cases were not appealing. A woman not married, and with children, was in a difficult position if the father opted out of his responsibilities. I remember one Christmas a group of carol singers being not at all amused when, upon being asked who they were collecting for and replying 'unmarried mothers', I offered to take the box on the spot! It was such a Victorian title, like 'decayed gentlewomen'. Later, on a programme with David Frost, I pointed out that men got stuck with bringing up families on their own as well and they deserved as much help. The next day the Society for the unmarried ladies rang up and said they saw my point and had I a better name to suggest? On the spur of the moment the best I could come up with was 'The Single Parent Family', for that is how I regarded myself, or any other parent in a similar position. They didn't find a better name and have kept it to this day.

As a single parent, there is never much chance to save with two growing children, so I have lived always on a kind of knife edge where one could not afford to be out of work for a second or the subsequent running had to get faster. I certainly could not afford a hobby or obsession such as I now found myself caught up in. However, the picture was so important to me that I knew I had to find the means to go on. If I succeeded, I had a chance to change history in a small way, and that doesn't happen often. Also I wanted something for myself; my children were grown up, they didn't need me as much, if at all. I had enjoyed their childhood; now we had to face the fact that they were on their own and so was I. Without consciously realising it, I had reached the crunch point – I had to emerge from the family and learn to live on my own again.

This was the first thing I had done entirely for myself for years, and so it was not just a search for Gainsborough but for me as well. The theatre was still, and always would be, my first love and my profession, yet to crack a new and exciting world was a tremendous challenge. I wanted to take up that challenge on the highest level I could; it would also benefit the theatre in the end as well. If I succeeded, I would have the best of both worlds.

It was a fight worth fighting, whether I won or not.

December 5th–7th: John Hayes located the Admiral Vernon for me.

He had been sent for restoration and then loaned to Beningborough Hall, near York, which took him out of my way for comparison. I phoned Beningborough and they arranged for a local photographer to take pictures for me and, in particular, a detailed one of the sword and the hand which were so like my picture. During this time, more letters from Hayes brought the total of his turn-downs to six this year.

December 5th: I have decided to bring in my own X-ray unit.

I have waited a long time to get hold of the gallery's one, but they have never found the space for me in their appointment book. I phoned an X-ray firm from the Yellow Pages. No fuss; they arrived, took all the pictures I needed and were out before lunch. Why didn't I do that before?

I have also written to Laurence Olivier. He is steeped in Garrick, probably knows more about him than anyone in the world. If he thinks it is right, then to hell with the identification department as far as I am concerned.

The hand in the X-rays is quite beautiful, very special. Arthur is quite taken by it. I am amazed to find that very few of the gallery's pictures have been X-rayed, so I have no way of comparing the technique with any of the others. I had hoped Mrs Siddons' hand would have been on the files, but no – only if a picture is in doubt does it get any special investigation.

I had sent Sir Ellis all the material I could on the coat of arms – again a considered turn-down. He had taken the trouble to look it up, at least. As to Gainsborough, I was just going to have to find more to convince him:

December 15th, 1978

Dear Miss Corri,

I can believe almost anything about 'likeness' and the hidden coat of arms certainly makes it seem plausible that the portrait is meant to be a likeness of Garrick. Incidentally Rietstap gives more or less that coat of arms as 'Garrick (Middlesex)' i.e. David Garrick: and a substantially different, tho' related, coat for 'Du Garric (Guyenne)'.

The person who did a thesis on the portraits of Garrick I find was named Martin Anglesey (? spelling) and he is now at the Royal Ulster Museum.

The Gainsborough part of it I find much more difficult to swallow. The date seems about the same as that of Admiral Vernon, but such things as the way of lighting the drapery is completely different, as well as the way of painting the hands. I don't honestly feel that Gainsborough is possible.

Yours sincerely,
Ellis Waterhouse

I had begun to find links between Margaret Burr, Gainsborough's wife, and the Bedford family.

December 15th, 1978

Dear Miss Corri,

You have certainly made a case for it not to be unreasonable to suppose that Garrick might have been painted by the young Gainsborough! In view of the publicity which Garrick normally made out of any portraits that were done of him, it is odd that no record of it should have survived.

The Bedford–Margaret Burr suggestions are ingenious, but purely hypothesis. The only real parallel with any of the admitted Gainsborough pictures that I can see is the rather pompous and awkward stance of the figure, which resembles that of the father in the Gravenor family. It is perhaps not impossible that a life-scale portrait done at the time of the Gravenor family might not look altogether unlike the 'Garrick'. But I am afraid that I don't really believe in this.

Yours sincerely,
Ellis Waterhouse

In between the exchange of letters we had a few telephone conversations. I got the feeling that I might persuade him if I could come up with more than my own conviction. He is teaching me that conviction is not enough, it needs to be backed by work and fact. I must try to provide him with both. The great thing about him is that, stage by stage, he gives me valid objections based on more than just his own instincts. At least he now agrees it could be Garrick and that there is a reasonable chance they could have met at this date. Two small hurdles crossed. Through all this, however, I must hold on to my conviction; the facts are the bones, but the conviction is the blood and the soul of what I am doing, and what will sustain me and keep the whole thing alive.

After seeing the 'T' on the last self-portrait at the Academy, I wrote to Hugh Casson again in the hope that he might let me photograph their picture (the self-portrait) as there is absolutely no question about *its* attribution. I felt that the initial signature might be the most important evidence yet to back my claim for the Garrick. I wrote, and we fixed a date for early January.

A very odd evening just before Christmas. I was parking my Morris on a pavement when I saw a Rolls with the sinister number plate WAR 7. Out of the car got a rather dapper Indian guy, and we both realised we knew each other. It was Shiv Kapoor, one of the backers of the first movie I had ever done, *The River*, directed by Jean Renoir. He didn't look much changed after at least thirty years. We chatted and exchanged cards, then I saw the reason for the number plate – he was in munitions. It was a rather black, sick joke. He asked if I would like to come to dinner and, as Patrick was home, said he would be delighted to meet him. I arranged to phone his wife, Aisha, to make a date.

It was all extremely strange. Aisha (whom I had imagined to be small, frail and Indian) turned out to be a tall, Californian show-girl type with a degree in political economy. The other guests were: the man who had designed the Canberra bomber (the brother of the actor, Peter Finch); the man who had designed the Centurion tank; and one who had been responsible for a particularly lethal machine gun. They were all filled with charm and looked as if they loved their fellow man and little old ladies. The man who had the machine gun to his credit confided that he was a Catholic and regularly went into retreat in a monastery in Ireland – to ease his conscience, no doubt. Shiv told us that he had factories in Australia and if Patrick wanted any help I should tell him, and he would be delighted to twist anyone's arm if the need should arise.

Afterwards, he said of my son: 'Such a nice young man – he could have a job with me any time.' Patrick was vastly entertained by this brush with big business, but thought marine zoology seemed preferable.

Christmas 1978 ended on a rather better note than the year before. My son got a scholarship to Canberra University, which meant that he would spend the next three years in Australia and get the best facilities for his doctorate. Although I shall miss him, he was so pleased I couldn't let my feelings get in the way. We spent Christmas in the country and I met Roger de Grey, the artist and Royal Academician. I had my folder with me, of course, and he got the Gainsborough Lecture. To my delight, he seemed convinced and urged me to see Hugh Casson as soon as possible. I needed to find a new home for the picture and Roger looked at the photographs with an artist's eye. Strange as it may seem, most of the 'experts' and the heads of galleries are not qualified in the practical sense. Their knowledge is all theoretical and from the art history side; not one of them knows what it is to paint a picture. Roger's appreciation of the picture and the work I had done helped me tremendously. I needed encouragement as never before. He promised to have a word with Hugh, so at least he will know from a fellow artist that there is something there, apart from my conviction.

1979

Roger de Grey told Hugh about the folder and my other evidence. I desperately need encouragement. I am becoming very depressed, getting nowhere with all this.

January 3rd: I have gone back to my old agent, Tim Wilson. I always said I would if he came back into the business, and a promise is a promise.

Tim has sent a nice, woolly man with thyroid eyes round to see me. His name is Don Taylor and he is trying out a play at the Manchester Library Theatre and wants me to play the part of a sort of resistance lady or a terrorist or something. He doesn't have a copy of the play, but it was done on television and my friend, Zena Walker, played the lady he wants me to do. I saw a splendid piece of his on television about the Great Plague called *Ring of Roses*, so it can't be rubbish, this play. It has been expanded for the stage and he has hopes it will be brought into town. He is nice, a bit over-earnest, but I like him and have accepted it, sight unseen. The Library Theatre is opposite the Midland, one of my favourite hotels in England, cosy and they look after one, so I can do a lot of writing and put my research together. Perhaps this year will be a good one after all. There are two other outside actors as well as myself and the resident company, which is run by David Skase and his wife, who were with Joan Littlewood for years, so let us hope.

January 5th: I went to see Hugh Casson.

I think all my pent-up frustrations were boiling over – my folder gets heavier and more untidy daily. We met in the Committee Room which is pretty impressive, Constable's *Lock* among the pictures, a huge, dark, polished table – a quiet, tranquil room.

It was three in the afternoon and the sunlight was trying hard to filter through the windows. Within five minutes my folder was spilled all over the table and I had launched full spate into my, now, standard lecture. Hugh picked up the infra-reds and the transparencies and went over to the window to look at them in a better light. I carried on with my lecture, spreading all my 'proof' over the table, the Hanmer Shakespeare comparisons, the Garrick photographs, the letters from the College of Arms, photographs of the shield, the X-rays. My spate of eloquence ended at last and I turned to find Hugh was laughing helplessly. When he finally managed to speak he said, 'All right, Adrienne, I am convinced. What would you like us to do? Would you like us to show it?' That shut me up completely. I didn't know what to reply. Apart from Roger de Grey and Arthur Lucas, no one else had given me any encouragement. He looked at my turn-down letters and asked if they (the National Portrait) had given me any firm reasons, or any other attributions yet. I could only reply in the negative. 'We could show it with the letters,' said Hugh wickedly. In the end he agreed to offer the picture a home and he said he would help to show it at the Academy whenever I wanted.

I explained that in order to protect the interests of the theatre, I wanted to show the picture not only to all the gallery experts but to the commercial ones as well. Even if I cannot get official approval, I have to be sure that no one from the sale rooms could buy it and then confirm it afterwards. Hugh promised he would write to John Hayes to get him to come in and look at the picture again *and* to look at my folder. He is a saint. This is a much better start than last year, and it is only the 5th. I have arranged to get the picture brought to the Academy, where Garrick will remain until I get the final 'Yes' or 'No'.

January 6th: I have had a breakthrough at last!

Lester Collingwood was *not* Lester Collingwood. I have been researching the wrong family. The other day, in despair, I took down a *Kelly's Directory* for 1902 and found that an Edward Henry Parker, new owner of the Alexandra Theatre

Birmingham, from 'this time forth wishes to be known as Lester Collingwood'. I phoned Michael Bullock at once, and he had known all along! By the next post I got a sheet of paper with the history of the theatre and Collingwood's real name. I have wasted months in research which could not have led anywhere. It must be all part of this dread that someone will claim the picture. If I am ever to prove it, I need help from them, not this stupid hindrance. It is just silliness, I am sure; it is in their own interests to do everything they can and to tell me as much as they know. I have written to ask for the date of his death, which will help me find the birth certificate and trace the family origins. Back to bloody square one.

January 8th: Hugh has written a lovely letter to Hayes, very tactful and helpful.

In consequence, I have my first letter from Hayes that promises to think again. Of course, it is really to Hugh not me, but at least Hugh has opened up the question again and thrown his own opinion behind it. He is very kind. He seems to do so much and yet it never flusters him, nor does he ever seem to find it too much bother. I think there must be two or three of him. One person is not enough to do the amount he does:

> You may remember our exchange of correspondence last autumn about this portrait, which has been tirelessly investigated by an old friend of mine (Adrienne Corri) and is now in the final stages of restoration by Arthur Lucas.
>
> Since October two further details have come to light under his treatment –
>
> 1. A coat of arms (apparently confirmed by the College of Arms as Garrick's)
> 2. What seems to be quite clearly the two letters T.G.
>
> These details seem to add plausibility – to put it mildly – to the suggestion that this portrait is of Garrick by Gainsborough. Those who have seen it (including Roy Strong and John Kerslake) or photographs of it (Ellis Waterhouse) seem baffled. The Wallace Collection derided the Tate's guess that it was a Verelst. You, I know, remain unconvinced from the photographs and evidence.

Roger de Grey and others here agree it is a very handsome picture, certainly good enough in our view to be shown somewhere publicly – captioned with appropriate caution! – in this, Garrick's bicentenary year. Could you possibly find time to go and see it? Arthur Lucas has it in his care and can fix a time to suit you. Adrienne Corri can provide all the evidence of her researches plus transparencies, X-rays, etc. on request.

Please forgive my pestering you but as the bicentenary year is already two weeks old it would be marvellous to get the puzzle at least partially resolved before Easter. I know you would not find the time wasted.

Sir Hugh Casson

January 10th–February 24th: Manchester. Oh Lord! The famous Snags again.

Different kind but bad enough. The set is 'too elaborate' (built for London – oh yes?), so we are to play in the Library's other theatre at Wythenshawe. Where is Wythenshawe? 'Où est Wythenshawe?' There goes my staying at the Midland and casually sauntering over two minutes before rehearsals start. I shall go up by train and look around. The theatre has booked me and the others at what they swear is the best hotel near the theatre. Is it *that* far from Manchester?

This diary entry begins 'BIG MISTAKE'. Wythenshawe is ghastly. The theatre is one of the civic centre numbers, plus a library, swimming pool, et al.; almost as bad as Billingham, worse I cannot say. It is fiercely for *the people*. Who are the nits who plan these places? Millions of little Birminghams proliferating all over England.

No matter, I am stuck. The hotel is dreadful; aggressively ugly, different, awful wallpapers on each wall, in foul colours. It is run by a little man with a camp, refined Lancashire accent – 'All the Best People stay here.' Lead me to the worst! The first read-through is disheartening. The resident company is what one fights to escape. I knew at the age of thirteen that staying with a repertory company would be death to me – what am I doing here?

The other imports, apart from myself, are Frank Barrie and a lady called Marilyn Taylorson. He looks as if he has a sense of humour, at least. She, I suspect, has none. The play is a bit like two teams. It is based, apparently, on something that really happened around 1840 in Hungary. A troupe of actors arrive at a remote estate, get taken in by the Count and his family, and after eating them out of house and home, perform a quite terrible Greek tragedy for them and then shoot them all because they represent the aristocrats and oppression – and a very jolly evening for all in Wythenshawe. It has a sort of Baader-Meinhof parallel and the res. co. is very enthusiastic about it (in a dull sort of way). After the read-through, during which my heart had sunk to the lowest point it can ever reach (this will teach me to take a play without reading it first), we dispersed to the wardrobe and to inspect backstage. The wardrobe is workmanlike – they seem to know what they are doing, the designs are good; I *could* be wrong. The dressing rooms are municipal, too. I imagine there is not much to choose between them and the cubicles in the swimming baths. There is a green room of sorts, very grotty, messy and dirty; this is the fault of the res. co. which seems to think that dirt is democratic. I can think of no other explanation. What is this insistence on ugliness being somehow a virtue? The res. co. is dressed as the 'workers'; they will bring out the worst in me, I know. I am wearing my dark mink coat – they sneer at it amongst themselves. I shall arrive in gold lamé if they keep this up!

We are to be picked up every day in the company van. This is a dank little number filled with coils of rope and other mouldering goodies, two benches – the kind of lift a hobo would refuse. We returned to the best hotel in Wythenshawe. Barrie has said nothing, but he looks profoundly depressed. M. Taylorson (a sensitive girl of uncertain age) has stayed on to see the play now being performed by the res. co. (she *would*). I would rather be dead. I will find out what they are like soon enough; it is some jolly little divertissement by Brecht. The proprietor would not serve us a drink until 6.00 p.m., so we wandered into the television lounge. It had a glass roof, like a fish tank, and one solitary commercial traveller watching football. The chairs were all lined up like a cinema. We watched glumly with this wretched man, hoping the news might come on with a world catastrophe or two to lighten our gloom, when Barrie began to laugh helplessly. The man became furious; the angrier he became, the more Frank laughed, and the joke of the situation hit me too. By this time, more irate gents were there, intent on watching sport, so we left before they threw us out, got a taxi into Manchester, found an Italian restaurant and had a decent meal.

I did not last long at The Best Hotel In Wythenshawe. After a dreadful, sleepless night in an uncomfortable bed, I was confronted with the worst, greasiest breakfast I have ever known. The owner was even more voluble in the morning about the charms of his rotten hotel. I am not very good first thing – the family has long ago learned not to speak to me until at least 11.00 a.m. Marilyn Taylorson sat opposite me eating (sensibly) health food she had brought with her. I do not know exactly what causes me to lose my temper, nor what my trigger point is. If I did, presumably I would have led a quieter life, but I was staring at a plate of peculiar ugliness while this little man droned on. It occurred to me that someone had actually sat down and designed the nasty thing, and that such design should not be allowed. Following this thought, I picked it up and smashed it. It was very satisfying; then another and another. I began to feel much better. Marilyn Taylorson, quite wisely, went into a yoga-inspired trance, and I left the hotel when I could get its terrified owner to make up my bill. I took a taxi and booked into the Midland. I couldn't afford it, but nor could I afford what that awful place would have done to me. Frank missed the whole episode. The owner told him that he had never had such a thing occur before, except when Sir Michael Redgrave was once there. I have never been able to find out what misfortune had brought Michael Redgrave to that dump. One day I must ask him.

Later, at rehearsal, Marilyn Taylorson offered to pray for me. The company leading man, eyelashless, with sandy hair, knew his lines at the first rehearsal (they melted away like snow on contact with an audience). Everyone works differently – I prefer to know how people speak *their* lines before I know how I will answer them. Miss Taylorson was going to opt for the spirited approach as the Count's (Frank's) daughter, Frank for panache – we needed a bit of that – but the Countess! A performance I will long cherish. After the first day Frank said, 'I wouldn't have married anyone like that, would I?' 'Pretend you married beneath you for her money,' I replied to console him. She was splendid, a new recruit to the company from the local amateur society, and she grasped her opportunity with both hands. All through Frank's long speech pleading for the lives of his family, before one half of the cast shot the other half, she prayed loudly and fervently, added to which she looked like an elderly, not too amiable, horse. (Don told me just before the first night that it was her first professional appearance – I begged him to keep this news from Frank.)

'You mustn't worry at the end if people faint,' said Don, seriously. 'I will have nurses standing by.'

The weather had not been good – now it became abysmal. I thanked God for the warmth of the Midland Hotel, and spread out all my work and continued my correspondence with the galleries. Frank used his spare time to write a one-man show on the Victorian actor, Macready. We both decided that we must make this awful time work for us, not against us. It was a very hard job.

It was the winter of discontent in more ways than one. In Manchester even the undertakers went on strike. So, as we were part of the Corporation, did our front-of-house staff, members of NUPE. I hoped God was being kind and that the wretched play was going to die a small, still death, but Don Taylor, particularly keen, had the audience smuggled in through the stage door. As the only lavatories they could use were backstage too, there was a great deal of true audience participation. Sian Phillips and Robin Sachs nobly came up from London, as did Frank's agent. I told mine to stay in peace at home.

I have omitted the title of the play – it was called *When The Actors Come* and began with a catchy little Magyar song, 'Fly, Peacock, Fly'. My only bit of fun in the piece was a flirtation with Frank's character, which made the audience feel that there was some larky sub-plot pending; and making my last speech very, very long and slow, to the great discomfort of the mass deaths. Those who came did not faint, nor did a London management clamour for our services. However, Frank wrote his show, which he now performs all over the world, and I did a great deal of work in the Manchester Art Gallery whose new curator, Tim Clifford, was most helpful. He also liked the look of my photographs and was very encouraging on Garrick *and* Gainsborough. He had just been given the post and was full of enthusiasm. I wondered how long it would be before fighting for money and the Manchester Council would break his spirit. He had brought another of the British Museum staff with him, Martin Royalton Kish – they had both been responsible for some of the best exhibitions in the prints and drawings department in London. I behaved like a fan when introduced; they were quite put out. I realised that I was just a museum groupie.

January 22nd: John Hayes DID go into the National Gallery to see the picture last year.

Arthur Lucas was away and Hayes said in his letter (still a firm 'no') that my folder was 'not available'. He doesn't seem to have looked at the picture for very long.

I wrote a rather irate letter suggesting that he might consider looking at it a little longer and taking a more kindly view. I was angry and it showed in the tone, I suppose. I didn't have an answer to that letter until the Christmas and New Year holiday when the picture was already at the Academy; a very huffy, ruffled reply it was, too. I got the feeling that if he had not heard from Hugh I would not have had a reply at all.

We have got to letter number seven in our exchanges.

Cooper's had taken more pictures of the little shield and some had come out rather well, so I sent some of them to John Hayes, plus a copy of Mr Dennys' letter and a further one on Garrick's claim to arms. He was still unimpressed.

February 5th: Lovely letter from Olivier and we talked on the phone.

He has no doubts *at all.* In fact, he has suggested that the British Museum hang the picture as part of the bicentenary exhibition on Garrick. He is lending them a suit of Davy's clothes and the 'scratch' wig he wore as Abel Drugger. An ancestor of mine (Luigi Riccoboni) saw him play Hamlet one night, and Abel Drugger the next, and refused to believe it was the same man.

Damn it! I *know* he is David Garrick; the man was almost part of the family.

Important plus – Olivier's letter mentions Garrick's *private duelling sword*:

Darling Adrienne:
The letter and the photographs you sent to Shirley Luke are most interesting indeed. I do applaud you for your interest in this great man.

I have a few articles belonging to him which will, one day, I hope, be of interest to you. At the moment they are in Brighton, where we are about to pack up in order to move up to Chelsea... We might have settled in, I think, with all pin feathers in place, some time in March. In the meantime, all is a shambles, but I shall eventually be able to show you a Reynolds portrait, a Zoffany, a red coat – possibly Macbeth? – a cream waistcoat with a red edging to go with it and a goldy coloured stripey silk waistcoat, plus his private duelling sword and what I think must be the earliest theatre wig – a very ordinary scratch wig with an adjusting buckle in the back of it which, I am sure, was for Abel Drugger.

Please drop me a line in a couple of months or so, and I shall love to show them to you.

I am returning the photographs and, of course, with regard to the detail of the hands, how possible it is indeed for them to grow up in the quite a bit older hand in the Reynolds portrait...

I should so love to see you again. I remember so much enjoying our association in that ill-fated *Shifting Heart* – was it?

All love – ever,
Olivier

Carl Toms saw the Garrick at last and loved him. I was able to have him put on an easel in the Committee Room. He thinks the picture looks right. As for costume, the wig is the most useful thing for dating purposes, according to Carl, as the rather harsh 'scratch' wig went out soon after the early 1740s, and a softer one took its place, especially with fashionable young men.

Carl observed that only someone who was a really good

painter knows how to set the head on the shoulders with such assurance. The set of the head has always seemed to me to be very like Lady Mary Howe, although I know it is a typical pose for a picture of this date; it already has a grace and ease about it that shows in the high Bath style. I love him. Such a lively eye! He is a charmer, perhaps he *was* more than the usual actor. He is everything I love about the theatre, that is certain – such panache.

February 15th: Another event happened which went into our family archives.

I got a note asking if I remembered a girl called Annabelle from my schooldays. As it happened, I did. A thin, gangling girl, a bit myopic, who liked poetry. She lived in Manchester and wondered if I would like to meet for lunch. I went as usual to the gallery in the morning and rushed back a little late. As I was asking at the desk if anyone was waiting for me, I became aware of a monolithic figure heading purposefully in my direction. It was Annabelle. She was a thick-set matron in tweeds and very sensible shoes, grey, crimped hair; in no respect could I find the schoolgirl under the layers of time, which clothed her like foam rubber. It was hard to believe she had ever been a child at all. We had nothing in common, and I looked in amazement and horror at this woman who was exactly my age – my mother had looked younger. And yet I knew she was the norm, not I.

Once, in an African village on a location, some very old women had asked my age. I was thirty at the time, so I told them through the interpreter and they began to laugh. They didn't believe me – they were around that age, too.

The same gap was apparent between me and Annabelle. There were two dishy young footballers in the room, who had been quite jolly when I walked in; it now made me feel uncomfortable. Yet she felt very sorry for me. 'It must be terrible to live in hotels,' she said. She showed me pictures of her family. She kept up with girls at our old school. After lunch we went to the ladies' room and I noticed a white hair pushing its way through my freak-out. 'Why does a white hair grow more strongly than the others?' I wondered aloud. Annabelle patted her grey curls with satisfaction: 'Oh, I decided to grow old gracefully,' she said.

As she left, I told the head porter, who is an old friend, 'That woman and I are the same age.'

'I shouldn't tell too many people that,' he replied gravely.

The family have promised to tell me if I show any signs of growing old gracefully.

While I was in Wythenshawe, Michael Bullock and Edmund King came over to have lunch with me. They have infinite faith that I can produce the proof of the picture, and are pleased that it is going to the Academy to be shown to the other 'experts'. They don't seem too dashed that I have not come up with rave reactions, or even agreement yet. At least I have Hugh's letter to show them. I have asked them not to say anything to the papers until I have something to tell them. As it is, at the worst the picture is much more valuable than when hanging on that dingy wall; at least they would recover their investment on the research and cleaning. In the dining room at the Midland there is a lovely Lely of Catherine of Braganza in middle age. I pointed her out to the manager years ago, and now she is beautifully cleaned and restored, and heavily insured, and the wall is decorated in her honour. This appears to inspire even more confidence in Michael and Edmund – they calmly light up cigars and drink their brandy, and seem to think the whole thing is a walk-over. They don't want anything in the press either, in case it gets in the way of the grant the theatre is getting, so at least I feel I have more time.

I was interviewed by the guy from the *Mirror*, who was so disappointed that I did not have any scandal for him to print, or say four-letter words every five minutes, that he didn't do an article at all. It was funny to watch his face – he was baffled. As far as he was concerned, I was a dead loss. I am doing the most exciting thing that has ever happened to me, but it just is not the same formula as before, therefore not copy. He did send a photographer over to the gallery while I was working on a small Gainsborough there, and I obligingly let them take pictures of me up a ladder, showing lots of leg, but I knew nothing would be in the paper.

February 28th–June 16th: Ten Times Table *with Irene Handl. I think she is the best comedienne in the world.*

After the winter of discontent, what a pleasant surprise – I love comedy. 'A serious business,' as my good friend David Garrick said, and he *is* a good friend by now, he and Tom Gainsborough. The Snag is there, as usual – very little rehearsal time. Bill Kenwright is the management again. The actor, Tenniel Evans, is our director. He was in the London production and knows what Ayckbourn wants, and the rest of the cast are excellent.

Irene exceeds expectations. I thought I would like her, I didn't know I would become devoted to her.

I have to play the lady quite differently from Julia Mackenzie. The part I have to play can be quite funny if I turn her into a sort of Mrs Thatcher – she is very high Tory, a beautifully observed bit of writing. Irene's part is quite small on paper, but as someone said, there are no small parts, only small actors. She has been very ill and doesn't want to do anything too demanding just yet. Her concentration is superb. Even at rehearsal you can see her building up the old girl's character, piece by piece, like some lovely bit of embroidery. We have no scenes or even exchanges in the play, but my woman is acutely aware of the old lady all the time. The idea of the play is simple – a group of people get together to stage a pageant which becomes a battlefield for the opposing Socialist and Tory factions, Tories personified by me, Socialists by a young comprehensive schoolteacher, played by Colin Spaul. The whole thing gradually falls apart and the last Act is total chaos. The last Act is the least good, but it does have a lovely bit for Irene to play the piano serenely while all hell breaks loose. I had forgotten how happy I could be on stage. Irene and I have a marvellous unspoken rapport; it is a little like having known her all my life. Her old lady is very benign towards my woman, which makes her even more nervous and wary of impending disaster.

Like all very good actresses, Irene gives so much, consequently you become better. The play is easy to learn – good writing always is, half the work is done for you. It is formula stuff, but of the very best sort, reflex laughs but nearly always springing from the character; only once or twice does Ayckbourn indulge himself in the wisecrack joke and it jars, but does not spoil, the end result.

Snag Number Two. Bill has somehow 'made a mistake' about the booking at Guildford. We have to open a week earlier; that means only ten days' rehearsal, including the dress and technical runs. He is the end. There is no way it can have been a 'mistake' – the bills and the programmes are already printed. It is a fait accompli. However, it says much for the cast that we all know our lines.

Wythenshawe is over! The rest of the dreary cast must have cheered when Frank and I left, but I can't swear to it. I don't think we will see any of them again. I will *never* go back to Wythenshawe and they will never leave it – enough said.

The opening at Guildford went well. It will, of course, get better when we are less nervous. The audience is a very Tory one, Ayckbourn country. I can tell from my first line to the Socialist schoolteacher what the audience will vote this year. The play is clever in that the public takes sides and either way the laughs are there, for or against. Labour like to see me get my come-uppance, Tories laugh with me. Irene is wonderfully helpful. The way the set is arranged, she sits on the left side and is always in my eyeline, and she sees everything I do. She has already given me a couple of tips on how to make a line or two work better. What more could I ask for? A master class each night. The temptation to play the whole part just for her is overwhelming. She does nothing, apparently, and yet the audience is with her every look or slightest move. It is all to do with something Angela Baddeley told me years ago in my first London play. The audience gets what you *think*. Irene thinks all the time, and in character. I am going to love this tour.

March 21st: I have an appointment to meet John Hayes at last.

The folder is in order, with the extra pictures and attempts to get up the shield and the letters, so we shall see. I don't expect much, but I would rather know who I am writing to, face to face. He can't be worse than his letters.

Well, of course, he wasn't; rather shy, not much social flair, not like Roy Strong – but then Roy must have been very difficult to follow.

I don't think he knew quite what to expect from my letters either. Someone much bigger and more formidable, a battleaxe, I suppose. He almost looked relieved. He peered at me rather in surprise. He was very nice altogether. He doesn't look convinced in any respect. I shall just have to go on digging. Still, at least the ice is broken.

As I was leaving, I glanced at a sketch on a shelf by the door. 'It's not Gainsborough,' he said quickly. I hadn't thought it was, not enough substance. 'Gainsborough Dupont.' (Gainsborough's nephew and pupil; much more likely.) I didn't really have time to look at it, but I do wish they would not always behave as if one is going to make mistakes. (Wishful thinking, perhaps?)

March 26th: Foul weather again. Suddenly, blizzards in the north. After Guildford, Billingham. Let me try to describe it.

I think they trained the architects for Birmingham there. Not a real community but an industrial town, brought into being by ICI. It has nothing whatsoever to do with the surrounding countryside; it is a concrete slum slapped down like some child's abandoned, broken toy, so built that it is a wind trap, and a rain and dirt trap.

There is a shopping centre for the people who work for ICI, and it is the only place they have to go for entertainment. In fairness, they have built a large sports and leisure centre; apart from that, it must be like living in Siberia. The shopping centre itself is built on a lot of confusing levels, impossible for young mothers with prams, or the old, should they live that long. All concrete, a uniform, uncompromising grey. There is a statue in the middle of a pathetic square, with a burly mother holding her infant's hand and braving the rain. The pavements don't drain properly so there are always puddles, even on the occasional dry day. On wet days, they flood.

There is only one restaurant and that is on a second-floor level, which was difficult for Irene to get to, and you don't feel like Chinese food every night. In the square is also a block of flats, known as Stalag 17, providing cheap accommodation for the actors who can't afford the pub, which is quite expensive. That is Billingham. The air is not very good either, as the smell from the giant plants around gives an impression that there is something nasty in the drains. The play went quite well. Irene is very popular (Labour vote I would say, by their reaction to me).

I could not face the local pub, so I found a large, comfortable place about ten minutes' drive away. It was lovely, in between three race tracks and the bar was open until all hours, filled with local farmers and trainers. Not a mention of the theatre. A lovely holiday. I felt a bit mean about abandoning Irene, but she likes to stay within walking distance of the theatre. I used to walk back with her every night because the sight of her battling alone against the cross winds, clutching her little dog Beulah, was terrifying. The weather was even worse than it had been at Wythenshawe – snow drifts and floods. One night I just got away in time before the whole concrete mess was marooned.

Irene and I had dinner together a couple of nights at the Chinese joint and noticed that the poor Chinese waitress was so depressed there that her eyes had become quite straight!

One bonus for Billingham. I managed to find Irene's books there, in the library. They are out of print and I have never been able to get them. They are extraordinary, the books of a wicked, precocious young girl; so very modern, quite unlike anything else I have ever read. I pursued her, trying to find out who the men were. 'I don't have to tell you the story of my life,' she said. I think she was quite pleased I had enjoyed them so much. She doesn't have to be told how good they are – she knows they are quite brilliant. Not in a conceited way, but the way you know when the work is good – Good is Good, and that is all there is to it. They would make a marvellous film. I think that would please her most of all, but really just to see them in print again would mean a great deal to her. They seem to have been timidly marketed on their first publication. Mind you, they are nothing like the image of a dear, sweet, little old lady that she projects. 'Some of my fans didn't like them,' she says. I am not surprised. People who liked *that* Irene Handl would have been shocked by the books; and those who expected a sweet old lady rambling on shouldn't have bought them. Maybe her image conflicted with her persona as a novelist – perhaps they should have been put out under a different name. Every now and again, when I have been talking to her for some time, I find I am surprised to see she is quite old. I have a mental picture of a young girl. Her mind is so young, so unexpected and fresh, and wicked.

Wolverhampton, then Sunderland. I had promised to give Philip Bond, who plays my husband, a lift and then I found out that Irene was going to try to travel all that way on her own on a Sunday with Beulah. So I bundled her and Beulah into the car as well; if we take our time it won't be too bad a journey. It would have been impossible by train; she would have had to change twice.

We started early and were doing very well (Philip getting withdrawal symptoms without his lunchtime Guinness), when I suddenly saw signs to Lotherton Hall and remembered that the Sargent exhibition had opened there. Squeals of complaint from Philip and Irene, but I wasn't going to be cheated from seeing it and I turned off, in spite of all protests. Irene did her pathetic bit with a lot of gasping, saying that she couldn't leave Beulah in the car and that she couldn't manage the stairs. Philip just sulked at seeing his booze recede. I told them it would be good for their souls, and that was that. There was a light rain falling, which added to the complaints. Once it was a fait accompli, however, they both quietened down.

I bounced through the door saying I hoped there was a lot of white satin, and there was; enough to satisfy even me at my greediest. It was a most beautiful exhibition in a marvellous setting, a perfect house for his work, lovely and atmospheric; the pictures belonged there. As soon as she was through the door, Irene's legs took on a wonderful turn of speed and remarkable agility. She was up and down the rather steep stairs like a determined cross between Paddington Bear and a mountain goat!

She was a fund of information about the period. She told me how the ribbons were put in the hair of the Edwardian hairdos, threaded on a big flat needle so that they didn't flatten the hair; she had watched her mother having her hair done as a child. She was lovely to be with; she almost knew the people.

The settings for the pictures had been carefully chosen to complement them. *La Carmencita,* for instance, in all that yellow satin, was in a room with black furniture set with mother of pearl. The picture of the children with the great Chinese vase was in the music room. We stayed over two hours and only left because it was getting dark. Irene had a wonderful time, not one complaint about her feet or legs, and Philip seemed not to notice his habitual thirst. 'It was a lovely day,' said Irene, happily. Beulah had slept quite contentedly and hadn't missed us at all.

The whole day was a sort of jewel, the very rare occasion when everything joins together to be absolutely right in every way, like a special gift. I think it made us all feel grateful.

June 11th: Our last week is at the Alexandra Theatre, Birmingham.

The theatre is even shabbier than it was in 1977. There was a heavy thunderstorm during one of our performances and rain dripped on to the stage. We had to move Irene's chair and alter some of our moves to avoid the worst wet patches, but we were all caught at some point during the evening. The only real protection would have been umbrellas. The dressing rooms are grubbier and shabbier, too. The whole place seems more run down. It is very depressing to work in such surroundings.

I met the board and gave my progress report, not that it is much progress. I have to explain what a difficult date the picture has turned out to be, and why I need more time than the year we first thought would be enough. They seem to understand, although trying to explain the academic *annoyance* and lack of interest is not an easy job. They really can't grasp why no one will come to see the picture (any more than I could, at the start), but they are reassured that it is in the Academy and that it is being well looked after. They don't seem to want to see him much themselves. I try to get them to make a firm date to come and see him now he is cleaned, and meet surprising apathy. It is the result, and that means cash, that is the really interesting thing to the board in general. The theatre certainly could do with some money being spent on it. I cannot give a definite date as to when I will get an agreement, if ever. Edmund King says 'take as long as you like'. One of the board can't understand why I have to research the early life of Gainsborough so much.

Derek Salberg, the previous owner of the theatre, has been in to see the play but we have not met. Somehow it has been prevented, and more relatives of the first owner, Lester Collingwood, have also been deflected. I cannot understand the attitude of the theatre board. I might have learned something of value to my search and so speeded everything up.

I make a stab at explaining that if I can find out more about the early years, the easier it will be to fit their picture in. Also the more I discover that the experts do not know, the better chance I have of beating them at their own game. That seems to make a bit of sense to them all. The lunch ends in the usual haze of cigars, and I have to leave.

I tried to stay in all the hotels and digs Irene was in on the tour; she wasn't very well and I didn't think she should be on her own. Some of the places were very rum indeed. As she likes to be near the theatre, it narrows the choice down considerably. (I gave up theatrical digs years ago, so it was all a new experience for me again.) One place in Southsea was very strange. The owner announced that 'All the luminaries of the British Stage have stayed here', and he had photographs to prove it. Irene told me that he painted – my heart sank. I am a bad liar and I hate to disappoint people, but to my surprise his pictures were marvellous. I wanted to buy one but he wouldn't sell. It takes him about a year to paint one landscape. He paints light beautifully. I was very pleased to have seen them. Life is full of surprises.

The tour ended and Irene and I have remained firm friends and see each other regularly. She is very interested in the progress of the Gainsborough. We have Chinese meals together and I give her the latest news. In turn she reads what I write and gives me great encouragement. I always find that, out of nearly every play you do, you manage to retain one friend at least, so the theatre family grows.

While we were in Bath I stayed at the Garrick's Head, as did Irene. Splendid food, kippers for breakfast, as many as you liked. I got a picture of the Head by hanging precariously out on the ledge in front of the pub – I might have broken my neck. The local newspaper loaned me a camera and developed the photographs. They came out very well, and so go into my identification kit. The photographer sensibly stayed on the ground and took some others, but mine were best.

Back in London with the Royal Academy at my disposal and a very kind secretary called Hans Fletcher in charge of me and the picture, I was able to have the Garrick set up almost permanently on an easel so that people could view him whenever I could arrange it. I set about coercing everyone I could think of whose opinion would matter. Consequently, I approached Agnew's, Leggatt's, and all the commercial dealers, as well as John Jacobs of Kenwood, Miss Einberg, John Hayes, Ellis Waterhouse and

Sir Oliver Millar all over again, hoping I could tempt them to come and look at the picture. They were bound to come to the Academy for other purposes and might spare a moment for the Garrick. I kept on asking the theatre management to come to see him in his new state; so far no response. It is so disheartening; I would have thought they could at least come in to see what I am trying to do. I have had little luck on the other fronts, but I shall keep on trying.

I can also continue to try different techniques to photograph the shield and letters. God knows what I would do without Hugh's help. Apart from the Academy being a marvellous place to show the picture off, I am being given all the help possible in every other way. When he is not on show, he is kept in a vault in his case so that he is safe and under lock and key, which means I don't have to pay too large an insurance premium, and when he has to come out the porters cheerfully carry him to an easel, not only without complaint but, I think, they are genuinely interested in any progress. Their opinions are divided, but after so many years of looking at all sorts of pictures, well worth listening to.

At last I get to see the Marlborough House Gainsboroughs. I have been away for so long, Julian and Osmond Bullock have arranged it for me. Osmond has got a bit bored on the genealogy side, but he did introduce me to all the first stages – for that I will always be grateful.

The Marlborough House pictures were ravishing – Colonel Bullock's hand very like Garrick's; Lady Mary Bate-Dudley was wonderful, and so was her husband, with his badly-painted arm and silly dog. I came out very happy, and then we went to the Academy to compare the detail. Garrick was looking well. Then Fortnum's for tea. Lovely – Gainsboroughs all day.

An absolutely unsolicited letter from the British Library about the identity of the Alexandra portrait, inspired by Olivier. I really don't see how the NPG can go on denying it after this.

Dear Sir,

David Garrick Portrait

We understand that there was in recent years a portrait of Garrick, probably by Sir Joshua Reynolds, hanging in the foyer of the Alexandra Theatre. Can you tell me, please, whether you still have this portrait, and if so whether it would be possible for us to inspect it at some convenient time?

We are preparing an exhibition here to commemorate the bicentenary of Garrick's death. It will be mounted in the King's Library from 30th November, 1979 until 18th February, 1980.

I should be grateful for any information you can let me have about this portrait.

Yours faithfully,
John Barr
Exhibitions Officer

June 21st: Otto Preminger is in town to do another film – Graham Greene's The Human Factor.

My friend, Rose Tobias Shaw, is casting it and has suggested me for the part of Richard Attenborough's wife. She rang up to say that Otto has been ill and is now very deaf, and not to get upset if he doesn't remember me. Apparently, the old boy had not recognised some famous actor who had worked for him, and the guy had got very cross. I am sorry to hear age has at last caught up with him. I always liked and admired him; one of the last of the old school.

Otto remembered me. He was sitting with hearing aids in both ears, round, pink and shiny like an old Buddha. His wife, Hope, doesn't look at all well; she is still so beautiful; it seems she has got some blood virus and no one can quite pin it down. She looked harassed and worried and far too thin. Rose is splendid, blooming as usual. I am playing the part – it isn't very big, just one short scene, a tantrum; and I can go to Jean Muir for my dress. The last time I got one of her dresses for a film with Otto it was so expensive that there were German shouts of, 'Vot is it made of – gold?' He had promised to give it to me; Hope beat me to it. She said it was the only good dress in the film. That was the ill-fated *Rosebud*.

On the way down in the elevator, Rose asked me who I thought could play Nicol Williamson's mother – none of the actresses she had thought of were available. I suggested Anne Todd. I had just met her again at the theatre, and she was looking great. 'Is she still acting?' said Rose. I was pretty sure she was, and Rose thought it a good idea. Next day she rang me. Anne Todd is playing the part. This is a rotten profession for women; men have a better deal as they grow older. An actress like Anne Todd should never be forgotten, she is such a good age, there ought to be lots of parts she could play. One trouble is that young directors are terrified to use people of her calibre and reputation in case it shows up their own inadequacies.

The scene didn't take long – one day – but it was complicated. I thought afterwards I was worth my money. It was a difficult tracking shot where I had to weave around cables and tracks and arrive in the right place just at the right time to deliver my tirade. We got it in two takes. Attenborough is on the board of the Tate; he has promised to put in a word for me there. Natch, he got the Gainsborough Lecture, but he is so preoccupied with his long projected film of *Gandhi* that I doubt he will remember.

This time I got to keep my dress.

I think the old boy is in trouble on the money side. Some backers have let him down. I thought Shiv Kapoor might be persuaded to put in some cash from those armament deals; the meeting I arranged was a disaster, mishandled by some idiot business manager from the start. Shiv felt he had not had enough fuss made over him, so no cash.

The film nearly ruined Otto – he had to sell some of his art collection at rock bottom prices to finish it; it was a damned shame.

July 5th: A nice letter from Richard Attenborough.

My dear Adrienne,

Thank you so much for your sweet note which I received this morning.

As you know, I am away on location next week and then I have to go to India, but if I have a spare moment I will do whatever I can to get in to see the picture.

In any event, I will talk to Martin Butlin about it: he is the Keeper of the British Collection at the Tate.

It was wonderful seeing you the other day.

Fondest regards,

Dickie A.

Gandhi took over and the 'spare moment' never came – still, he remembered.

In July, my son left for Australia to take up his place at Canberra University, and my daughter went to the less distant location of Clapham to share a house with some other art students. For the first time in twenty years I was alone, and it was not lonely. I had expected to feel lost; instead I found myself enjoying the luxury of solitude. The end of the close family ties was the beginning of my own life again. I felt an almost guilty pleasure in the silence and the choice of what I should do each day, without having to consult others. Gradually, this feeling wore off. My freedom did not last long – the pursuit of Thomas Gainsborough and David Garrick saw to that.

June 20th and July 5th: A letter from the British Library and another letter from Olivier. (He thought it was a Reynolds.)

5th July 1979

Darling Adrienne:

Thank you so much for your lovely letter. I imagine by now John Barr and/or Helen Smith of the British Library will have contacted you, as I advised them very strongly to do so.

If Sir Hugh and Dr Hayes would only hurry up and agree about the authorship of your lovely painting which, darling, I don't have to see. I got such a lovely idea of it from the photographs you sent me. It is quite clearly an infinitely better piece of work than the one in the National Theatre restaurant – part of the Somerset Maugham legacy.

My Shirley will have told you that I have already lent all my Garrick memorabilia for the Garrick Exhibition, got together by Mr Barr and Miss Smith for the British Library, to be held in November, or thereabouts, and I don't feel too keen on parting with them for more than this particular term. All the more, then, do I hope that you and they can get together on the Gainsborough portrait. To my shame I am not sure of the painter of the one at the National.

I should think that if your picture goes to this exhibition it will be the best imaginable thing for the Alexandra people, much better than offering itself to the disinterested gaze of their patrons. I should imagine they would see the importance of this particular showing as thereby may hang their hopes for keeping the theatre upstanding.

Much love and all my warmest possible wishes.

Ever yours, Larry

No matter, his opinion about it being Garrick is what matters most, and he would not tell the BL about it if it were not correct as far as he is concerned.

I went to meet John Barr, who is the exhibitions officer; very nice and enthusiastic; he is from New Zealand and is a film buff. We went round the library together, just taking the books from the shelves – lovely, none of that waiting around and filling in forms. He seems to know where everything is, a form of heaven to be allowed to get around that library on your own (maybe they would have me on the staff). I told him all about the Garrick and the identification search, and he thought it would be a splendid idea if the picture could be shown for the bicentenary. I would love that so much. He seems to think Olivier's word to be enough, but Miss Smith has the final say as she is arranging the whole thing. I made an appointment for them to come to the Academy to see Davy. I came away on a cloud; at least it looks as if something will come of this.

July 12th: I reckoned without Miss Smith.

She was not charmed by my friend; he was not her idea of Garrick, whatever Olivier and I might think. The flirtatious look of my man almost annoyed her (she can't have met many actors). She seemed to think Garrick would be far graver, not nearly so flippant and larky. She did not believe in the duel either; not becoming to the image. Her Garrick seemed almost Wagnerian. Poor Davy, done out of an engagement at the British Library by a dour blue-stocking! Well, she wasn't his type anyway. He would not have called her a 'sweet, witty barbarian' as he did my ancestress, Marie, and sent loving messages; but then Marie had brains *and* looks and was very feminine. Poor Miss Smith – she reject Davy? It was almost the other way round.

John Barr was very upset and apologetic, but it wasn't his

fault. We are going to keep in touch. Good to have a friend there anyway.

July 13th: It's a good year for exhibitions – Hudson at Kenwood.

John Jacobs, the curator there, knows a great deal about the eighteenth century so I might as well combine business with pleasure and take the folder. I now feel lost if I go anywhere without it.

I liked the pictures a lot; nice portrait of Garrick, older than mine, a mezzotint with a funny, fashionable French wig. On the whole excellent for me, from the reference point of view. There is a formality in his work which I feel sure young Gainsborough copied.

Gainsborough's brilliant conversation piece in the National Gallery, of Mr and Mrs Andrews, is more disciplined than those of Francis Hayman, although even Hayes uses him as a comparison. I feel that Gainsborough aimed higher, even in the early days. The two young people are portrayed in a cornfield of almost surrealist crispness and detail, the young man in the guise of a country squire holding a gun, his wife in a ravishing blue silk dress seated on an ornate garden bench which is, for some reason, taken from its home in the garden and placed in a field. The Andrews picture is dated around 1747–48. Another conversation piece, the Gravenor family, put at about the same date, has much more of Hudson's quality, too, than Hayman. Hayman always has an informality in his work, as if all the sitters were friends – he doesn't remove himself from them. The Andrews picture can never be said to be like that. I love it, but it is a sinister picture in a way. I don't feel Gainsborough liked that couple much.

John Jacobs was pleasant but very sceptical over Garrick. I do get so sick of being treated as if I know nothing at all. What is the matter with these people? Years of going to galleries all over the world have trained my eye very well (whether I knew it was happening or not). I have seen most of the Gainsboroughs in America, in out-of-the-way museums – Omaha, Kansas City – which is more than they have. Anyhow, he is going to come to the Academy so I can chalk up another official opinion.

July 20th: I have met a lovely lady from America, Babs Craven, who is good on identification (she is an adviser to the Lincoln Arts Center Library, in the theatre section).

Like Jean Anderson, she specialises in porcelain, memorabilia and so on. She is extremely knowledgeable about Garrick, having seen his face endless times on snuffboxes, commemorative plates and the like. I took her straight into the Academy where, to my great delight, she fell in love with the picture. She was amazed at the trouble I have had – she is in no doubt herself. She suggested I ask an old friend of hers, George Nash, who was in charge of the Enthoven collection for a time. He is cataloguing some pictures for Harvard with Sir Anthony Blunt – I will ask him to help me get *his* opinion. I have not been able to contact him so far, he is quite elusive, but a great scholar. I admire him, I wouldn't even mind a turn-down from him.

George came to the Academy, liked the picture too, and thought it was young Garrick and says he will try to bring Sir Anthony in if he can. He likes him – I think he finds him distant and a little hard to know, but he admires him and thinks he would be interested. I hope so.

Cooper's were too expensive and too busy for me to go on plaguing them, although they genuinely cared about the project and took endless trouble with the different experiments. I had sent some of the photographs to the forensic department at Scotland Yard, and a splendid gentleman there, Ken Creer, had become interested in the problem. As well as being a photographer, he had invented a method, used all over the world, which tests whether a document has been altered. He thought there might be a way to bring the letters and the shield up more strongly, and came to the Academy with all kinds of filters and highly sensitive film. He had been impressed by my identikit tracing of the Hogarth portrait over the Birmingham picture, and convinced by it – 'A job for you here any time,' he said.

Ken Creer came from Scotland Yard today and we tried all sorts of new filters on the shield and the initials. The light was bad and the results poor. We are going to take the picture up to the forensic lab later in the year (which means hiring it for the day) to do more tests. None of the new photographs brings up the shield or underscoring more clearly, but they all show it.

After nearly two years of fruitless experiments to improve the quality of the photographs, I returned at last to the first process with the help of yet another photographer. By putting the transparencies on a light box and photographing them in black and white, we were able to print very good pictures of all the underscored letters. The trouble is that if the pictures are blown up a great deal, you blow up the grain of the canvas, too, and lose definition.

July 23rd: Mirrington of Agnew's came in today.

He reacted (as they all do) as if the picture were a strange animal, not fitting into the known scheme of things.

John Jacobs of Kenwood arrived, too; it was unfortunate that they were both there at the same time as (like prize fighters) they warily sparred, each unwilling to make a statement. Jacobs finally retreated with the cry of, 'It says Suffolk, but I am not committing myself'. Mirrington admitted it baffled him and could not reconcile himself to the dating or the style. I gave him my lecture on early work, etc., and he replied faintly, 'We do have our own Gainsboroughs, Miss Corri.' He suggested I let them have Garrick for their showroom in order to study him further, but I can't do that as there are others who must see the picture.

Spent more days at the Witt Library; masses of information assembled. The amount of work attributed to Gainsborough is phenomenal; if all the pictures *are* his, he can never have slept. There are one or two obvious mistakes – a drawing, for instance, supposed to be of Garrick by Gainsborough, is by Van der Gucht, a study for an oil-painting – I have seen this picture. Hayes says this drawing has disappeared and that he never thought it was Gainsborough but, somewhere along the line, it was sold as one, identified by the auction house from some bit of family history no doubt: 'Great Aunt Martha always said it was right, and so it must be.' It is amazing how gullible the auction rooms will be if it is in their own interests; also, they are so very lazy. It is appalling, with all the work that goes through their hands, that they have not set up first-class research departments; but that can be said for the galleries, too.

I am being horribly impatient – how many first-raters are

there in the world, in any field? Too few.

I shall not meet Sir Anthony Blunt! Suddenly the papers are filled with scandal. A book has been written naming him as the fourth man in the sordid Burgess/Maclean affair. It is terrible to see this clever, and very private man, humiliated. If he was so guilty, why was he knighted after his confession? Why did he continue in a position of trust? Is it perhaps that he had not done too much harm? No one except Blunt himself appears to try to answer these questions. He gave an interview of great courage (desperately painful to watch) on television in which he tried to deal honestly with these questions; his rational approach was lost in the hysteria of the moment. He never gave an inch on principle, and tried to point out that it happened at a time when the Russians were our allies.

One day, perhaps, I shall meet the professor, but at the moment must give up all hope. For all his political or emotional errors, academically he is a real first-rater.

July 24th: Today there is something I dread.

An actors' protest march to Covent Garden, the Opera House, to hear speeches, then to the House of Commons to lobby our MPs. All in order to get VAT reduced on theatre tickets. It won't do a blind bit of good; VAT is a European tax. We are, as usual, out of date in our gesture; it should have been made when the tax was first proposed, then we might have won some concessions, as did the French and German actors (all more aware politically). Now it is too late; typical of our union. We were probably wrangling over something idiotic and so the issue was never raised. Still, I will march. I also dread the kind of bun-fight these things generally turn into, and the way everyone will look. I am going to be very conservative, in blue, but with comfortable shoes. We are to assemble at Marble Arch.

Worse than I expected. Actors, like vampires, should not be seen by daylight. The lunatic fringe predominated – are we really such a tatty lot? Why should people shell out good money to see tramps? Well, that was the general impression. I had a sinking feeling that the tax might be raised if Maggie or any of her lot saw us.

Thank God Geraint Evans was there, looking grand, and Ralph Richardson – a bit of class. I am proud of the theatre and hate to see it let down. Of course, there were plenty of serious, concerned members of the profession present, but they could hardly be seen for the fools in tinsel and funny clothes. I stuck close to Geraint and, to do the organisers justice, they did try to make the march look a sober affair – good blue coats and knights were shoved to the front – but it was not an easy job. I was pleased to see my Welsh friend looking in such good spirits; he has been very ill but today he was blooming. We have known each other since the 'fifties and Glyndebourne days. I was able to regard the whole thing as a pleasant stroll, and a chance to catch up on news. However, half-way down Piccadilly he started to look in his pockets. 'My God' (that lovely Welsh accent), 'I've forgotten my heart pills!' I was so worried. He decided he could make it to Covent Garden then go straight home. By that time, whatever impact the march made would be over and recorded for posterity.

When we marched past the Arts Council I noticed they had a police guard. What did they think we were going to do, storm them for grants? All the office buildings had people at the windows waving encouragement and spotting their favourites. Shaftesbury Avenue, the heart of theatrical management, the people whom we were also hoping to benefit, had done nothing ('Nothing shall come of nothing'). My bank waved, and I looked at the street name, 'Goodman's Fields', above the Dean Street sign – it means so much to me, that name, not just my overdraft. God bless the National Westminster.

As we reached Soho, actors began to drop by the wayside at their favourite pubs, there were serious worries that no one would be left. On the whole most of them stuck it out and came on to the Commons after the speeches, some jollier than they were when they started out, it has to be admitted. Geraint got home safely. I telephoned his wife, Brenda. 'Oh, the fool,' she said, 'he's always forgetting his pills.' She had seen us on television and one of her sons had said, 'Dad's done all right!'

Of course the tax stayed. The arts, especially the performing ones, get very short shrift in this country, in spite of the money and prestige they have earned. Foreigners can never understand our government's attitude – I think the puritan streak is at the heart of it all, in spite of everything my friend Garrick tried to do.

July 30th: A commercial with Charlie Drake.

I have to sit, playing the piano, while he uses this new miracle commodity made out of waste matter (they don't say what) and redecorates the room around me. Money for old rope, you might think. There is going to be a big campaign, they promise. We shall be rich, the whole country will want this miracle stuff, ads in the papers, colour supplements, you name it.

On the morning we are to film, my sinus is at its worst; I can hardly open my eyes and my head is splitting. I do everything I can before the car arrives – ice, allergy drops, nose drops, eye drops, pills. I succeed in managing to look like Henry Cooper after a bad fight; at least my eyes are open. The make-up lady is kind, but cannot suppress a shudder; she knows a difficult job when she sees it. She slaps more ice and witch-hazel on the swollen thing in the middle of my face that should be a nose, and it starts to subside. She is very, very good; so is the hairdresser. Between them they work a minor miracle; by the time the director arrives, I not only look human, I look good. I love them both, others less strong would have screamed and gone home; my heart is theirs for ever. All this before 8.30 a.m.

Now the problems begin. The STUFF is meant to be a malleable paste which spreads over any kind of surface (in a variety of colours), not only painting the surface but re-contouring and filling cracks, smoothing bumpy surfaces; it is really what I needed on my face early this morning.

Looking unbelievably glamorous, I start to play the piano, and Charlie starts to slap this stuff on the wall. In the first place it won't come off the board it sits on; it is pink, looks a little like ice-cream, handles like chewing gum and porridge mixed together. Charlie struggles, the watching executives look grim – there are four of them. They seem to think Charlie is doing it on purpose. Each time he dislodges a glob of this thing, it either recoils on to the tray, or slithers off the wall, should he get it that far. Twelve takes and Charlie is sweating and exhausted; the floor is covered in stalagmites, unyielding and unmoving. They cut to hold a conference. The floor looks like Francis Bacon's studio – maybe they should have hired *him*. After the break, a sturdy chippie (or carpenter) is delegated to slap the stuff on and then the director will cut to Charlie making it look as if he has done the work. I will continue to mime playing the piano. The chippie fares less well than Charlie; he gets it on to the wall but then the wall peels off. Another conference. At ten that evening, by a series of cunning fakes and trick camera work, they have managed to make the two and a half minute film. I will not buy the stuff. I am nervous in case it sells and people blame me for it.

I needn't have worried. Various acts of God kept it from the public and Charlie and me from our fortune.

I had wanted to be at the Academy when Sir Ellis saw Garrick, to personally back up my arguments on the 'middle' style, but luck was against me.

August 12th: Sir Ellis has seen the picture!

He just popped in, as he was giving a lecture next door at the Society of Antiquaries. He didn't see the folder. I feel suicidal over the whole thing. I know it wouldn't change the canvas, but if only I had been there to explain exactly what I see in the portrait. I must get him to come and look at it again.

One concession in my favour – he agrees it could be Garrick:

August 15th, 1979

Dear Miss Corri,

I had to be in London today and I looked into the RA and saw the portrait. I am quite prepared to admit that the sitter is probably Garrick, but I am afraid it seemed to me utterly impossible that Gainsborough, at any stage, could have had anything to do with it. It doesn't, in fact, seem to me to be the work of a young artist – though I admit this is a question of feeling rather than something demonstrable. In fact, I shouldn't be surprised if the waistcoat were not the work of a professional drapery painter. Stylistically, it is much closer to Hudson – though much less competent – than Gainsborough was ever likely to have been.

I hope to be in Yorkshire this weekend and will try and have a look at Admiral Vernon, but I have a strong suspicion he will confirm this unfavourable view.

Yours sincerely,
Ellis Waterhouse

August–November: At least the autumn has begun quite well.

A nice part in *The Mitfords*, or rather the version of *Pursuit of Love* and *Love in a Cold Climate* – Thames Television. All very grand and pre-sold to America, decent fees and directed by Donald McQuinney. He looks like Jacques Tati and is damned good. I have worked for him several times.

August 15th: The Snag struck again!

I don't believe it, the biggest Snag of all, a strike of technicians. The Snag has now a form in my mind; like a sneaky, nasty yeti, it lurks and strikes with vile regularity. This time everything seemed lovely, should have been lovely; it really isn't funny at all. We are all under contract, cannot work, will not get paid and cannot take any other jobs. The strike is an indefinite one and seems to be hardening. One of the reasons we do not get paid is because it affects the accountancy side and no cheques can be made out. A 'Catch 22' situation. Christmas coming up, the commercial will not be shown either – one Snag at a time please, not *multiple* Snags!

While the strike lasted I returned to my job of research full time. At least I didn't have time to sit around and mope. I kept up my barrage of letters and my rounds of the galleries. I left poor John Hayes alone, for which I should think he was grateful. Ten turn-downs from him so far, and five from Sir Ellis Waterhouse; not a brilliant record. At least I could concentrate on the genealogy side and Edward Henry Parker's origins.

October 20th: Today the picture goes to Scotland Yard.

I have never been there and I am quite looking forward to it. The building is large and grim, like any government department, faceless. It could be the BBC.

Up in the lab they have kindly pinned sheets of paper over the more grisly pictures – nice of them to think about it. They have a splendid crop of house plants, or so it seems. I comment on them and ask who the gardener is (I can never keep plants). 'Miss Corri, don't you know marijuana when you see it?' I don't. They think it is very funny – I have been admiring a haul which they have to keep healthy until the case comes to court.

The Yard photographs do show the shield a little better; on the whole the transparencies are still the best. I resent having to prove what, in the end, is only a minor part of the picture's identity, when to me the whole speaks for itself. So far, however, it seems only to be heard by me and Arthur Lucas.

I did get a lovely official album stamped with the Metropolitan Police seal, with all the photographs.

November 29th: The Garrick Exhibition opened at the British Museum. Small and rather poor.

I didn't note that with any satisfaction at all. Nothing else has been done this year for him. Without a theatre museum, of course, there are few facilities; even so, this was unimaginative. I am glad that the Garrick portrait didn't make his début here. Garrick himself deserved more attention. This was bookish and staid, nothing much of the flavour of the theatre about it. Miss Helen Smith was very reverent and very boring in her approach. There was hardly anyone there.

Christmas at Sian Phillips'. She married Robin Sachs this morning, they appear to be very happy. It was a lovely way to celebrate, the first Christmas for years where I have been among adults exclusively; a wonderful change.

The technicians' strike went on. There were a lot of meetings which got nowhere and for any actors already signed to do a television show it was murder. We were in a workless, unpaid limbo.

I buried myself in research and tried to make the most of the spare time. Then, just as suddenly, the strike ended and we rushed back, none of us quite remembering what we had rehearsed; so Christmas and the New Year blurred into one and January 1980 saw the end of the Mitford Saga.

My count of turn-downs at Christmas in this Year of Grace 1979 totals:

John Hayes, National Portrait Gallery	Turn-down, full and positive
Sir Ellis Waterhouse	Turn-down but might be persuaded
Elizabeth Einberg, Tate Gallery	Turn-down flat
John Ingamells, Wallace Collection	Turn-down flat
Malcolm Cormack of the Mellon	Turn-down flat
Sir Oliver Millar	Turn-down but has not yet seen the picture
Roy Strong	Wavering, can't be positive either way (suspect he's being kind)
Michael Levey, National Gallery	Turn-down but that Zoffany guess was plain silly
Tim Clifford, Manchester	Maybe, but hasn't seen the picture
John Jacobs, Kenwood	Turn-down but retreated saying, 'It says Suffolk, but I'm not committing myself.'

Of all this list, only Sir Ellis Waterhouse, John Hayes, Roy Strong, John Jacobs and Michael Levey have seen the picture. The others have turned it down on the photographs.

If I can go on after all that, I may have to be committed, in a different way. I shall, however, go on in spite of it all.

1980

No reply was forthcoming from the theatre about Parker's exact date of death – around 1910 was all they seemed to know. Perhaps they couldn't find it, so I steamed ahead on the little information I had. At Somerset House I found his will, 1911. He appointed his brother, a Robert Gunning Parker of Bristol, and a John Lewis Jones as executors.

Starting from wills is considered the wrong way round in genealogy practice, but I had no alternative. I went to the General Register Office at St Catherine's House, Holborn, to look for his birth certificate. The names of his two brothers on the will meant I could be sure when I found the birth certificate that it was the correct one if it connected with other members of the family. The theatre had given the date of his birth as 1855 and the place as Bristol. His brothers had used the double-barrelled name of Gunning Parker in the will, which perhaps meant he was registered under that, so I had to look him up under both names. A couple of elderly relatives had lived in Bath – so far so good.

A day of research in London has to be very carefully planned. All parish records are supposed to be at the General Register Office (GRO), although ones for Kent are in Canterbury. The records not at the GRO are scattered around in an almost haphazard manner; some are in the library in Buckingham Palace Road which has the ominous sign: THERE IS NO PUBLIC LAVATORY IN THIS BUILDING. If the call of nature hits you during your research you have to go across the road to the bus station. The staff have a pretty smug look on their faces as they watch you whizz out.

There is also the Guildhall Library, the British Library, the Public Record Office, the Court of Arches, Lambeth Palace and Kew Record Office. These are the main ones to begin with, but there are many other smaller caches tucked away all over London. For the Welsh and Cornish records you have to go to Taunton (Debrett brought out a very useful book in 1981 which lists all the record offices in Great Britain). I had to find out the hard way.

The original registers and documents are ultimately the most reliable sources. Few researchers ever make notes absolutely verbatim and you invariably find small discrepancies creeping in. The best thing to do is to search out the originals yourself and work from those.

At least the Society of Genealogists can cut a few corners to begin with.

Back to the genealogy and *Kelly's*. In the will, Edward Henry Parker's brother is described as a tobacco merchant; in *Kelly's* as a vendor of fishing tackle. His other brother was a John Isaac Parker, a pawnbroker, also of Bristol. No age was declared on the will, but the document sent to me by the theatre said that he was born in Bristol in 1855.

At St Catherine's House, in Kingsway, all the births, marriages and deaths after the Great Census of 1837 can be found. Wills are at Somerset House. This is all considered 'modern'.

Although all parish records should be at the GRO, many parish priests are quirky customers and I soon learned that quite a few preferred to keep the old registers in the churches where they belonged. I really can't blame them, they are lovely personal records of the districts and should be in the local parish if they are well looked after. In the Devon area, all the records are deposited at Taunton; many were destroyed during the war, which is as good an argument as any for leaving them in the local churches and simply copying.

There was no birth registration for any Edward Henry Parker in Bristol in St Catherine's records for 1855, nor any Gunning Parkers. So, bearing in mind he was an actor and might have lied a little about his age, I started on the earlier books of births. Nothing in Bristol, the theatre had apparently got the town wrong, too. I turned up a few other Edward Henry Parkers, sent for their birth certificates, but they, too, ended in blanks. For the hell of it, I simply took *all* the possible Edward Henry Parkers within a fifty-mile radius of Bristol, between 1852 and 1858, and sent for *all* the birth certificates. This was expensive but it seemed the best way to find him, providing he had been born in that area. There seemed to be an awful lot of them.

One registration finally fitted. In Kilmersdon, Frome, Somerset, October 16th, 1855, Edward Henry, son of a Moses Rennolds Parker and his wife Mary Ann, formerly Giffard! On his mother's side, then, if this was correct, Edward Henry was a Giffard. I hoped that somehow I could tie him in with Garrick's first actor-manager, Henry Giffard. This seemed pretty unlikely because, as far as I knew, the early Giffards had no children; still, their property must have been left to someone, and the name of Edward Henry's mother gave me a little hope that they might have been distantly related.

Every book I had read stressed that Henry Giffard was Irish. He was also treated as a relatively minor figure in the theatre of his day. When Goodman's Fields Theatre opened, *Gentleman's Magazine* gave more space to the decorations of the building by Edward Shepherd, and the stage designs of Francis Hayman, than to the owner; and to the fact that the Lord Chamberlain would not grant him a licence, which meant that every performance at Goodman's Fields Theatre was technically illegal. All this had made me feel Henry was some sort of renegade; as he did not figure in Garrick's life after the first seasons, I had assumed he must have returned to Ireland. The Gunning name held a ray of hope, as they were a well-known Irish family. Osmond Bullock (of the Marlborough House pictures) offered to help me; his bet was that the Gunning side would turn up the answer. He spent months on it and turned up masses of quite interesting, but irrelevant information, and gave up in despair.

January 15th: There is a new curator at Gainsborough's House in Sudbury, Stephen Jones, and he is coming to see the Garrick at the Academy.

Curiously, his letter is the most considered; still, he sounds quite young, plenty of time for him to grow biased. I would just like to get the picture shown and have a few other opinions. It is time it had an airing; it is also interesting to note that he thinks he should see the picture:

> If it is by Gainsborough I do not think it can have been

painted earlier than 1752 which would make Garrick at least thirty-four or thirty-five in the portrait. I am not very clear as to the point at which Garrick's fortunes really rose but obviously this portrait would have been painted after he became a success because, in the first place, he would not have been dressed so elegantly and, in the second place, he would not have been able to afford a portrait of this kind.

Stylistically, the painting seems a little conservative for Gainsborough; I am thinking in particular of the treatment of the hair and of the ruffles at his wrists. Comparing the photographs with the works we have in the house of the Ipswich period your painting seems to lack the impressionistic brush work of Gainsborough's early portraits, and the figure also seems a little too solid for early Gainsborough. On the other hand, thinking of our portrait of Lambe Barry, which is similarly posed, though reversed, half length, there are certain similarities in the general treatment. Obviously, I should like to see the portrait in person before committing myself to any judgement at all. You will appreciate that where scholars as distinguished as Dr Hayes and Dr Strong have paused for thought, I, as a very junior art historian, do not wish to rush in. It is a very lovely portrait indeed and I am sure that when the truth is established it will prove an important and interesting work.

February 11th: Stephen Jones came to the Academy and the picture goes to Sudbury in June.

I was able to show him the last self-portrait and the signature out of its frame, as we had been doing more photographs with yet another photographer, this time Major Steadman, trying a variety of colour filters. 'What's this one worth?' he asked Hans Fletcher, who was supervising the session. On being told around £100,000, Major nearly fell over. He rallied a bit and told me he didn't like it nearly as much as the Garrick. Hugh's halo is even larger in my eyes.

Stephen Jones hinted hopefully how nice it would be to show the last self-portrait and the Garrick together, and Hugh agreed. So the upshot is they both go to Sudbury. The first time they will have had a chance to see the self-portrait in Sudbury; almost like Gainsborough going home on a visit.

I don't think that Stephen is convinced about the Garrick, but he is not a fool and knows it will help his exhibition (on Joshua Kirby) to have the two pictures there. He is young and has great enthusiasm and enterprise.

My letters to Sir Ellis continued. It was rather nice to have someone to write to who knew what I was trying to do, even if I couldn't get his agreement on stylistic reasons alone; I needed his opinion. I had begun to find quite a lot of interesting information on the Gainsborough front which seemed to be new and exciting, even if it had nothing to do with the picture of Garrick. For instance, one day in the Buckingham Palace Road Library, I took down the Harleian Register, and while looking at the entry for the Gainsborough marriage, it occurred to me that Dr Keith's Mayfair Chapel records might *not* have disappeared. I could not find the marriage register of Dr Keith's clandestine Chapel at any of the record offices, nor was the Gainsborough marriage among the Fleet Marriage notebooks (tiny diaries carried in the back pockets of the clergy), so I took a look at a map of Mayfair in 1746. The only church still standing from that time was St George's, Hanover Square. I reckoned that any papers not at the record offices must have gone to the nearest church for safe keeping, and so they had. Dr Keith's register is there in the safe, as are all the other local records.

At St George's (where I was married myself), the vicar disapproves of Dr Keith no end, and doesn't even really think you should want to look at the books. 'I have no time for dead people,' he said crossly. If you turn the register round and begin to read from the back, upside down so to speak, you also find birth records. I had no idea I had such an involved mind, but I quickly discovered the eighteenth century didn't waste paper. I thought the register romantic – all those runaway marriages. But I had to keep this view to myself.

A sad little note emerged on St Thomas's Church, Holborn, given by Gainsborough as his parish on the marriage register. March 1st, 1747, is the entry of the death of an infant, Margaret Gainsborough. The first child born to the Gainsboroughs had died and was buried there. From the date of this entry it is obvious that Margaret Burr was pregnant at the time of her marriage. Some of the early books had contained unflattering remarks about Gainsborough's morality, mostly made by William Wyndham, who later became the Secretary for War in the Pitt administration, and Gainsborough's own letters hint at various amatory escapades. If the seduction and marriage had been a piece of gossip and scandal at the time, the reason for these remarks would be plain. A not very auspicious beginning for them both, but touching and human, and certainly more believable than the silly story about her appearing from nowhere and being sketched into a drawing in sunny Suffolk (this is Walter Armstrong's version).

I wonder why no one has bothered to look at this register before me? In those days it was almost inevitable that there would be a child born within the first year, and one each year afterwards, with depressing regularity. The children's births are always on the records of the father's church. From the entry it is clear there were *three* daughters, and that the young couple did not immediately settle in Sudbury, as has previously been thought. The following year another daughter was born and registered there in Suffolk, but then no more entries until 1752. Either poor Margaret had suffered a series of miscarriages, or she had been left in Sudbury with his family while Gainsborough returned to the pleasures of London. The more I researched into his life, the more unanswered questions appeared. If my picture was correct, and he could paint so well in 1742, it is logical that he would have found plenty of work in London; it also made sense of the fact that his picture of the Charterhouse was accepted by the Foundling Hospital with the other established painters of the day.

The Garrick was the key to an entirely new view of Gainsborough's life, if I could prove its authenticity. The hunt was revealing side issues I never dreamed were possible. The entry also made me wonder if he had met his wife in London or Suffolk. On the register for the marriage she gives her church as St George's, Hanover Square, an unlikely local church for an obscure country girl. For the meeting to have taken place in London was more probable.

March 4th: At last a Dr Who.

That will make the children in the road have some respect for me, and all my love of science fiction can be indulged.

I was solidly bitten by the bug of pure research into original papers, and began to think any time not spent on it was wasted. Nevertheless, I had to go on earning a living to pay for this lovely new occupation. One consolation (to me at least) was that I could continue the research wherever I happened to be – a view not shared by directors I worked for during this time. They seemed to feel they were not getting my undivided attention when I arrived at rehearsal with bundles of birth, death and marriage certificates, not to mention wills. No play, unless you are on the stage for every second, *needs* full-time attention, and hanging around with nothing to do at rehearsal is soul-destroying. One actor I know is an authority on Rowlandson, Gilray, Cruikshank and others, and researches them during his breaks; another studies Army history. These are the sane ones.

March 20th–April 20th: The Dr Who *was not so much fun as I had expected.*

Tom Baker was tired and moody. He had been doing it for a long time, but then it had paid him handsome dividends, and it is such a good programme. There is no pleasing actors!

Lalla Ward, who played his assistant, was unhappy, too. My only real fun was a weird make-up and lots of special effects – instant ageing and a hammy death scene. Apart from that, and a nice director and crew, pretty miserable.

Anyway the children in my road were impressed for five minutes, and I was able to hand out *Dr Who* photographs and a few reject space helmets which the property master gave me.

During the *Dr Who* rehearsals I met Vivien Merchant once more. The restaurant at the BBC rehearsal rooms is a nightmare – we all know each other, have probably worked together, and can't remember each other's names. It can be very embarrassing. One lady I know was confronted with the sight of two ex-husbands and an ex-lover all crammed together in the lift, and forgot *all* their names.

Vivien still looked lost, but she was working again, in *A Tale of Two Cities*. We had lunch together – it was the last time I ever saw her.

My ex-husband was there, being directed by Don Taylor (Wythenshawe) in the Arthur Miller play, *The Crucible*. Don told me that the early English settlers had really worn top hats, not those Welsh numbers we usually associate with the Puritans. He dropped the idea when I pointed out that it would make my ex look just like his father, Raymond Massey, as Abraham Lincoln.

Bouts of depression began to hit me very badly, and I thought I really could not go on with the search, although my conviction about the authenticity of the picture never wavered.

May 7th: It is now nearly four years and I have not produced enough proof to satisfy the experts.

I think I am going mad. I mutter George III's words to Fanny Burney, 'I am not mad, Miss Burney, I am not mad!' to myself, but am I? No one else believes in the picture; I have missed two summers being stuck in libraries. For what? I am almost too tired to go on. Arthur Lucas is right, I shall never convince them. I am even sounding less convinced myself. I can hear an hysterical note in my voice, almost as if they *must* believe me if I say it long and often enough. I have begun to notice a bored look on people's faces, or one of pity and disbelief; or worse, a kind of humouring kindness, as shown to a child or someone in their dotage.

I am going to see David Carritt at his gallery tomorrow. I set great store by his *reaction*, not so much as by what he will *say*, for why should he agree before it goes for sale? It would be against his interests. Yet I will know by the degree of interest he shows, or at any rate the time he spends with it, what he thinks. He is probably, like all good dealers, pretty enigmatic; after all, that is his job; why should he confirm when the others will not?

I had left David Carritt until last. A very sharp man with one of the best eyes in London, or perhaps the world; certainly the commercial world. I had great respect for him. It was he who had bought the Mentmore Fragonard the National Gallery paid so much for (I believe the representatives of the gallery at the same sale had confined their bidding to a very doubtful Rembrandt).

I rang up, explained the situation yet again. I could hear the desperate tones coming through and tried to quell them. He had a very smooth voice, but pleasant, and I made an appointment to see him the next day, Friday. My folder was now a bulging dead weight of transparencies, infra-red photographs, the Scotland Yard file; all inessentials in my opinion. The picture speaks for itself, if they could only *see*.

When I had talked to Ellis Waterhouse about Carritt he seemed wary of him, but said that he had given one of the best lectures on Chardin he had ever heard. The line between commercial and academic expertise is so fine; with the exception of Waterhouse, all the best brains seem to be in the auction houses or galleries, perhaps because, as one elegant dealer said rather inelegantly, 'We have to put our money where our mouth is.' Unlike the public galleries who, of course, have public funds.

May 8th: The interview with David Carritt was classic.

His 'salon' (it could hardly be demeaned by calling it a shop) – smoked dark glass in Duke Street, one Angelica Kauffman-ish type of picture in the window, discreet and awe-inspiring. A very nice American was thanking Mr Carritt profusely for being allowed to spend a great deal of money with him (he was accepting this with great grace). An assistant (who smelled rather strongly of beer, rather letting the image down) asked me to wait, and I watched Mr Carritt's sales performance with great interest. It was impeccable. He was a slight, good-looking man, in appearance as smooth as his voice; shrewd eyes.

I was to be interviewed in the flat upstairs; the beery gentleman was left to mind the store. The upstairs had a carefully geared image. Expensive furniture, tasteful beige and cream, a rather (to my mind) indifferent Boucher, the right bits of Roman pottery, the right, but not ostentatious, Italian Renaissance drawings, just enough to inspire a certain awe and reverence for the owner. A good set – Carl Toms could not have bettered it.

Mr Carritt settled himself under the Boucher and prepared to give me an audience. In his honour I was wearing the audition mink (so-called because I used to lend it to friends when they went to interviews, the theory being if you looked as if you didn't need the job you might get it – it often worked).

Although it is a bit frayed now, it still has class. I had not been invited to remove it, but it was hot so I peeled it off and began the Lecture. What was good enough for the rest of them was good enough for him. Half-way through, I noticed he was looking a bit stunned; perhaps the ambience usually worked differently. I was beyond being impressed by anything. He shuddered at the X-rays and said he didn't need to see them, but took the transparencies over to a light box and studied them closely. When he next looked at me, I thought I detected rather more in his manner than the wish to impress. He had become business-like.

The interview ended with Carritt agreeing to come to the Academy to see the picture, and heaving a sigh of relief to see his immaculate room restored to order. A very, very bright man. Mr Carritt is like a sleek, well-fed, intelligent cat who hunts for fun as well as food. He would not give me the time of day if he did not think I was right, and, if he does, it will not stop him filching the picture from under my nose – with charm, of course.

I rate him a good deal higher than the other commercial gents I have met.

Nineteen eighty was almost totally dominated by my research. Small, unimportant jobs came and went, most of my diary tersely noted reference rooms. A concert here and there, or the theatre, were my occasional relaxations. Most of the time I was too tired when I got back at night to do anything except sort out my notes of that day. No job of real interest remains from that year, in my diary or in my mind.

May 12th: David Carritt came in to the Academy today, apologising.

He was late – his mother is ill. He doesn't look too well himself. He was amazed at the stuff hanging backstage at the Academy. A self-portrait of Cotes, for example, finished by Gainsborough after Cotes' death. He spent nearly an hour with the picture – in the life of that busy man, it meant a great deal. His verdict was (safe because there were no witnesses) that I was right and that there was no reason in the world why it should not be by Gainsborough. He thought the head 'magnificent', parts of it patchy as might be expected for a first attempt at a large portrait, but in all a wonderful picture. As there was no one else there, he didn't have his dealer's face on and was openly enthusiastic. Here was something that I had not been allowed to see at my first audience, a man who loved paintings, not just the cash. Arthur Lucas has cleaned many pictures for him, so I know he will probably talk to him about it. I had only been able to get a small, dingy office for this showing of Davy, but it didn't seem to make much difference. Garrick lit up the small room and the works we had passed, including a Gainsborough landscape, did nothing to detract from the way he affected Mr Carritt.

At the end the dealer, of course, reappeared, pound signs in his eyes. He smiled and said that I needed 'to get documentation'. However, he had restored my sanity a little; even if he never says it publicly until after the sale, he knows and I know that we had both had the pleasure of looking at the first 'grand' portrait by a great painter.

May 22nd: Lotherton Hall again.

Jean Muir is having a very grand retrospective exhibition. She asked me if I could lend anything, but she had examples of the dresses similar to mine; my very early Jane & Jane ones went too far back.

It is strange to see the house under such different circumstances. The rooms upstairs have been beautifully arranged. I am used to the mechanics of the fashion industry, but it must be interesting to other women, who don't know how much goes into the frock they finally buy, to see the process. Endless fittings for the theatre also gives one more insight. Half the battle of whatever character you are playing is fought on the first appearance. This makes actors become more aware than most people as to how they look and how to create a certain impression.

Looking at people in the street, I am terribly conscious that it takes an actual decision to dress as they do. Acting gives the excuse to observe, and I am afraid, I use it, as does every actor I know. Anything I see which is singular or interesting might be good for a certain role. There is always a bit of you that stands aside and watches, no matter how involved you may be, rather like a doctor dissecting. The most conventional people tell you about themselves, whether they know it or not, in the clothes they wear; even if they are trying to be self-effacing that is, in itself, a statement.

Being there early is fun, the last of the stands just finished; we all have time for a drink before 'the public' arrives, and then they are there and Jean is doing the receiving. Large matrons squashed into her dresses that they bought years ago, 'This is one of your Jane & Jane ones!' Lots of little buttons, I remember those. The influence of clothes can never be overestimated; they can raise or lower a person's morale; the right colour can give so much pleasure, and they express the times so well. That is what it is all about.

Jean was rather touched at the response, and very pleased. It was a good day. One of the exhibits had a particular edge – a red trouser and tunic outfit belonging to my friend, Jill Bennett, with the appropriate little card: LOANED BY MISS JILL BENNETT, and a portrait of her in the same gear, painted by Patrick Proctor; lovely picture. This had a card saying: LOANED BY MR JOHN OSBORNE. The story of a marriage in those two items.

June 3rd: The picture has gone down to Sudbury with the Academy's self-portrait, and I am going to give a talk on him.

I would really rather wait until all my work is complete; still, it is nice that he will get a showing at last. The talk is to the Gainsborough Society, but it is very difficult when the question of whether the picture is authentic or not still hangs fire. I am far too over-anxious and defensive about him, and I really am sick of people being – the only word – indulgent with me. I am at the stage when I feel they are tapping their foreheads behind my back and humouring me to my face. This way madness certainly lies.

Apart from a few personal entries, my diary became filled with cryptic statements which consisted of: PRO all day; GRO; St Catherine's; Somerset House – and so on. My diary entries had been supplanted by my discoveries, which went into notebooks that seemed to multiply by themselves. Nowadays I lead a life which belongs more to Garrick and Gainsborough than to myself.

June 25th: The V & A gives rather grand, mini-Glyndebourne type evenings for their supporters, the Friends of the V & A.

Ham House had just been redecorated and Frank Barrie and I had been coerced, willingly, into being the entertainers, reading letters and papers to do with the Lauderdales in the seventeenth century. There is something rather marvellous about speaking the words of the people who owned the house, with their portraits looking down at you.

It was all at very short notice and with too little rehearsal, but it went so well that we did another performance the next night "by request". We started in evening light, but it gradually got darker; as I am long-sighted, I couldn't get the script far enough away to see. Frank shamelessly dragged his chair over to the window! The next night we had lights. Eddie Kulukundis arrived and sat beaming in the front row, which was about three feet away. It was a bit difficult to try to pretend to be Lady Lauderdale with Eddie's cheerful face there.

Eddie is a Greek shipping magnate with a passion for the theatre. This passion led him to assume that thankless, but necessary, role of an 'angel'. No matter how much he loses, he seems to count it a privilege. He can be relied upon to take me to a play any time I ask him to; he doesn't always stay awake, but he sleeps quietly.

I want him to put on Frank's one-man show of *Macready* which is extremely good and very moving. Frank has bookings to go all over the world with it – he has had a tremendous success in America. Wythenshawe was certainly productive for him in that way.

I only wish to God I could bring my Garrick/Gainsborough project to a satisfactory conclusion. It has been going on for so long now, sometimes I lose heart and think that Arthur Lucas was right and that it will never end. I only wish I had someone at home who took an interest in it. I need encouragement, and not just from kind friends and neighbours.

July 18th: I didn't do a very good talk at Sudbury. Over-

anxious, I knew it. Stephen Jones was kind and threw the right questions at me, but I need more time to research; I don't know enough yet.

The show at Sudbury was good in many ways. Garrick looked well in the little museum. The Gainsborough self-portrait loaned by the Academy looked as if it were visiting country relatives. I still don't feel as if he lived in the house. It is charming, with a pretty garden, but there is something wrong. It has the air of a set in a play, as if designed for the 'story' of Gainsborough, not the reality. The last self-portrait is the only one, apparently, that he wanted reproduced in engravings. Why? Because the others still show traces of the countryman? The last is a man who has arrived, and a gentleman – was it so important to him? Had he had to fight for that position? None of the present books show much of a struggle. They are all cosy and idyllic, yet the marriage was not happy; he says in letters that his wife is 'weak but good and never much formed to humour my happiness'. Yet poor Mrs G. seems to have had a difficult husband, and the letter to Cosway, who lived next door to him in London, shows without much doubt that they were enjoying the favours of the same lady. He emerges from his letters as a randy man, given to bouts of extravagant remorse after committing an indiscretion, and just as soon back to his old habits. A man of appetite. His writings smack of the theatre and *Tom Jones*, as if his education had been from plays and novels. Was that it? Did he pick up his schooling in the streets and theatres of Covent Garden rather than the fields of Suffolk? I think that may have been the case. Whatever it is, I shall do my best to find out; I cannot accept the versions I have read, nor this country setting for him.

The Mayor of Sudbury was Indian and opened the exhibition. The mixture of cultures was interesting. He was very English – India was alien to him. In 1977, I saw a small Indian boy at the art gallery in Wolverhampton, looking with wonder at an eighteenth-century explorer picture of a boy his age in India, and he looked just as removed. Two more generations and it will be like all those colonial British who talked of 'home' but had never been here.

Tom Keating was there. He liked the Garrick and thought the

picture looked right and (knowing Gainsborough's brushwork) could not think of anyone else that it could be. He is a rakish old boy, actorish and flamboyant, very sad in a way. I saw some of his own work. It isn't very good and he knows it. He can't stand the 'experts' and was not surprised by the trouble I had been having. Looking at the Vere portrait in the hallway, we were both sure it must have been painted not long after my picture. Keating made an interesting remark as he left. He said, 'They didn't know my fakes, why do you expect them to know the real thing?'

Every dealer in London sent someone down to look at the picture when it was at Sudbury. Elizabeth Einberg and Mary Woodall had a look at it, too. They were rather circumspect, I gather from Stephen Jones. From their conversation, they could not agree it on principle, but they seem to have kept their options open. However, I never heard from Miss Einberg that she had seen it, although we corresponded over some photostats I sent her some months later.

August 8th: A friend in the Genealogy Society told me the Earl of Halsbury, descended from the Devon Giffards, has done a full family tree.

I got his phone number and had a very helpful talk.

The Giffard branch from that area of Devon is a legal one and the present Earl of Halsbury is a keen genealogist and gave me a very complete family tree. They have always been in law, the present title stemming from one of the family who was the judge in the famous Tichborne Claimant case. No mention of Henry Giffard anywhere. The most fascinating part of the family tree was, however, the split in the Giffard family made by the Civil War; one side was for the King, the other for Cromwell, and the quarrel remains to this day. Therefore, you find names like Charles and Maria in one branch, and Puritan ones on the other. This gave a faint ray of hope. Mary Ann's father was called Isaac, her husband's father Moses Rennolds Parker.

Isaac Giffard's description of himself as a 'yeoman' made a genealogy friend of mine assume that he was a sort of farmhand. However, his will gave his address as the Manor House in the parish of Swainswick. I took a day off from the reference rooms and drove down to look at the village.

Going to an actual location can often be a hundred times more useful than all the reference books in the world. The Manor House turned out to be a good solid one, rather soberly grand, that of a man of means; his description of himself as a yeoman was in the tradition of Puritan families. The church at Swainswick, where his daughter married, is lovely. The village is on a hill two miles outside Bath, and the area was sharply divided in the time of the Civil War between the King and Parliament. In this division lay the key to the Giffard family.

The Genealogy Society have a very good Irish section, where I had another piece of 'shelf luck'. On the register of Saint Werburgh's in Dublin, the marriages of two young Thomas Giffards are recorded in 1698. They turned out to be young cousins who had run away from England to join the Irish Militia; one was from the Chittlehampton side, the other from Ashburton. The family feud had meant nothing to them, and their marriages were celebrated on the same day. The entries are incomplete, as many Irish records were destroyed by fire, but there is a birth entry – Henry, son of Thomas Giffard – in 1699. No mother's name, nothing more at all; however, this was the link I needed. Henry *was* connected with the Devon Giffards, and his father's brief career in the Militia gave him the right to the claim that he was an *Irish* officer's son. Neither father nor son appears on the Earl of Halsbury's family tree, although there is a Devon baptism for a Henry Giffard in the same year in England. After that, nothing more is known of the child, but the ages and background would seem to confirm he is the actor-manager.

Perhaps the Irish marriage was simply not recognised by the English side, or the young family returned to Ireland. I could find nothing else about Henry Giffard until he surfaced as an actor-manager in England in 1730.

As Henry had no children by his wife, Anna Marcella (Mrs Lydall, the actress), I had to locate the owners of the painting in the years between his death in London in 1772 and the picture's last home, the Alexandra Theatre in Birmingham, 1911–1977. I had to plunge into more than church records if I was to find out how the Garrick portrait had come into the possession of Edward Henry Parker.

Although I was finding all the research fascinating, it did have its drawbacks. Having been trained all my life to develop my voice, I now had to forget I had one. In all the record rooms, especially at the PRO, no one speaks; noise is frowned upon, and so you quickly learn to speak without sound. Indeed, so much does this become second nature that sometimes you continue to do so in the outside world. At dinner one evening I noticed that the man I had been talking to looked puzzled, and I had to ask him if he could hear me. 'Well, no,' he admitted, as if his hostess had landed him with a mute or a lunatic. I didn't explain, I just asked him to tell me if I got inaudible again.

After two weeks, I became 'accepted' in the search rooms. Although no mention was made of the Garrick picture, I was getting to know the Giffards very well as a family.

A regular 'searcher' came up to me one day and mouthed, 'We're very impressed.' 'Why?' 'You've found out more in two weeks than most of us have in two years – you can have a job with us any time.' He worked for Debrett.

I *had* found out a lot, but still not enough.

My next step was to work on *all* the wills of the Giffards and, while I was about it, the Gainsboroughs and anyone connected with them. I now had a full and thorough set of files on church records. I had to try to fill the spaces left here and there and hope some kind of inventory might come to light, or that a will would list the portrait specifically.

The Public Record Office (the PRO), contains all the really early stuff back to the Domesday Book. Modern, or anything after 1700 (apart from wills), means you have to go to Kew. After 1837 (the year of the Great Census), you can check all births, marriages and deaths at St Catherine's House, Holborn, and any wills after that are at Somerset House across the road. My feet became quite bruised by the cobblestones on the forecourt there, through nipping backwards and forwards to check things out.

The PRO, Chancery Lane, is architecturally a joy. A Victorian Gothic pile, freezing in summer, marginally more so in winter. It is ideal for research as other places are not too far away, unlike the extension at Kew which requires a day's journey and there is no possibility of quickly checking a fact or two at the Law Library, Somerset House or elsewhere in London. It is also, in its very awkwardness, labyrinthine corridors and tortuous stairways, more conducive to study. There is a pretty library, a rotunda like a miniature version of the King's Library in the British Museum, the staff is splendid, helpful and patient, and the whole atmosphere helps concentration wonderfully.

You have to learn a completely new language there, otherwise you are lost. The first day I was a complete ass. Wills have their own codes: Probe. (for Probate) II's or Admins. (when there is no official will), Probe:12's, I.R. 22's, and so on. Once you discover which you need, you fill out a form with the details and wait for the document to be found. As most of the records are now on microfilm, whenever possible you are given a tape, sat down at a fiendish machine, given rudimentary instructions and left to muddle through. I never mastered the things. Time and again I would do exactly as I had been taught, and it would unravel the film in the opposite direction, letting out screaming noises as it did so. Machines, like children and dogs, have an inbuilt instinct for the inept. I was invariably rescued, panic-stricken, by the staff or another researcher, as I tried to stuff the film back. Eighteenth-century writing is difficult to decipher at the best of times; on microfilm (I know it must be filmed to preserve the documents) it is almost impossible. After a few days they found that it was easier to give me the great books containing the wills, rather than risk having all the machines broken and a protest riot from the other searchers.

The real problem lay in the fact that I had set myself too many lines of research to follow all at the same time, but because so much of my time had been wasted by the Collingwood side-track, I went ahead with the Giffard/Garrick/Burr/Gainsborough families simultaneously. While at a record office, it seemed a good idea to look up all I could, rather than to make four separate excursions.

I went around with huge bags of notebooks containing whatever I could discover about *all* the families. On more than one occasion I found it paid off handsomely to work in this seemingly haphazard way, although it was not much appreciated by the unfortunate person who chose to work at the same table as me.

I started again with Henry Giffard and his wife's wills. This was technically putting the cart before the horse, as the proper way is to continue with direct relatives. There were so many Giffards, however, that I thought it best to find out if there was even a hope of connection with the early ones. If that led nowhere, I would just have to face the fact that the picture had nothing to do with the early Giffards and was a random acquisition of Edward Henry Parker to decorate his theatre.

My hunch turned out to be good, and it immediately cleared up a lot of problems. Although Henry and his wife had no children, there was a son, William, by a 'former marriage' and a grandson of eleven years in 1766, called Joseph. The first will is cautious about William, as he appears to have debts; in the last codicils in 1772, the year of Henry's death, he seemed to have reformed and Henry left him a handsome legacy. Maddeningly, the pictures are not itemised: 'All my family pictures' to William. In her will, his wife, Anna Marcella, left her house in Windmill Lane and the rest of the pictures to William; again they are not itemised, although everything else is listed to the last spoon and tablecloth.

The location of Anna Giffard's house in Windmill Lane interested me. The various wills give different parishes: Ealing, Turnham Green and Acton. Windmill Lane ran down the edges of all these, from Uxbridge Road to near the river at Richmond. I needed to get out of libraries for a while, so I made a pilgrimage down Windmill Lane, in the vain hope that something might be left of the house mentioned by Anna Marcella Giffard. Nothing of the countryside remains; it is urban sprawl, unrelieved except for Osterley Park. I got a good idea of the location of all my people's houses from this trip. The Giffards and Gainsboroughs appear to have lived within a five-mile radius of each other and of Garrick. I wandered into the little churchyard at Heston; lovely, pre-Elizabethan. A very grown-up girl guide emerged from the pews and offered to give me a guided tour. 'We have a very interesting grave,' she informed me ghoulishly; 'the last man to be flogged to death in the British Army.'

We found the old part of the graveyard and there, almost side by side, lay the graves of Gainsborough's daughters, Mary and Margaret, and those of my early Giffard family. It was terribly touching, they must even have worshipped in the same congregation. I stood there for a long time, thinking of their beautiful portraits and the lonely, lost old ladies they must have become.

It seemed so sad, compared with those little girls chasing the butterfly in the National Gallery. I am glad they can still remain those children on canvas.

The executor of the wills was most important: Sir John Chapman, who was MP for Taunton. There was the real link back to the Giffard Devon roots. The Giffard wills were surprisingly substantial. Henry was a rich man of property; he mentions that his wife 'through her employment in the theatre as an actress' and her careful management, brought him money, and stresses that it was during the first twenty years of their marriage. His son, William, was born in 1721, being eighty-three when he died in 1804. Henry's first marriage could have been in Ireland. I could find no trace of it here. In Fitzgerald's *Life of Garrick*, 1868, he tells how one of the Giffards, 'alive in this present century', used to boast how the great Garrick played Osric to his Hamlet. William would have been old enough to have been that Hamlet, and amongst the family pictures surely he would have taken great pride in one of Garrick.

William's will is maddeningly short and uninformative. His property went to his son, Francis. His daughter, Lucy, got little but presumably that is because she was married to a successful young lawyer called Alexander Copeland. William married three times and is buried at Hammersmith with his second wife and fourteen children. His son, Francis, died in 1821, and *his* son, Francis II, in 1827; and the property reverted to the Devon side of the family, there being no direct issue in London. Still no specific mention of the Garrick picture, the only picture mentioned at all being one of 'Miss Chapman, to go to Sir John Chapman' in the will of Anna Marcella, Henry's wife. She died in 1777, and by this time the executor was a lawyer called George Gostling. Sir John Chapman died the following year, leaving his property to his brother, who died a year later and all his property was dispersed by sale. This meant I could not trace the Chapman portrait and it could have been just what I needed, as in Sir Walter Armstrong's Gainsborough Index the portrait of a Miss Chapman is mentioned: 'curiously tightly painted', which would describe the style of my Garrick. George Gostling, the new executor, owned several Gainsborough landscapes and was a man of importance with a large house and grounds, Whitton Park near Twickenham. He left a huge will with many codicils and some of them were witnessed by both Francis Giffard and his son. I could not find mention of them in the Law Society, so they were perhaps in George Gostling's firm in a civil capacity, for he had a large property empire and both Francis Giffard I and II left substantial estates.

The theatre seemed to have been abandoned by the Giffards for the law (where an acting talent is always useful). Even the wives are lawyers' daughters, so it would seem that the theatre died out in the family until young Edward Henry Parker revived it. The background of the picture seemed quite a logical one, now I could trace the Giffard family back directly to Henry Giffard, but the Gainsborough attribution was as far away as ever.

September: Peter O'Toole has made every headline in the world with his Macbeth.

Trades unions, wars, strikes, everything swept off the front pages, and all because the critics hated it. I think the notices were almost as bad as *The World of Paul Slickey*. I am going tonight. I wanted to miss the first night; it sounds as if I have lost out on one of the great moments in theatre history. I feel a bit sick now – how will the audience react? Can it really be as bad as they say? Not possible. Anyway, Peter cannot be dull whatever he does. I just hope it doesn't affect his nerve or that of the rest of the cast. I shall never forget our second night in *Slickey*.

I needn't have worried. The theatre was surrounded with television units from all over the place – Italy, France, America – unbelievable. The evening papers were still headlining it. We could have had a revolution, no one would have noticed. The theatre was packed and the curtain went up very late. When it did, it was worth every moment. The witches were pretty, vampire-type Hammer Horror girls. Well, so what? When Alec Guinness played Macbeth, they were black like the Supremes. Peter's first entrance was magnificent. He strode down to the front of the stage and delivered 'So fair and foul a day I have not seen' straight at the audience. The whole place burst into a spontaneous ovation. From then on, nothing mattered. Peter went through the evening, blue eyes blazing, and although it *was* terrible, it was also wonderful. It was full Star Time, terrible in the way Orson Welles could be.

Every other actor came on to the stage, dropped on one knee (generally) and faced upstage where Peter stood in a spotlight. One little man tried to play it for real in the scene after Duncan's murder, but Peter just glared at him and his voice died in his throat. The rest of it didn't matter. What we watched on the stage that night was THEATRE. Critical judgement had no place, nor was it wanted. It had nothing to do with the 'good taste' we have all had shoved at us from the National Theatre and the rest of them, it was unabashed HAM. It was not dull, nor was it what I had dreaded – embarrassing. Something happened on that stage that night; it may not have been *Macbeth*, but the hell with it, we could all see *Macbeth* done somewhere else some other time. Tonight was special.

I forget how many curtain calls he took. I nipped out and backstage while they were still going on and Bryan Forbes (eyes also blazing – it must be catching) was trying to make a speech. Nanette Newman, impeccable in beige cashmere, was standing in Peter's dressing room, a sheaf of roses in her arms (I never did find out why), looking slightly glazed but beautiful as usual. She is the kind of woman who must look good first thing in the morning, or in a hurricane or a shipwreck. Tonight wasn't a good night, but she still looked great and decorative, but slightly displaced, as though no one had told her what was going on.

Peter strode in at last and gave me a great hug. He is far too thin. All I could say was, 'Well, you certainly don't do things by halves.' The next day I got a note from him:

> Idiotic dear,
> Halves? We haven't even started yet!
> Love,
> Peter
> P.S. Sou'sou' west?

Dear God, shades of Wilfred Lawson; and in the same theatre.

Macbeth made more money for the Vic than it has ever made before, but so stupid are people that the grants for the theatre were withdrawn and it closed at the end of the season. There is no humour left in the world. It was lovely to see that an actor could still make such a stir. And a nice change from the usual fearful or boring headlines.

During October I continued to send my research to all the experts in the hope of keeping their interest in Garrick.

October 3rd: A letter from Sir Oliver Millar.

Dear Miss Corri,
Thank you for your letter. The material on Gainsborough's life and the matter in Mrs Gainsborough's will is very interesting. Is it in fact unpublished, because if so there should be somewhere in which it might see the light of day, possibly in a publication associated with Gainsborough's House and Sudbury. Do the 'oil drafts' appear in the sales of Gainsborough's effects after his death?

If Professor Waterhouse and John Hayes saw the picture you would really have to accept their opinion, as they are very experienced indeed in this artist. And Dr Hayes would have to be taken very seriously in assessing whether or not it is of Garrick.

If the picture is still at the Royal Academy I would be happy to see it; but I am very busy indeed at the moment, I am afraid, and can do nothing before the beginning of November.

Yours sincerely,
Oliver Millar

October 8th: The theatre board, which now included a man whom I had not met before, rather ferretty and sharp, at last came down to see the picture.

I showed it to them in one of the Academy's committee rooms, surrounded by other splendid works. It looked very much at home. The same could not be said of the theatre board, apart from Edmund King. Out of the context of Birmingham, they looked ill at ease, rather overwhelmed by the surroundings of the Academy; it was interesting and illuminating. I wondered why I had been so surprised by their lack of co-operation. The picture and what it stood for was outside their range of vision. They knew where they were in the Midland milieu of 'where there's muck, there's brass', but this was not in their country. The picture meant 'brass' all right; there it ended. They could not wait to get to the nearest restaurant where they ate a huge, rich meal, drank wine and brandy as usual, and practically kippered me in the smoke of their fat cigars.

The new member of the board suggested that a rich friend of his might be willing to buy the picture and give it to the city. This seemed like a good idea, in that the theatre could have an endowment and the city would not have to pay to own a picture which would be a great draw at the gallery. I did not like this man much, still, I had to admit his plan was sensible. I was disappointed in their lack of real interest in the picture. At one point, when I was showing them some of the family tree I had put together, the new man said, 'But what has this to do with the picture?' The need for a correct provenance to be established had completely eluded him, it seemed.

October 17th: Went to the Festival Hall for the first time in ages – have not heard Abbado except on record.

He is a very strict conductor, not happy with frivolous pieces it seems, but with the Berg Violin, near heaven. I wanted to leave immediately afterwards, I didn't want anything else in my mind, but I had to stay. The next piece was Rossini – Abbado practically rapped his knuckles.

The Berg was so beautiful, a desolate, moving work. No hi-fi system in the world can convey the immediacy of a live performance, thank God. Nor the excitement of the participation of audience and orchestra when, unexpectedly, perfection occurs.

What combination of circumstances takes over and raises the good to the sublime is one of the great mysteries of the theatre, and one of its terrors, because there is no way it can be predicted; and once achieved, no guarantee that it can be produced at will. When Paul Scofield played Lear, some nights he was incredible, on others just an actor. He said he knew it was no use trying if it didn't start to happen in the beginning – on other nights he *was* Lear. You can only gauge what your performance must not fall below in those cases, but you can never say what heights it might reach. Old Wilfred Lawson was like that – some nights in *Peer Gynt* Saint Peter would walk on to that stage, on others a sad old man. Garrick's last performance was Lear, for George III. All the way home in the carriage afterwards he was worried because the

King had not seemed to appreciate it and he thought he must have fallen short of his own standards. How was he to know the irony that he had been playing a mad King to a mad King? Even other actors on the stage with Garrick were terrified by him, so real did his performances seem. I look at my portrait and I know all that is ahead of him. I wish I could go back in time, just once. I don't think I would be disappointed. The stuff of legends does not change.

October 20th: The Devonshire exhibition at the Royal Academy is beautiful.

My favourite Van Dyck is in it, a lovely man in brown, Arthur Goodwin, 1595. I wonder if he really was so good-looking? What luck to be born in a time when a painter like that was around. The exhibition ends up with Lucien Freud. No one will linger over those in future and fall in love with them. A most wonderful little drawing by Rembrandt of a fat actor learning his lines. Of all the drawings there, it is the one I would want, so beautifully observed. I am glad the old boy had a sense of humour; I think it is the only funny drawing by him I can remember seeing. Costume drawings by Inigo Jones. Strange, almost Victorian lady attributed to Velasquez; a curious picture, I would like to know its history. I bought the catalogue; foreword by *Sir* Anthony Blunt. I commented on this and the young student selling them leaped to his defence, quite without cause. I was pleased to see that, in his own world at least, he is still properly treated.

November 11th: I have had to sell a couple of pictures, including the Marie Laurencin.

It didn't fetch a great deal. The really rotten picture (waves rolling in on a beach, which I had bought on tour) did very well. So I was able to get rid of a few bills.

Most of the month was spent in the search rooms at the PRO.

Those doing the Elizabethan or medieval scrolls have the documents brought up in tiny wooden coffins which emit clouds of dust when opened, and a bout of muffled, suppressed sneezing breaks out. Gradually, through the grapevine, if you are finding interesting stuff, other serious searchers will look over your shoulder and mutter approval; then you know you have arrived. Sometimes faint indications may be shown when *they* have found an interesting fact. It is difficult, even in these quiet surroundings, not to want to communicate an exciting find. One young man, working on Elizabethan Customs and Excise, began to make what would, in any other place, be regarded as choking sounds; knowing better, I went to look at his work. He had found a lovely document where the scribe had made rude caricatures in the ornate title letters of all the magistrates conducting a smuggling case.

I started on the Gainsborough wills. It is revealing how character comes out in that 'Last Testament'. Gainsborough emerges as not too pleasant. His first move is to leave only a hundred pounds to his nephew and assistant, Gainsborough Dupont, and any paints and brushes he may wish to have. 'But should he make any other claim or claim any work in the studio, this shall be forfeit and he shall be made to pay for Board, Washing and Lodging, for the time he has lived with us.' The rest deals with stocks and shares. He insists that, after small bequests, everything must be sold from his studio and as his brother, Robert, received half the estate, this was implemented with almost indecent thoroughness. Mrs Gainsborough, in some of the earlier books, has been censured for the speed of this sale, but the will makes the reason very obvious. In contrast, her will is kind and charming.

In fact, Mrs Gainsborough was starting to come out of my research with a much nicer character than she had been allowed before, either in her husband's letters or the many histories. She is very intriguing altogether. As Mrs Gainsborough had arrived on the scene just after the '45 rebellion, I started to look up Scottish records and her family under her maiden name of Burr. Later in life she had hinted at 'a Prince's blood in her veins', etc. This had been taken by most writers to be a harmless bit of snobbery on her part, perhaps to cover a less romantic situation, but behind every rumour there is usually a grain of fact, even if it has been distorted by time. If she really had been an ordinary local girl – the daughter, says one book, of one of

Gainsborough's father's commercial travellers – there would have been no difficulty in tracing her birth. Also, the remarks about noble birth would have an element of silliness in them, in that everyone would have known who she was.

She had an income, or annuity, of two hundred pounds a year, which led others to believe, because it came from the Duke of Beaufort's estate, that she was an illegitimate daughter. The Beaufort family have never fully confirmed or denied this supposition. After further tracking, it became clear to me that Margaret had good reason to believe herself the daughter of Frederick, Prince of Wales.

I felt a little like the lady in the Thurber story, 'The Macbeth Murder Mystery'; because she reads the play as if it is a detective story, she manages to come up with some marvellous new twists to the plot. The way I had chosen to search for the Garrick/ Gainsborough connection seemed to be producing equally surprising and unexpected results.

Sir Ellis became far more fascinated by the new material on Gainsborough's wife than in whether the Garrick was actually by his hand or some other artist's. All the new finds did indirectly help the case for the picture, for if I could fill in the early years fully, there was a greater chance of my convincing the art world that my opinion was worth something. Indeed, even if I never found any more documentation on the Garrick, my search had made everything written so far about Gainsborough's life inaccurate in many respects. Rather than too little fact on Gainsborough, as in other books, I was starting to find too much.

I also became rather too interested in the new background that was emerging for Mrs Gainsborough, and for a time I fell into the fatal error of letting it distract me from the business of establishing the Garrick portrait. There seemed to be new avenues which promised to shed an entirely different light on Gainsborough's whole life, much more complex and interesting than anything I had read in any of the earlier works.

Other distractions surfaced, too. One day I saw the will of the son of Grignion, the engraver. It said: 'My father's plates, that are with my aunt, to go to my son.' Where are they now? That would mean the early plates of Reynolds and Gainsborough, and engraving plates are no easy matter to dispose of. They might still be in some attic or cellar. I will look for them when this is over.

'What a pity you have no one to tell all about your discoveries at home,' said a lady, hearing I lived alone. Is she mad? There is not a shopkeeper, passing stranger, postman, chemist, grocer, the man who sweeps up the leaves, within a five-mile radius of St John's Wood who has managed to escape the Gainsborough Lecture. I can bring him into any subject, and do. My neighbours are very patient but their eyes do glaze over a bit. They are starting to cross the road when they see me coming. My chemist is also a genealogist. I go in and report any new finds. They are all very patient with me and kind; it's like having a large family.

November 12th: I went to a couple of auctions to see what the prices were like.

Why must the person bidding for the best pictures always sit next to me? It puts the fear of God into me. At Phillips a Cotes went for £90,000 to the man on my left. I was afraid to blink. Then at Sotheby's, a Turner, £300,000 – this to the man on my right.

One day I shall sneeze and find myself stuck with an expensive masterpiece.

November 26th: The Dr Who *was very successful for me and a large article appeared in* TV Times.

All about Gainsborough, of course. Good photographs of the Garrick and me at my desk researching, assisted by my pet squirrel. Not a word about science fiction.

By the end of the year I could not call it a spectacular result for all my work. I had the infra-reds, the photographs of the shield and the 'T' and 'G', but they did not seem to count, and the Giffard background and genealogy. I needed papers, a receipt, some kind of bill or note, and none seemed to remain.

Sir Ellis agreed that the Gostlings also had Gainsborough landscapes, although it did not necessarily mean that the Giffards patronised the same painter. I had been able to establish that Henry was more than just an Irish actor-manager; he was a man of substance with wealthy friends, lived near the Gostlings and had re-established his respectable Devon connections.

I continued to research. George Gostling, the second executor of the Giffard wills, turned out to be a great help in an indirect way. He had been a member of an ecclesiastical legal body called Doctors' Commons. This gave way to the Prerogative Court of Canterbury. They were extremely important men, having a kind of monopoly on land conveyancing and divorce. There is only one book on them, by a Mr Squib, which I duly read. The practices were hereditary ones, and to George Gostling's anger (so it seems from his will) he had no one to follow him. He doesn't list his landscapes, although he left a great deal of his library to the Law Courts.

George Gostling had been so important, I thought the best thing to do was to try to find *his* papers; as he had taken over as executor, there might be something left. I sent down an enquiry to Hayes (the town not the man) where all original papers are stored by the PRO. Again nothing. The only other place I could look was the Court of Arches, which is in Lambeth.

'You're not a researcher,' said a scornful boy who opened the door. 'You look too cheerful.' When I got inside, I saw what he meant. Of all the research rooms this is the quietest, and that is saying something. Rows of elderly lawyers, no other women at all, except the one who got the documents after you had decided what you wanted from the index. 'Shelf luck' again. I found a litigation (1760) being dealt with by a John Fitz-Frederick Burr. By pure chance I had found Margaret's brother. Gostling was dropped for the afternoon while I tracked down more on John Fitz-Frederick.

When I went back to the Public Record Office I looked up his will. It is cryptic and mysterious, but he also had an annuity of two hundred a year which he left to his wife; the same amount as Mrs Gainsborough's income. The witnesses and the executors were all friends of the late Frederick, Prince of Wales. Sir Ellis was fascinated by this turn in my research; in deference to the Garrick portrait I abandoned it for the moment and went back to the Giffard search.

On the bottom of the codicils in Gostling's own will, I noticed other names as witnesses with the Francis Giffards; these were a Mr White and a Mr Ainge. I took them to the ever-patient Mr

Richardson of the Law Library, and within a few days he had sent me a complete genealogy of the firm, which began as Blake, White & Ainge, went through many permutations to the present day, and is now known as Gilmore, Naylor & Gunnery. If an inventory had been made of either Henry or Anna Marcella's wills, they would have it.

The firm is now in Golden Square, so I just got into my car and went straight there.

Impulse will get me nowhere. The office was shut for the day, but there was a sweet old caretaker who had been with them for years, and he couldn't have been more helpful, although he nearly broke my heart in the process. The firm had been in Essex Street since 1680 but had moved in 1962 because the original building was falling down. In the move, all the original papers had been thrown out and destroyed: Sheridan, Scott and God knows who else. It is publishing as well as legal country there, so it doesn't do to think what might have disappeared. They had called the PRO, but no one had bothered to go and look. If an inventory had been left, it has gone with everything else that could have even included a receipt. I can't bear to think about it.

When I spoke to the present firm at last, they knew very little about the move or what had happened to the papers, but they suggested a Mr Gilmore (now retired to Switzerland) could perhaps tell me more. I got Mr Gilmore's address and he replied at once. He is coming over for Christmas and will come round for a drink and see if he can give me any help, although he thought it unlikely.

December 2nd: A letter from Elizabeth Einberg.

She said she was extremely grateful for the photocopies of the church register that I had sent to her, showing the marriage and the child's birth certificate. She thought it all sounded utterly fascinating and said she would love to have copies of the other data. She was glad my work on the portrait was progressing well as it was a nice picture, Gainsborough or not. There had been a couple of articles in the press. One had repeated a comment of mine about art historians appearing to listen only to other art historians but, said Miss Einberg, 'they most emphatically do not! They listen to their eyes and the sweet crackle of authentic documents!' Well, in spite of the odd metaphor, I understood what she meant, and so I continued to dig for those 'authentic documents'.

December 12th: At last managed to persuade Sir Oliver Millar to see the Garrick (on parade, as he put it).

Harassed, and looks less grand and imposing out of his setting. I had asked the porters to put the Garrick up near the Devonshire Gainsborough of Georgiana Poyntz (Countess Spencer) – the colours were complementary.

I have changed indeed. Two years ago I listened meekly, although bewildered by adverse remarks.

Sir Oliver said the buttons were wrong. Out of everything right, the *buttons* made the picture wrong. I behaved badly. I heard myself saying, 'Negative criticism, that's all people like you ever give, negative identification.' I really lost my temper; I didn't mean to, but I am so sick of fatuous remarks like that. The buttons are *not* wrong, I have been to the V & A and looked at endless suits of that date. They are quite a usual, common type of the day.

I can't remember much more that I said, except that it was a stupid reason to give to reject the whole picture. He fled the Academy. I felt very ashamed. The porters had disappeared behind the easel when I blew my top. They re-emerged, wreathed in smiles; they are so nice. They took Davy back to the vault assuring me that, no matter what anyone else said, *they* liked him.

December 15th: The Gainsborough Exhibition at the Tate, one that is to go all over the world to represent him.

Wretched. Badly chosen and horribly lit; wrongly dated, at least the early ones. Someone seeing him for the first time would think the man subject to brainstorms. Why should he paint like an angel one day and an idiot the next? I must say, when he is bad he is awful.

Saw the exhibition the first time with David Walker, who got enraged by the way Gainsborough *will* put the figures too close to the bottom of the frame, leaving a great gap to be filled with sky and unconvincing trees at the top. He kept wanting to push them all *up*. The second time I went there, I met little Maurice Binder, who does the screen titles for the James Bond films. He was looking bewildered – a very good artist, he could not make out the datings. 'Tell me, Adrienne,' he said, 'why should a man do a sketch for something ten years *after* he has painted the picture?' He had never seen a lot of Gainsboroughs all together before and was terribly disappointed. Afterwards we had tea and poor Maurice was subjected to the Gainsborough Lecture and a blow-by-blow description of my fight for the Garrick. He did not hold this against me and, as it was near Christmas, made me a present of a red Tate Gallery shopping bag; ideal for carrying some of my folder as it has now spilled out of its original container.

I had a funny moment with Maurice a few years ago. I was making a Hammer Horror, *Vampire Circus*, and he was working on another stage with white Persian cats, doing the titles for *Diamonds Are For Ever*. I went to see him and found him fed up, dripping with blood where the blasted things had scratched him, with the owners of these savage animals looking indignant. The cats, it seemed, did not like having diamond necklaces stuck around their necks, and Cubby Broccoli had specified that he wanted 'diamonds around a white pussy'. I met Maurice in the bar later, heavily bandaged and very depressed. 'How was I to know he didn't mean a cat?' he said, miserably.

December 19th: At last Sir Ellis Waterhouse has agreed to see me.

He lives in Oxford. I am going to take down the whole folder, plus all the photographs. I feel I have *got* to make him see what I do in the picture. I think I have my work cut out.

It was such a cold day, threatening snow. Sir Ellis opened the door. He looked fierce and younger than I expected; very aware, no nonsense about him. I realised I had all of five minutes to persuade him or I was OUT. 'Take your coat off and leave it there.' A command, not an invitation.

'No, don't.' His wife had appeared, a very pretty, smiling woman. 'It's freezing, the Aga has broken down and the heating is off.' She caught sight of my Tate Gallery shopping bag and it amused her, 'Look Ellis,' but by then he had led the way into a large and indeed very cold living room, man-handled a gas heater into a corner, and my interview had begun.

'Don't tell me about marks on pictures,' he said before I could open my mouth. 'There is a man who can find the King of Bavaria's signature three million times on the Last Judgement in the Sistine Chapel.'

'I don't think I am as mad as that, Sir Ellis.'

I had no sooner produced the photographs of the signature than they were out of my hands and he was looking at them in the clearer light by the window. 'Ah yes, there it is,' he traced the 'T' and the 'G' with his finger. He could see them, I didn't have to go to great lengths to show them. I couldn't believe it. He examined the comparative one on the last self-portrait and appeared to accept this also. 'How do you think he did it?'

'With the end of his brush on the base coat, then painted over; it's the top paint filling the groove made by the brush that gives the delineation, and that's why it doesn't show up on X-ray.'

'Why did he do it, do you think?'

I explained that I thought he had worked so much with other artists, he wanted to distinguish the work that was entirely his own.

'Is it on all his work, do you think?'

I explained how rebacking flattened the indentation marks and so it was very possibly obliterated on many works. This seemed to satisfy him. By now he was looking at photographs of the complete picture again. He picked up a photograph from a large pile on top of the piano. 'What about him?' It was by Kyte, a travelling country painter; heavy, workmanlike, too literal, none of the lightness I could see in Garrick.

'No, I don't think so.'

'Why not?'

'It's a different man, a different way of seeing; also the style is completely formed, I don't think the Garrick is.'

He put the Kyte back on the top of the other pictures. 'No, and it's none of them either,' and he pushed them all away dismissively, and looked again at Davy. 'He looks like an actor.'

He went on to talk about the convention of gesture being handed down from the eighteenth century; how one could still see it in opera. He, unlike the others I had contended with, did not seem to be a one-sided man, nor, with his background, should I have expected him to be. Also, he was the first one not to talk down to me and treat me as a complete fool. We talked a little about the theatre, and then he abruptly left the room to reappear, a moment later, holding a folder. In it was the catalogue of the sale of Garrick's house after 'La Violette's' death in 1820. Luigi Riccoboni's book *The History of the Italian Theatre* was there. Did its author give it to Garrick personally? Probably, because the books that remained after Garrick's death were his private ones. It is not likely that he would have given away the book that was the gift of a friend. I wondered if it had been inscribed. Seeing my family name there made me feel more at home, and I told Sir Ellis of my connection. It seemed to please him. His wife came in with tea for us and we continued to talk. He did not mention the Garrick much again. He thinks visually – when he mentioned a picture I knew he was also looking at it in his head. It gave me great hope. I had felt some of the others were blind. I also knew that when (if) he finally dismissed Garrick, he would have good reason and be able to tell me exactly why.

We talked for nearly four hours. I had not realised how late it was and was appalled. I apologised for taking up so much of his time. He saw me to the door. 'Well, I've been wrong before, I could be again.' It was the nearest to hope I had managed to get in the last three years. As he was closing the door he suddenly said, 'When is Garrick's bicentenary?'

'We have just missed it,' I replied.

'Still, nice to do something for him yet,' he said and the door closed.

He is going to America and will not be back until the spring, when he promises to come and see Davy again. I have promised to go on with my research. I don't think he cares for Gainsborough's character much; he seems to feel quite strongly about him, as if they were acquaintances: 'Look at his friends, that ass Thicknesse!' I have said I will send the transparency from Sudbury of the Vere portrait with the similar waistcoat. I dare not think that it is a breakthrough, and yet it is the first encouragement I have had, apart from Hugh's great kindness, Roger de Grey's interest and the sympathy shown me at the Royal Academy. And I liked him. I already thought his work the best I had read so far, and he appears to be interested in mine. I won't mind being wrong half so much (of course, I don't *want* to be). Equally, if he agrees, how much more it will mean.

December 23rd: Mr and Mrs Gilmore came for drinks.

He was quite calm about the loss of the papers. When I explained (as well as I could through clenched teeth), she rounded on him and said, 'There, didn't I tell you? You should have looked through them.' He was so complacent about the chucking-out of two hundred years of history that I got rather snappish. I don't think he had ever thought of the papers as history. He is a very successful businessman and it is today's deal that obviously interests him. To be spiteful (which I felt), I did point out that the papers could have been worth a small fortune, and to get someone in to catalogue and sort them out might have been an investment.

That kind of money seemed to be in the chicken-feed department for Mr Gilmore, and he may have gone to Switzerland for business reasons, because he was not retiring age. However, he saw how upset I was and, in order to calm me down or mollify me a little, he offered to give me an introduction to Hoare's Bank, where the firm has had an account from 1698. Being a man of money, he had come up with a monetary solution, and though I had no great hopes I took his suggestion. So I ended Christmas 1980. Still no concrete evidence, for all this work.

1981

My year began as the last one had ended – with a letter from Sir Ellis.

January 3rd:

Dear Miss Corri,
The transparency has come from Sudbury and I have sent it back to the curator direct, as he wants it. It is certainly the same tailor as your picture – and very similar in style of execution. But the coat is rather smarter!

We fly off on Tuesday and I am having no letters forwarded. I am told the temperature in LA is now in the '70s and '80s!

Best wishes for Garrick in the New Year.
Yours sincerely,
Ellis Waterhouse.

I liked this letter in particular. He said Garrick, firmly and without question now.

The transparency he referred to was the Vere portrait I had noticed on my first visit to Sudbury. Stephen Jones had sent it to Sir Ellis for comparison. Sir Ellis is an odd, academic bird, but he is not in the least insular like so many of them; in contrast to his quiet life in Oxford, he seems to love America.

January 5th: My next move was to follow up Mr Gilmore's lead about Hoare's Bank, so I wrote to make an appointment.

While I was on this tack for research, I thought I might as well write to the other banks to see if they also had records. Coutts, I have heard, is excellent and has all its old ledgers, and many papers besides. I remember once my manager at Barclays, Pall Mall, showing me a most beautiful watch and some other jewellery which had come to light when they opened one of their old boxes. It had been in the bank for over a hundred years and they were trying to trace the owners. That was a comparatively modern bank, so heaven knows what the old ones contain. Most of the banks responded kindly to my letters, except for Coutts who seemed to be admitting no researchers and gave no reason; still, as I had quite a lot to do and learn, I could leave them until last.

Although so much time had been wasted in the early stages of the search, I now had the components I needed which, if I could fit them together, would give me the 'documentation' required for the Garrick portrait.

I was completely familiar with the world in which Garrick and Gainsborough moved. I had the Giffard family tree and history. It was up to me to fit the pieces together and to find out if the picture of David Garrick belonged there. I had a collection of names known to all three men, and my love of eighteenth-century letters and diaries began to pay handsome dividends. Now I had a reason to bring what had formerly seemed useless (although amusing) information into a coherent whole.

January 8th: My first day at Hoare's Bank.

The banks all have a separate character. Hoare's is very grand. All the porters are in a kind of livery with top hats which sit on a rack next to guns, used to defend the bank during the Gordon Riots. There is such a muted feeling that you can't even get up courage to raise your voice, and women seem out of place.

I couldn't have chosen a worse time. The archivist had just retired and Mr Rennie Hoare, whose chief interest seems to have been the museum and the bank books, was ill. Mr Henry Hoare was threatening, in a vague way, to close the whole history side (too expensive, he said). However, Mr Gilmore's introduction helped, and a Mr Lloyd of the tax department was seconded to show me around.

The filing system seemed pretty comprehensive. I selected some accounts – Gainsborough's, Mr Robert Andrews, Sir

Thomas Hanmer and the Beauforts, just to start; and I was then left in peace to get on with my work.

January 10th: At Hoare's; working bank hours, nine to four.

I didn't make much progress at first. I have never been wildly good at figures; this system seemed to have very little to do with modern banking practice. To get my bearings, I went ahead to 1762, when Gainsborough had opened his account at Hoare's, in order to get some names to refer back to, and to find out just how well he was doing in Bath. His account was peculiar, to say the least. The credit side seemed mainly to concern Mrs Gainsborough's annuity; on the debit side he did not appear to pay his bills directly through the bank, and I could not believe that all his other transactions were cash. He did pay quite large sums to Gainsborough Dupont in the early 1770s, which would seem to be for work, contradicting all I had read about Gainsborough painting every inch of his canvases himself. This money was clearly paid as a salary, so his nephew was an assistant as after the not-so-kind references in Gainsborough's will, the money did not appear to be given but earned.

The account was very simple: sums going out to Isaac Gossett, wax modeller and frame maker; to his relatives; to Mary Gibbon, his sister and to Richard Gardiner, his brother-in-law; regular money to an Edward Parker; and he bought stock. In 1768, £21 to Francis Hayman. He received £50 from the will of Quin, the actor; £10 at intervals to his brother, John. The accounts were in no way complete and posed many questions. I was quite sure that they had been seen by others studying his life, and on face value would seem to support Philip Thicknesse's claims that he was not at first successful in Bath. Yet why would he pay such large amounts to his nephew when he was scarcely making the same amount himself? In 1762 he was a man of thirty-six; how had he banked until then? Did he (as Sir Ellis asked) keep his money in his stocking? It seemed unlikely. None of the figures quite made sense.

Back to the filing cabinets. James Unwin, Gainsborough's friend, had an account at the bank, and here I found large payments to him *through* Unwin. Unwin also seemed to make and take payments for others. In fact, his figures looked more like those of a small-scale banker or notary. A little more work on his account and I realised this is exactly what he was. He started to handle money for Gainsborough around 1754, ending regular dealing for him in 1759.

James Unwin's figures were a trading account, apparently using the large bank as a clearing house. Other people seemed to operate in the same manner. Mr Robert Andrews had three accounts at the same time, handling incredible sums, larger than I had thought possible for a private country gentleman of that time; of course, when I delved further I found that he was a great deal more. Mr Robert Andrews is one of history's dark horses; his interests and his money spread like a large net, encompassing, among others, the future King, Frederick, Prince of Wales. Indeed, all the Prince's household seemed to deal with him at some time or another. It was Mr Andrews' account which began to show me the outline of a complicated puzzle, very political and intricate, and every person on it was connected to my research in some way.

Through Mr Andrews I saw that all Gainsborough's early patrons moved in the same circle and knew each other. When Mr Andrews died, his son took over his financial empire, continued to make loans and to take handsome interest. The two young people in the cornfield gained a new significance; they were powerful, and controlled others. The idle moment of the country squire in Gainsborough's picture was, to some extent, a pose. Mr Andrews had a great deal more on his mind.

I looked at Sir Thomas Hanmer's accounts and, as I expected, the payments to Hubert Gravelot and Francis Hayman were there at the time they would have been working on the Shakespeare; no payments to Gainsborough, although Joshua Kirby, his great friend later in life, does figure largely on this account. This was unexpected as he is only supposed to have been a humble house painter in Suffolk in 1742; yet from the payments he is clearly far grander and is, in fact, quite well off and living in London. A different picture of the whole society began to emerge.

January 19th: I had not reckoned on how tiring the bank book research might be.

I developed an almost permanent stiff neck and aching shoulders from hauling the books around backwards and forwards from the shelves. I don't think that the staff quite knew what to make of the maniac in their corridors. After a whole day, my legs and ankles were horribly swollen from standing at a high desk with the books. I persuaded Mr Lloyd that I needed a table, and now have a little room, which I vacate when customers arrive.

The names collected from the wills and churches helped me to understand the bank books more easily. Groups of people tended to stick together, and the artistic world, as today, was quite small. A successful portrait for one rich man would lead to one for a friend, or to a landscape. One name would connect with another, rather like discovering an old address book or diaries, and even though the Child's bank books had been destroyed in this century, taking with them the accounts of David Garrick and the Bedford family, it was possible to reconstruct them to some extent by cross-referencing names connected to them on the smaller bankers' accounts.

As I went through the books, I made other notes on the well-known artists, singers, musicians and writers of the day. It was quite fascinating. In the case of foreigners, you could tell who came here and when they arrived or left the country. As most of the documents for Covent Garden were destroyed during the war, and there are none for the many small theatres like the Italian Opera House and other places long since gone, I realised I had stumbled on to the most complete form of art records that still exist. It was also possible to work out a pretty exact guide as to how much was earned for a commission. Taking well-known artists – Hudson, Highmore, Thornhill, Wootton, Andrea Soldi, Batoni, Kyte, Scheemakers, Riesback, Jervas, Mercier, Goupy, Gravelot, Hayman, Hogarth (lamentably few payments) and Arthur Pond (many), for example – and matching the payments up to projects you knew they were working on at the time (the Hanmer Shakespeare, for example, or the Charterhouse) it was possible to work out an accurate scale which looked something like this:

£25–£30	A head or small overmantel size
£40–£60	A three-quarter painting
£80–£100	A full-length portrait

This could be based on known paintings by these artists, which were easily identified on certain accounts.

Using this as a general rule was useful, and the payments did not vary too much. Hudson, perhaps, commanded a slightly higher price. Arthur Pond did very well indeed, 'all in all', as George Vertue, the diarist and artist, writes, but of course *c.* 1740 they were modern artists being bought by fashionable, modern men, so their prices remain comparative and competitive. It also became apparent that one set of books was not enough and that, ideally, I should be able to cross-reference with the other banks. Most of them could not have been nicer, except for Coutts where the books remain untouched, uninterpreted and not at all understood.

The porters (if these grand gentlemen can be given such a mundane title) provide the human element at Hoare's. They all think I am funny and behave accordingly. At least I am a bit of light relief. The young female secretaries are marvellous – they all look impeccable and make me feel like a walking slum. They are forever in the ladies' room, chatting about their boy friends and correcting their already perfect make-up. The conversations give a sample of the side of the bank that I don't see:

'I told him, if you think I'm typing it again you've got another think coming, three times is enough.' This from one pert blonde who would have been daunting to argue with – I could just see her despondent boss. Or the wedding and engagement chats:

'I think I'd like a three-stone one like Mavis had, two diamonds at the side and a ruby in the middle.'

Woman's Own litters the lockers; women's lib is as dead as a dodo in the City. I wonder what will become of them all.

February 15th: I have taken to having a Chinese or Indian meal every other Sunday with Irene.

I look forward to them very much – she is marvellous to be with and to talk to. The other night when I had been going on too much about Gainsborough, I apologised, saying, 'Sorry to be such a bore, but it has become a passion with me.'

'Don't apologise,' she said fiercely. 'That's what it is all about, you can't do anything without passion. You must be passionate about everything you do, that's how I wrote my books.' She is more proud of them than anything in the world, she said they just had to be written. She went to the Midland Hotel and wrote the first one in three weeks.

I think sometimes our conversations rather faze the other occupants of the restaurants. Irene has a turn of phrase not really associated with the lovable little old ladies she plays. Sometimes we find there is a deathly silence while the other diners listen. She has a very black sense of humour which brings out the worst in me, and I always feel refreshed after an evening with her, even though we never finish until at least midnight. I get very worried about her health – it irks her so much to be in the throes of the discomfort of being old. Unlike me, she does not take a wild interest in medicine and refuses any vitamins or wonder pills I want to give her – she is probably right.

At last the children in my road, having seen *Dr Who*, are a little more polite to me. Up to this moment I have been the funny grown-up who liked to roller-skate.

I had been longing for a pair of skates when the new multicoloured ones came in, and I had dropped a lot of hints but none was taken seriously, so I bought a pair for myself, only I hadn't the courage to be foolish in daylight and waited until dark – I should also have waited until midnight. As I took my first turns outside the house and, more adventurously, up and down the street, various doors opened and children came out to join me. Next day they came round to see if I would like to come out and play.

Well, it was the only exercise I was getting, the bank books having got in the way of everything else. My social life and my sex life have receded into the background. I knew I was a goner when I forgot a lunch date with a very attractive man and my diary simply said, 'Forgot X – wonderful day, FIVE Gainsborough entries!' What the hell, I was discovering and changing history, you can't do that every day. The truth of it was, none of the men I knew at that time knew much, and cared less, about my research, so in the end it was just Gainsborough and me, and of course David Garrick.

I told one of the grand porters at Hoare's about my skates and I have promised to bring them in and give a demonstration in the corridors. Mr Lloyd was shocked. 'What, at your age?' I'll show him! I haven't quite got the nerve to do it yet – I would hate to cannon into Mr Henry and be barred from the bank. The porter, Roy, is very funny – now, when he passes my door, he changes his usual sedate walk into a skating glide, and then back to dignity.

February 11th: I received a letter from Edmund King.

Dear Adrienne,
We have not met since Bob Oulsnam, Mike and I came to see the picture.

I feel that it is time I dropped you a line so that we know what is happening – very much, of course, in the interests of the Alexandra Theatre, which, in a small way, is a 'D'Oyly Carte'. I do not really mean this, but the success of the picture is becoming of vital importance.

Mike and I reported to our board on our trip to London to see you and to find out how things were going, and they were very pleased with all we told them.

Could you now drop me a line to say how things have progressed since we met? I saw from the press that there has been a big Gainsborough exhibition in Paris, which shows that the 'old boy' is still commanding a fairly big interest.

How did you get on with your investigations in America to trace one of the people you think might have been an owner of the picture some time in the past? If you could drop me a personal note to bring Mike and me up-to-date I should be most pleased.

Incidentally, thank you very much for the Christmas card you sent me. It was much appreciated. I did not send any out this year, or you would certainly have had one!

With kindest regards and the best of luck with our project.

Yours very sincerely,
Edmund
E. H. King
Chairman

Although they had given me so little help in terms of information, Michael Bullock and Edmund King still seemed to have all the faith in the world that I could pull the whole complicated piece of research off, and in doing so, help save the theatre. They were a little like children in their lack of comprehension. In one breath they would tell me how vital it was to sell the picture, and in the next seem to think they would lose their grant if they did. Edmund assured me all expenses would be paid for the research, but at the same time I never felt I could ask as things always seemed so desperate from their end. At least what I had done had raised the picture from its initial value of £20 to a great deal more, even if I never found the definitive proof. It was a ridiculous situation. I was selling my own things in order to carry on the search, and their difficulties made me unable to ask them to help. It was all my own fault for not having been more practical to begin with, and I also felt responsible for not letting down their hopes, which were so clearly pinned to the success of the venture.

Edmund's letter made me even more helpless in explaining to them how much this was costing me; my only hope was to get an agreement on the picture as soon as I could for all our sakes. It was hopeless to try to explain to them how many bruised egos I would have to clamber over before the final decision; in turn, they could not understand why it was taking so long. Either the picture was a Gainsborough or not – what was the problem? I had a simpler approach in 1977; now I knew better, but I still believed in the picture and I was making headway in that I was finding out a great deal of new information about Gainsborough and his life, although I still had not managed to connect it to the Garrick portrait directly.

During February I also went to some of the other banks to follow up my entries at Hoare's. Gosling's, an old bank taken over by Barclays, was nearest and I could dash down there and back to the books at Hoare's without inconveniencing everyone too much.

February 19th: Gosling's, Barclays branch in Fleet Street, has a set of wonderful books.

There again, I was given all the help I could have wished for; there was one snag. The books were in the main bank vault and it meant having to trouble them every time I wanted to get another volume. 'Just leave me in here,' I said hopefully. 'Miss Corri, do you see those boxes?' 'Yes, what of them?' 'They are filled with money – we can't leave you in here alone.' I saw their point. One day while I was working, I looked up to see a large trolley, stacked with cash, sitting next to me. I had become part of the staff. It didn't interest me at all; it was something quite abstract and had no reality. Indeed, the more I worked in the banks the odder the whole system seemed. That people could want money, kill for or covet it, seemed absurd.

Some of the clerks would chat to me (Gosling's is more informal than Hoare's).

'I prefer really old history myself,' said one young man. I had just given myself a treat and was looking at Sir John Evelyn's books. 'This man saw Cromwell's funeral, the Fire of London, Charles II, knew Samuel Pepys and Christopher Wren, etc.,' and the poor young man got an impromptu lecture, but it did catch his imagination and after that he regularly popped his head round the door to find out if I had discovered anything new.

Giggles and jokes in Gosling's. Squeaks of terror (simulated) when the young clerks turn the lights out on the girls in the big main vault next to my little room. High jinks, I think it would all be called; rather Dickensian and larky.

The basements of the Fleet Street banks go back to the Elizabethans; as you go into the vaults, so you pass down through centuries. The first banking took place in pubs – hence the sign of the Black Horse for Lloyds, the Golden Bottle for Hoare's and the Three Squirrels for Gosling's. After the Great Fire, the new buildings seem to have been built straight on top of the ruins, and I managed to catch my heels in the great old flagstones of the basements. One of the vaults at Gosling's was being re-dug and strengthened while I was there, and the earlier buildings, almost back to Roman times, showed in the rubble that was being exposed.

I had never thought of banking as remotely romantic, but the books were the most wonderful reading. Gosling's was a literary and university bank – they were also publishers. Thomas Madox's *Firma Burgi*, written to give George I some idea of his new country, was published by them in 1726. Benjamin Franklin had an account with them, and for Gainsborough it was very valuable for his time in Bath, where he sometimes seems to have taken payments through his friend Shute Adams, at the same time as he banked at Hoare's. John Plampin also banked there, but I could find no record of a payment to date his portrait (also an early one) properly. This was because I needed to work at the banking system a little longer to understand it fully, and look at many more books.

The bank books all have different problems in a purely physical way, apart from the size and weight (they are as large as an average suitcase). The paper at Hoare's Bank is oxidising, and suddenly I found my hands were bleeding as if I had been rubbing them in ground glass. There is not enough moisture in the cases and I have spoken to them about humidifiers. If I give Henry Hoare another lecture on his books I think he might throw me out. I had to remind myself the other day that it was *his* bank.

The books at Gosling's are in a very good state – the paper that is – but they are very dusty. Poor Mr Roberts had been getting filthy by being gallant and carrying them from the vault for me. I do it myself now, and wear overalls. The dust can give you a rash, so now I take a medicated ointment with me to wipe my hands as I work. I also keep the pages clean by dusting them all the time. It would be awful if too many people handled them without care. I have got quite possessive about them. They should all be microfilmed; a Museum of Banking and Commerce is what I would like to see; however, banks are not banks because they *spend* money, and all they say is: 'Who would pay for it?'

I have never seen history brought to life as vividly as in these books. Daniel Defoe, Smollett, Hume, Benjamin Franklin – you can see the War of Independence coming up simply by the names of the people going out to the Colonies. I find myself wishing I could warn the ones I can see buying South Sea stock. They are so alive to me, and the houses – all the artisans are there, too. Walpole is reputed to have destroyed all his payments for Houghton because he did not want people to know how much it cost. I could, given time, reconstruct those payments.

March 5th: I have accepted another tour.

This time *An Inspector Calls* by J. B. Priestley. Alfred Marks is to play the Inspector, a part originally created by Ralph Richardson. I worked with Alfred in a series of Feydeau farces for Granada Television years ago; he can be a fine straight actor, and ought to be very good in the part. We all meet for drinks and a chat before the rehearsals are due to start, and the cast are very good. Peter Vaughan is to play Mr Birling; all very promising. We rehearse in London and as my part is not a very strenuous one I can carry on with the banks as well, until we go away.

March 9th: The first reading of An Inspector *boded not at all well.*

The director was not really in command and Alfred needs a firm hand (as do most actors). I am not needed every day; perhaps I will get a lovely surprise at the next rehearsals. We are working in a place which also houses the Irish Genealogical Research Society, and the Ormonde, Ossory & Butler papers are on the shelves there. I can retreat to them and work if need be. The V & A is not far away. I must make the best of things.

March 11th: Lunched with a banker friend, with a view to getting an introduction to Coutts.

He was very helpful and showed me around his bank's offices and the records they had, but being comparatively modern (early nineteenth-century) sadly, not much good to me. He promised to do what he could about Coutts, but over luncheon, having seen my file and evidence, he and a couple of others rather wickedly suggested that I should persuade the theatre to part with the picture at £100,000 now, if they were so in need of cash, and he and his friends would commission me to go on looking for the evidence. I relayed the message to Edmund King, advising against it, as I know, if they will only wait, I will eventually come up with the documentation. If not, at least that offer is now there for them. At the moment, I must go on alone. I can't ask the theatre, in its present financial state, simply to back my word against all the experts in the world.

March 18th: The Bank of England.

I had gone down to the National Westminster Bank archives in Lothbury to see if they could help, as they had taken over so many of the small local banks in the Sudbury/Suffolk area.

I couldn't find anything on the records they had left, but as I was next door to the 'Old Lady', with my ever-present folder and a lot of my bank notes, *and* I had already got a parking ticket, I thought I would see if I could make an appointment to look at *their* books. I have always loved Sir John Soane's grandiose building, so it was fun even to go inside.

The Bank of England has Beadles! Or so it seemed. Or the Lord Mayor was visiting, I wasn't quite sure which. Grand though Hoare's was, it had nothing on this. I finally got up the courage to approach one of these decorative gentlemen and was asked to wait on a marble seat while he made suitable enquiries.

The architecture inside was as imposing as outside, so I was enjoying myself hugely, when a nice, preoccupied man from the library came down to the foyer to interview me. He was clearly busy and I had not made an appointment, so I launched into the Gainsborough Lecture (before he had too much time to think), which was now coupled with eighteenth-century banking, and out came all my notes, photographs, etc. I stressed how kind the other banks (except Coutts) were being, and he started to look at the notes I had managed to make from the other accounts. One name caught his eye – Friedrich Kaendler from the Gosling books.

'He was here, at this date?' he said in surprise. Thank God, a kindred spirit. I started to babble about the information that it was possible to get from the books if you read them, as I was doing at the other banks; that is, not simply as private personal accounts but as merchant bankers dealing with each other. He looked very doubtful. 'No one has ever had permission to look at every account,' he said. 'That is why no one has ever understood them or got so much out of them,' I said with what I hoped was great firmness, although I squeaked a bit in the marble halls. He still looked very doubtful. We went up to the library so that I could spread my folders out properly and explain the cross-referencing. Finally, he said if I could get proper recommendation, acceptable to the governors, he would see what he could do.

I walked out very happy – they had *all* their books, from 1698 to the present day, intact. Poor Hugh Casson was pressed into service yet again, as was Roy Strong (not a knight would be unturned to get me into those books). However, no others needed to be disturbed.

I got back from the bank to find the house had been burgled. Rather a shame as I had just managed to get my few bits and pieces of jewellery back from my classy pawn shop. Oh well, at least I had been wearing the audition mink.

They were tidy burglars on the whole. My living room, covered with papers and books, had defeated them and, apart from going through the desk and bringing to light a few letters I had thought lost, they hadn't done any damage – for this, much thanks. It is the feeling that all your things have been rummaged through that is so awful. They stole some of my property jewellery, too – that must have annoyed them. What they made of my collection of Victorian dresses and corsets I can't think. Some of my junk stuff dated back to my first plays in the theatre, and a ring Irene had given me on the last tour was amongst it – damn!

March 23rd: I sent copies of all the banking information as I found it to Sir Ellis, so that he returned from America to find a mass of unsorted material waiting for him.

I had made lots of notes on Reynolds, too, especially for him. I had continued my letters even though he was away. I needed to tell him as I went along; not many other people wanted to know, or indeed would understand all that I was unearthing. As it was, I was just starting to understand it myself:

Dear Miss Corri,
I am afraid I have kept these some days – but I have been coping with two months' mail!

The Evelyn payment to Reynolds in 1747 is interesting and puzzling. Gainsborough's payments to Dupont also are very interesting. I don't in the least understand the occasional payments into the account by Lord Howe or Lord Hardwick or Mrs Langston as they are never enough to pay for any picture. Also I don't understand Doctors' Commons at all.

You will have to publish the fruits of your business researches.

I have to be in London one day this week but am occupied

the other end of London from the RA all the time – and I am not sure when I shall be able to come and see the portrait again.

Yours sincerely,
Ellis Waterhouse

April 1st: Finding another picture with as clear an underscoring seemed a tall order, always providing the museum or owner would let me try.

I was pretty certain about the landscape in the Tate but, after my interview with Miss Einberg, did not feel too inclined to ask. The Royal Academy landscape was on loan, and John Jacobs at Kenwood was so sceptical I hesitated to ask him.

It was also an expensive business. All the experiments at Cooper's and the Yard had drained my resources and I wanted to be sure of the results. I needed another picture as clear as the self-portrait. By this time, I even dreamed about the problem. At three one morning I woke up as if I had been spoken to. 'The little girls!' Why hadn't I thought of them before? The two heads in the V & A. Roy Strong would surely give me a chance to see if they were signed.

I got up and went to the museum as early as I could before rehearsals. There in the corner, clear to the naked eye, without any special processes, was a 'T', this time even better for my purposes than the one at the Academy. It was in his younger hand, less elaborate, exactly like the one on the Garrick – a kind of 7 in shape.

Roy allowed me to have photographs taken by the V & A photographer, Sally Chappell – some more evidence for my folder.

These photographs also showed the brushwork clearly, and the great similarities in the way the paint was handled in the Garrick and the children's faces, the painting of the eyes particularly. Even though there was at least fourteen years in between the pictures, they had to be by the same hand. They were a bonus I had not expected.

April 4th: I seem to go to a lot of weddings these days.

Eddie Kulukundis and Susan Hampshire are to be married. He rang me early in the morning; he didn't seem to be able to believe his own luck. Apart from losing my favourite theatre escort, I am very happy for them both.

The wedding reception was splendid. I went with Carl Toms. Colour scheme pink and white, food to match – lobsters, pink champagne and strawberries. Carl and I decided that we would, if possible, eat nothing else. Susan in a pink and white dress, roses and lilies on the tables. All Eddie's family had flown over from Greece and there are a lot of Kulukundi (if that is the correct collective noun). The theatre faction was minimal. Eddie held tightly on to Susan's hand all the time, like a small boy. He looked dazed and happy. The sight of all that family was a bit overpowering – Greek shipping families stick together. Susan coped with the whole thing magnificently; great poise. After the bride and groom left, the female relatives descended on the tables, fingers flashing with diamonds, and took all the flowers! An old Greek tradition?

One of Eddie's cousins pushed a great bowl into my arms; at my questioning whether we should, she said practically, 'Why not? They're paid for.' Why the rich stay rich, I suppose. I was on my way to visit a friend in hospital. I made a great entrance although I was worried that, for someone who had just had an operation, she laughed too much.

My flow of letters to Sir Ellis continued unabated. The reference to porcelain was because I mentioned the many entries I had found at Gosling's mentioning Friedrich Kaendler, who had later become head of the Meissen factory; like the man at the Bank of England, I too was surprised that he had been here at the dates I had been examining on the bank books.

April 5th: Letter from Sir Ellis.

Dear Miss Corri,
What a mass of fascinating material you seem to me to be finding. Gainsborough must surely have banked somewhere else as well, or did he keep most of the money paid him in a stocking?

Alas, I know nothing about porcelain and am not seriously interested in it.

Reynold's accounts are pretty confusing, but much fuller, but it is clear that he quite often didn't record payments.

By all means look in here whenever you find yourself in the neighbourhood. I don't think we shall go away much for some months now.

I shall be in London on the 14th ... so I could look in and see the picture in the afternoon. I don't think it is necessary to have the other picture there as well. I wish the portraits of Sir Onesiphorus and Lady Paul would turn up. They might be quite curious.

Yours sincerely,
Ellis Waterhouse

Sir Onesiphorus and Lady Paul have disappeared. I found the payments in the books at Gosling's. They were supposed to be a very funny-looking pair and their double portraits had caused some hilarity when Gainsborough painted them.

April 16th: Alfred is playing this play for comedy, too. I don't think Priestley actually intended it this way. I fear the whole thing is another mistake.

We opened again in Lincoln, which pleased me, and I went to find George Stowell, the old verger, at the cathedral, but he is dead. The librarian has left, too, and the Dean's books have been rebound with their proper titles. Damn; such a lovely joke lost for good. I went to see Mrs Stowell. They had been planning to come and see the play together; he died only a week ago. She told me a strange thing; George was responsible for winding the great clock in the cathedral tower, which booms all the time and is part of life in Lincoln (one reason why George was always looking at his watch). As he was being buried, the clock suddenly started chiming out of order and quite madly, then stopped and could not be rewound. They have had to put in a new electric mechanism. It would not go for anyone else but George. I can still see him nipping about in the rafters. I didn't have the heart to go up to the roof again.

As well as the chimes of the clock in the tower, our director put a clock effect (a miniature Big Ben) into the play. I nearly fell off the sofa laughing. It struck nine when Alfred entered and nine when he left, to denote, I suppose, that we had imagined it all (fat chance). I had worked for Priestley years ago in a play called *Summer Day's Dream* (1948), and because our director stamped his foot a bit at my hilarity I thought, rather than argue, I would write to the old boy to ask his opinion of this bit of gratuitous decoration. His reply was swift, concise and to the point, 'No, there should not be a clock chiming. If I had intended one I should have written it.' I pinned this to the notice board – we subsequently 'lost' the clock.

This play has been my hilarious introduction to the School of Coarse Acting. Alfred, as the Inspector, is a cross between Groucho Marx and Christ. It is the funniest performance I have ever seen; my jaw tends to drop with astonishment and wonder and my lines leave me completely. 'If,' he says ponderously, 'you will not move until after my line, I can get a laugh on "prostitute".' I wait obligingly. Utter silence. Peter Vaughan, not to be outdone, is being a Victorian paterfamilias, done up for all the world like Gladstone.

Alfred has persuaded our director that he is God as well, which means he pins himself to the back wall and does the most old-fashioned upstaging I have ever seen. One night, when my neck simply would not turn further round, I walked straight up to the back of the set and delivered all my lines from a pillar at the door. Being beaten at his own game brought the look of a hurt baby to Alfred's face, and he continued to address his lines to where he thought I should be. In the interval, one of the other actors took them their mugs of tea; both old boys were sitting in gloomy silence. 'Do you think she knows what she's doing?' said Peter finally. ' 'Course she bloody knows!' said Alfred blackly.

He hardly speaks to me now. I am so glad Priestley didn't come to see us, it might have killed him.

Poor Alfred – I did, once only, persuade him to do nothing at all on the Inspector's final big speech, instead of the crucifixion act he had worked up (looked a bit like the Christ on the mountain in Rio). He was marvellous, very moving, and the speech got the round it should, even with a small audience. Next night, however, he was back to the old tricks. I suppose it is too much to expect an old dog to learn now.

Fortunately, off-stage we all get on very well. Julie Dawn Cole is very much in love and her nice young man proposed to her in

York, very romantically in the cathedral. She burst into tears when we all met in the street, and we managed to find some champagne to drink their health. Now she sits on the stage each night in a haze of wedding plans and hardly hears her lines.

May 12th: The Inspector *plays at Bath this week, but Sir Ellis is due to come into the Academy to see Garrick again. I must be there, so I will commute for two days.*

He was not entirely discouraging, although still on the fence. He seemed to like the picture a little better than last time, but it is not likely that he will fully agree it unless I have more proof. Understandable – I have never seen another exactly in this style. It *is* a good picture. I felt quite cheered to see him again.

Neither Sir Ellis nor I had much time; I was terrified I would not get to Bath, and he had another appointment, and we both tend to be better in letters to each other than in person. I was a little disappointed, but not too much, as he was so clearly giving Davy lots of second thoughts, based on the new background I was starting to provide on Gainsborough's early life and career.

I wish this tour were over, then I could get back to work. The car broke down twenty miles from Bath and I had to get a taxi and only just got there in time for the performance. I had been belting the car too hard, and it just gave up.

May 18th: Edinburgh. The National Gallery.

Lovely to see the Van Dyck again, and the Tiepolo, not to mention the Hon. Mrs Graham. I know what I really want from life – the Edinburgh National Gallery. It is the most select collection in the world. They may only have one of a certain artist, but it is the best one. Rembrandt, Rubens, Vuillard, and on and on. It is more like a private man's taste than a public institution – I do love it. The cast lost me the other day; however they knew exactly where I would be, in front of the Van Dyck. I felt guilty. I had lost them deliberately; they had been so bored when I took them round. I didn't want to inflict my choice on them, but I had to see more of the Van Dyck.

I also went to the Royal Bank of Scotland in Edinburgh. Their librarian, Christine Robertson, was sweet; a great enthusiast with a real love of history. I think she found the idea of the picture rather romantic and did all she could to help. Her bet is that I will have more luck at Drummond's Branch in London, where the archives are almost intact, and she will give me an introduction to the archivist there; she says he is very helpful. I got the feeling that the Royal Bank found its museum rather a waste of time, but that Miss Robertson was hanging on because she believed in it. I found some very early accounts in the attics. Behind some Victorian papers were bundles of notes of hand in practically mint condition, the earliest dating from 1700, some large documents and what looked like an early charter, seals and all.

I staggered out, very dirty, crashing straight into two of the directors, and before they knew it I had them on hands and knees, looking at all my finds on the floor. Poor Christine Robertson, I think I rather embarrassed her, but maybe I also did her some good; perhaps they will now start to take an interest in the mine of information at their disposal. I stressed the monetary value of the papers, as I have learned to do with bankers. I hope I didn't overdo it; being Scotsmen they may be tempted to sell them. I did tell them that they could be photocopied and bring in handsome dividends (the bait I had used for Henry Hoare), and properly collated, they could. The information on the books is endless, not just for the arts but for social and economic history. If only I could make them all see what a marvellous chance they are losing in not being aware of it all.

At the Royal Bank, the notes of hand gave precise details of trade between Holland, Scandinavia and France; the names were obviously old merchant families dating long before the founding of the bank itself. Followed up, they could give great insight into the financial support given to various political factions: who was putting money into the '45 rebellion, and where their allegiances lay. So much so long neglected. It would have probably been thrown out if it had not been for people like Christine Robertson.

June 1st: We play in Bradford.

Not much you can say after that sentence. We played in a vast, mostly very empty, theatre; it has been marooned in one-way traffic systems and is almost impossible to reach even if you were the most avid theatre-goer in the world. I went out to the moors on most of our days off. Willis Hall, the playwright, phoned and he and his wife were kind and gave me a couple of splendid days. We have known each other for years, since his first successful plays: *The Long, the Short and the Tall,* where Peter O'Toole knocked the London stage sideways for the first time; then Albert Finney in *Billy Liar*. It seems so long ago. He lives in a seventeenth-century farmhouse and the turmoil of those days is past. I think it is rather a pity.

June 8th: Peterborough.

I found I could get a fast train, so I commuted this week. I had to get back to the banks. The introduction to Drummond's was important to me; there were so many clues to follow up at Hoare's. The next week, Eastbourne, was within reach of home, although it was tiring, but it meant I could get in a few hours of research a day.

June 22nd: Cardiff.

Too far to try the commuting game, so I was forced to sift through my notes instead.

June 29th: Belgrade, Coventry.

I was persuaded not to drive up but took a lift in one of the other actors' cars. Regretted it deeply. The next day my little Morris Traveller was stolen from my door in London and left wrecked in an underground garage. I loved that car; I'd had it for years. It was a miserable week.

July 2nd: I went over to see the Birmingham theatre board while An Inspector Calls *was in Coventry.*

I gave them copies of all my evidence to date. I don't think they really understood a word of what I said. Apart from Edmund and Michael, I don't like the others. I got back to Coventry so terribly tired and miserable. I don't know why

I wish they were different; Birmingham councillors are just that; if they were anything else they wouldn't be there, and that's all. If I hadn't done so much work and didn't care about it so much, I would hand the picture back and let them get on with it.

The research on the banks offered some compensation; all the commuting became worth it, and even the indifference of the board faded into insignificance.

As I had got sidetracked at the PRO, so I began to find more about Gainsborough's wife at Hoare's Bank. The whole of her family had sporadic accounts there, including John Fitz-Frederick Burr, her lawyer brother. It was significant that he did not use the Fitz-Frederick until after the Prince's death, and also that the bank accepted it as they did. In fact, there were so many links to Frederick in the Gainsborough history that they merit a separate book to themselves. Margaret Burr's annuity went through the Beaufort books because the exiled Earl of Arran (the bank allowed him his title until death) arranged for Frederick to have the money for annuities to his children through the Duke of Beaufort's accounts. George II, being mean to his son, created an excellent channel for the banished Scots to reach the heart and the pocket of the future King. The Scottish connection inevitably led me to Drummond's where Gainsborough had an account from 1784 until his death in 1787.

July 8th: Drummond's is lovely, very Scottish, so I felt very much at home.

One day while I was beavering away there, a funny cry came from the top of the stairs (I am generally placed in the basement where the books are kept). 'Adrienne Riccoboni! What are you doing here?' I couldn't think who it could be who knew my name before I had changed it (under protest); one of the clerks had gone to kindergarten with me.

I found Captain Robert Shaftoe on Drummond's books the other day – the Bobby Shaftoe of the song. I let out a squeal of pleasure and disturbed some clerks who were working on the modern files. I tried to explain; they really think me some kind of nut and it was a waste of time.

I worked in all about a year at Hoare's, three months in

Drummond's and, on and off, three months or so at Gosling's. I had to keep tearing myself away to work at what was rapidly becoming my secondary profession, the theatre.

July 11th: The tour ended and we all said goodbye in Oxford.

Julie is planning her wedding for the autumn, so we will meet again then. We had one horrendous day together in London looking for white taffeta, which, because of the Royal Wedding, was in short supply. David Walker drew a design for her dress, a romantic crinoline, and I went back to the banks full time, and to Gainsborough. National events came and went disregarded.

July 29th: Can't get to banks because of Royal Wedding.

August 2nd: Decided to take some time off to pay a visit to Gainsborough's grave at Kew.

I last saw it years ago when I had been at Kew Theatre. I was fourteen, in my first job, as Alice in *Through the Looking Glass*. Some of this search has made me feel very much like Alice all over again. Who is John Hayes? The Mock Turtle? Too much character – Humpty Dumpty? Just as opinionated. I can't fit him into any of the Lewis Carroll people, perhaps because he has no sense of humour. Elizabeth Einberg is very good for the White Queen.

I had thought the tomb to be more imposing, and that Gainsborough's name was on the side, like that of Zoffany, which is in the same churchyard, facing the road. It was a fine day and the tomb that dominated the churchyard was a very grand one, to a Thomas Gardiner. I discovered that he did not lie under this monument, as it had been moved when the church was altered, but beside the Gainsborough grave, marked only by a small stone. Gainsborough, as he had wished, lies just below the grave of his friend, Joshua Kirby. There is a cosy intimacy about the arrangement of the graves, like the care given to the seating at a dinner party.

During my work at Hoare's Bank one of the names that had recurred on the books of the Beaufort family had been a Thomas Gardiner, who seemed to act for them in a legal capacity. He, in turn, made payments to a Richard Gardiner; a yearly allowance such as a son might receive. It wasn't too difficult to link the accounts with those of Gainsborough. Richard Gardiner was the name of his brother-in-law, husband of his sister, Susannah. Another part of the Gainsborough puzzle began to be a little clearer. Not much attention has been paid to the marriages of Gainsborough's sisters; this family connection may well have been the link that introduced him to his wife, the mysterious young Scotswoman, Margaret Burr.

The other graves in the area are interesting; mostly legal families, some of the stones are very indistinct. I noticed the end of one name had the letter 'R'. Out of curiosity I started gently to clear the other letters. Old stone flakes as you remove lichen, and it is almost better to leave it rather than to clean it from the letters. By pressing the lichen flat you can sometimes get a better result; it tends to fill the indentation and you don't disturb the inscription. The surname was Burr. In this case, Elizabeth Burr. A Daniel was the next name to appear, and in the end I found that the ground at Kew contained not only the Gainsborough family, but those of Gardiner and Burr. I had always taken for granted that, as Thomas' brothers had remained in Sudbury and Susannah died in Suffolk, she had also lived there, but now the thought crossed my mind that this might be just another of the many misconceptions I had encountered in my search for the real Thomas Gainsborough.

In looking for the origin of Gainsborough's wife's family, I had come upon this entry in the Huguenot register:

121: Daniel Burr, son of Nathaniel Burr, by Sophia his wife, born in Amsterdam.

NATURALISATIONS

George I. 21.

Bill received Royal Assent 22nd March 1722–23

129: Elizabeth Burr (wife of Daniel Burr Esq.) daughter of Frederick Daucherbs by Petronella his wife, born Amsterdam in Holland.

Sofia Rebecca Burr, daughter of the aforesaid Daniel Burr, by Elizabeth his wife, born in Amsterdam.

Frederick and Daniel Burr (14 & 12 years or thereabouts respectively), by Elizabeth, etc.

124: Eliz. Burr, wife of Daniel Burr, late of Amsterdam, now of the city of London, merchant and...
Sofia and Rebecca Burr their daughters, and Frederick and Daniel Burr, their sons, born abroad, Patent Roll 4. George I, part 5.

Looking around that graveyard was more informative than all the books.

Frederick, Prince of Wales, had built his house at Kew and held court there. Kirby had been drawing master to his children; Quin, the actor, also a friend of Gainsborough's, had coached Frederick's children in amateur theatricals. The Bedford family also had strong ties with Frederick, and most of Gainsborough's early portraits were of his circle. An early visit to the Duchy of Cornwall seemed a good idea, to follow up this thread.

August 12th: At Drummond's I struck oil at last.

It was Drummond's that provided one of the most important clues. On the books of a firm called Warners & Blakeseley was a payment to John Gainsborough for £25 7/–. This was the only entry referring to Gainsborough's father I could find, and it was in 1742, February 22nd, around the date of my David Garrick; it would be during the first season at the Goodman's Fields Theatre and at about the time of the rumoured duel. Gainsborough's father had never, to my knowledge, been discharged of his bankruptcy and this payment would correspond with the amount paid for a landscape, if judged against the scale of payments I had worked out at the other banks. It looked very much as if the sixteen-year-old artist was helping his father. I found one other very significant entry on the later books: '1747, December 24th – by draft received, Shepherd's bill on Gainsborough, £90.' This was on the account of a silversmith, Henry Hutchinson. Shepherd the architect dealt through the Hutchinson books, and was using him to cash a note of hand from Gainsborough. It was the first concrete evidence I had found to link Gainsborough with Shepherd and the Goodman's Fields Theatre's architect; my first connection with the circle of people around both Garrick and Henry Giffard. The sums of money meant that Gainsborough was a fully fledged artist, and not just an apprentice. The earlier payment meant that it could just be possible for him to have worked at Goodman's Fields Theatre, and for him to have had the opportunity to paint the Garrick portrait.

August 18th: Duchy of Cornwall. One thing about research here, it is comfortable.

I had become so used to whatever space I could find in the banks that the pleasant surroundings almost put me off. Comfort and research didn't seem to go together. Confirmation of all that I had been finding on the bank books was there in neatly bound volumes. All the names of the accounts I had been working on, especially the Scottish ones; *and* the ever present Mr Robert Andrews emerged again, underwriting loans to Frederick, to the tune of £30,000 in one case in 1743.

In the household, Robert Andrews is 'Remembrancer'. French and Scottish names predominate. With the Pretender in the north and Frederick at Kew, George II must have felt like a king on a chess-board, one move away from check. Looking up the household on the bank ledgers gives it a proper perspective. Charming though Fred may have been, he was no fool and a very real potential danger to his father; he seems to have used the possibility to the best of his advantage. George's seemingly irrational outbursts against his son have a basis of more than lampoons and satires. Fred was a constant source of worry, with a strong political background. Not allowing him to lead troops in Scotland during the '45 rebellion was a sensible precaution – the danger of the Scots deserting the Pretender and going over to Frederick, against his father, was a distinct alternative. Wisely, George avoided this possibility. Even if Frederick had not gone so far, more popularity for him in Scotland had to be avoided.

At last I had permission to search the books at the Bank of England. Three months after I had applied, and when all living relatives who could be traced had been consulted, I was allowed to go to the record rooms at Roehampton.

August 19th: Almost as if to make up for the slowness of my early progress, the research began to inundate me with information.

No laborious search was needed at the Bank of England. I started to turn up extraordinary entries almost at once. Perhaps it was also the fact that I was now so conversant with the people I was looking up that it was easier to see the clues as they presented themselves. I found the Goodman's Fields accounts in the first week. It was wonderful – tiring, but wonderful.

Each entry at the bank, as in Drummond's, had a number which was supposed to relate to day-books that had long ago disappeared. Although this method seemed correct, after a fashion, I found I could not cross-reference the accounts by date as I could at Drummond's; unlike that bank, the numbers did not seem exclusive to one date. I asked the curator if he could help me, and we went back to the first books, 1698, to discover exactly how the numbers worked. My guess was that they were also the clerks' way of keeping tracks of larger capital sums.

The key to the books at the Bank of England lay in this number system. It was a kind of code. Looking at the account of William Pitt, for instance, it is remarkable that he never seems to pay a small bill; all the payments are in hundreds or thousands. This leads one to wonder how he paid his tailor or bootmaker. Following the larger sums, you find out how this was done. The large payments go to a merchant banker, who in turn pays the bills to the more humble men acting for Pitt as agents or brokers, so to speak. One banker deals with domestic affairs, one with shares, and so on. Tradesmen knew there would be credit at the appropriate account and presented their bills accordingly. The numbers, therefore, have to be broken down into stages:

1 The large day-accounts of capital sums passing into the bank itself;
2 The smaller sums which comprise these day-book totals;
3 Which debit or credit accounts they have come from;
4 The identity of the original payee.

The bank contains bankers within bankers and if, after a time, a trader proves his worth he is then allowed to open his separate account. Thus, you can find Gurney's, Coutts, the Royal Bank of Scotland, Hoare's, Lloyds and Gosling's, all using the mother bank many years before (in some cases) or at the same time as, they are trading on their own. The most involved accounts are the ones that deal in numbers only, without names, and here complete familiarity with the ledgers is essential. It is really like finding long-lost telephone books. Friends bank with friends, and use the note of hand system, where if you are owed £100 and you owe someone £20, you give a note for the twenty to be paid by the person who owes you the larger sum.

To keep themselves from going insane, the clerks put numbers to follow the payments, but it is essential to read ten of the huge ledgers at the same time, as ten are used for each financial year. If the bank is asked if they carry Garrick's or Gainsborough's account, they will say, 'No'. Yet you can find them on the interior bankers' books. The receipts for Goodman's Fields started on the books of Freame & Barclays, with the names of Hayman and Kirby.

August 21st: Giffard, Garrick and Gainsborough appeared for the first time together.

Credit No. 83, £60, March 22nd, 1742. It took me two and a half days to isolate the payment, but it led back to a banking firm called Hulls & Ellis (also within the main bank) and the account of Mrs Giffard, under the name of Lydall, her stage name. She used this to differentiate her banking account from that of her husband. It was an easily identified account as it listed her payments for the performances; these amounts, for her appearances, corresponded with known dates on programmes of the time. This rule applied to other actors of the day, including Garrick, Macklin, Mrs Pritchard, Peg Woffington and foreigners like the dancer, 'La Barberina'. So, on March 22nd, 1742 Mrs Lydall paid the sum of £60 to Gainsborough. At the end of March, the first London season finished for Giffard at Goodman's Fields, and Garrick was a star for the rest of his life, and part of the history of the Giffard family. It was not unreasonable to suppose that the payment was for that ebullient portrait commemorating the duel.

At last it seemed I had found an entry which fitted perfectly for the Garrick portrait. There was one real worry. It seemed such a large amount for a young artist of sixteen, although it was the standard amount earned by most of the other artists of the day. If he could command such a price, then he was fully established, and although I had found the payment to his father at Drummond's Bank in the same year (which crossed through to Shepherd on Freame & Barclays) it was difficult to believe from all the books I had read that he was so well paid at this date.

In the last week of August I sent all these findings, and all the evidence so far, to Sir Ellis Waterhouse, begging him to reconsider his earlier decisions in the light of the banking evidence and the new picture of Gainsborough's life that I had been able to produce, all backed by complete documentation. I had been able to photocopy most of the banking evidence, except that of the Bank of England where, strange as it may seem, there were no facilities to do so. To have copies made of the Bank sheets, I would have had to take the books up to the City and have them photographed there. The cost of this would have been too much for my already strained resources. I also sent him all the other photographs, including the new ones from the V & A which showed the comparative brushwork so beautifully, and waited for a reply. For once he did not reply by return of post. When his letter did come, I was afraid to open it. I left it on my desk for hours while I got up enough courage. Taking 'no' for an answer had become second nature to me by now, but this did not mean that I found it any pleasanter.

September 1st: Letter from Sir Ellis Waterhouse.

Dear Miss Corri,

I think you have made a very good case for the Garrick being a very early Gainsborough. I don't really set much store by the comparison with Mrs Lowndes Stone and other later portraits, but I think it makes sense as being *before* Admiral Vernon and other Ipswich pictures. What originally most worried me was its affinities in style with Hudson rather than with anyone else – and this you never find in later Gainsborough portraits. But, given the Hayman-Shepherd-Giffard milieu which you have discovered, I think it likely he would have tried to be 'fashionable' in this way. It must, I think, have been the connection with Hayman which got him into the Foundling Hospital series. At that date, he clearly *preferred* landscapes, but he certainly must have tried his hand at portraits.

You can't ever prove these things, but it seems to me you have got as far as one can – and the evidence is much stronger than it is for many pictures. On the other hand it is worth remembering that there are very few major artists about whose earliest works we know anything at all! The time may soon be ripe for exhibiting the picture – but not before you have got your findings at the banks into a publishable form.

Yours sincerely,
Ellis Waterhouse

I had to read it three times before I actually realised that, in many ways, he seemed to be saying 'yes'. In order to make sure I was not mistaken, I went next door to my neighbour, Joanna, who had endured a blow by blow progress of the proving of the picture for the last few years. She also had to read the letter several times. We were both a bit stunned. 'I think he is agreeing with you,' she said at last. Her next move was to bring out some champagne; by the time her husband came home, we were both slightly smashed. I tottered next door in a happy haze, only to find I had lost the letter. Joanna retrieved it from under the kitchen stove. At last Garrick could be said to be by Gainsborough. The long search was almost over.

God knows, grateful as I was to get that letter, I could not help questioning the assumption that Gainsborough preferred landscape at that time; he may have been trained to landscape, but a rather high-handed letter of his to Lord Hardwicke later in life, that I had read in the British Museum, rather contradicted the idea that he preferred it at any time:

> Mr. Gainsborough presents his Humble respects to Lord Hardwicke; and shall always think it an honour to be employ'd in anything for his Lordship; but with respect to real Views from Nature in this country he has never seen any place that affords a Subject equal to the poorest imitations of Gaspar or Claude. Paul Sandby is the only Man of Genius, he believes, who has employ'd his Pencil that way – Mr. G hopes Lord Hardwicke will not mistake his meaning, but if his Lordship wishes to have anything tolerable of the name of G, the subject altogether, as well as figures etc. must be of his own Brain; otherwise Lord Hardwicke will only pay for

Encouraging a Man out of his way and had much better buy a picture of some of the good Old Masters.

That letter seemed very revealing to me at the time; after all, he had to start painting faces somewhere. Now at least, if I can write a good enough article, Garrick will be recognised by everyone as that starting point.

As often happens in life, the anticipation of the event led to a kind of deflation rather than the elation I had expected. It seemed not so much the end, but another beginning. Now I really had to work. I sent a copy of Sir Ellis' letter to Sir Hugh Casson:

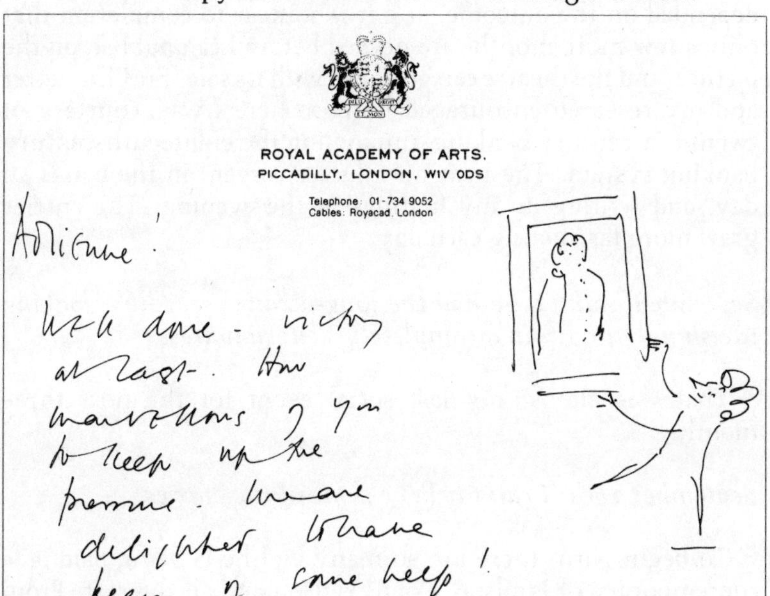
ROYAL ACADEMY OF ARTS.
PICCADILLY, LONDON, W1V 0DS

Telephone 01-734 9052
Cables: Royacad, London

Adrienne!

Well done – victory at last. How marvellous of you to keep up the pressure. We are delighted to have been of some help!

much love
Hugh

I don't know what I would have done in the last few years without his encouragement and the support of the Royal Academy, from the Academicians to the porters; they had all been interested, and were with my fight all the way. I can never thank them enough.

I took Sir Ellis' advice and started to write up my findings. I was aware that the Garrick payment was only a start, and that there was far more to be found on the books of the Bank of England. I went on with my search there. The whole project needed my full time and attention, so I had to go to my ever patient bank manager to ask for a further overdraft in order to finance the work I felt was needed. He turned a little pale, but he agreed. I promised to keep my expenses as low as possible, until the time when the theatre board would be able to reimburse me for the cost of the work I was doing on their behalf. He knew that I had committed myself so much to the project that I could not, and would not, turn back. I knew how much the theatre depended on the outcome, and it is so near to completion that only a few more months are needed before I can publish on the picture, and the theatre can go ahead with its sale. Sir Ellis' letter and my research encouraged him; so here I was, courtesy of twentieth-century banking, untangling the eighteenth-century banking system. The next months were spent in the banks all day, and writing up my findings in the evening. The entries grew more fascinating each day.

September 12th: Julie had the long-awaited wedding, looking ravishingly pretty in a completely Victorian dress.

That was almost my last social event for the next three months.

September 16th: I can't believe some of the entries.

To begin with, there are so many and he is being paid as a contemporary of Hudson, Pond, Wilson and all the rest. From the moment he reaches London, and from the bank books (this is compatible with the dates of 1739–40) that boy is earning money. I have checked and re-checked to see that it cannot be anyone else but none of the rest of his family is earning in this way nor do they bank in London. Also these payments link up in a clear unbroken line with his later ones at Hoare's Bank. Samuel Handley deals with James Unwin and Bertie Burgh in the later books, Gainsborough being handed on, as it were, first to Burgh then to Unwin, although payments to Burgh run parallel for a time.

October: It is very odd to find that I have an endless capacity for reading lists.

Not only that, remembering names – dead ones only; in life, I am as bad as ever. The method required to do the bank books is to store a list of *all* relevant names in your head, having first worked out *all* the possible connections, and then go through the pages letting your eye and brain select automatically. At least, that is what I think I do. I know I can look at a page now, however large, and the relevant names will come leaping out of it, no matter how small the writing may be, or how difficult to decipher. One entry for Gainsborough was right down at the bottom of a page, practically going off it – I still found it. I have gone back over stuff with my notes again and again, just to make sure they are correct. It is very tiring – sometimes I don't make sense for hours afterwards, and I can't talk to people while doing it. I must use complete concentration. You have to blank everything else out of your mind. After four or five hours, I am not in this century and find it hard to readjust. They must think me very strange in the bank. I have had toothache for weeks now, but the information I was getting was so good I managed to block out the pain. When I finally got to the dentist, he was so angry; I had nearly lost the tooth, yet I swear that when I was working I didn't feel a thing.

I don't take lunch breaks – I have a sandwich, or nothing. Bob, one of the staff at the Bank of England, brings me something when he gets back from lunch. They make a good beef sandwich, and a great cup of tea. It always seems like the best drink of the day. I know when three o'clock is coming up, like one of Pavlov's dogs.

Ray, another porter, doesn't believe me when I say I think the tea is so good. He is a keen marathon runner and, usually, I only see him in his bank overalls, grey and sober; a few days ago he blossomed out into blue and red satin running gear with a Union Jack on his bottom. I have never seen such a transformation. I fell about laughing – it was the surprise more than anything. Ray was furious with me.

Because the Bank of England is so large and has such influence, the books are very much more complicated than the other banks.

The link to it all is in the accounts that are solely debit or credit. Each week or ten days they clear large amounts to other bankers; tracing over the number attached to the sums cleared, you are able to identify by date and name where they have come from and where they go. Complications set in when the sums go outside the Bank of England itself, which is where knowledge of the other banks is essential – then you check by date and sum involved. It is not, in the end, as difficult as it sounds; that is, it is not too bad if you have spent a year learning who deals regularly with whom. So you get to know that Freame & Barclays deal with Hubbald and Doddington, who deal with Barber and Slade and William Poyntz, Martin's, Collett's, Hoare's, Child's, Drummond's and Gosling's, to name but a few. Taking notes on each bank as you go, you are able to make an index of the interior banking, and find that Admiral Vernon deals on Sam Smith, amongst others, the Gravenors with Benjamin Hill, Claude Fonnereau on Samuel Handley. The numbers will follow debits and credits until the whole of the large sum is accounted for, then each Quarter Day the system begins with fresh numbers. How I could stick to solving these complications seems, now it is over, almost unbelievable.

The deep conviction I felt about the Garrick portrait pushed me through this mental assault course. To stop at this stage would have made nonsense of all the preceding work. I was in so far in time and commitment that there was no way back. If I ever felt tired or like giving up, one look at the picture would revive my heart, one entry to Gainsborough in a week would be enough to re-fuel the search. Sometimes I would go through ledger after ledger and find no direct payment; all the time I made notes of the other artists or names relevant to Gainsborough and his circle. At the end of it all, I had thirty-eight notebooks covering the first twenty years. All the direct payments to Gainsborough will eventually be broken down. I have only done a few for the time being. Other early pictures overlap to other banks, and some to ledgers I have not yet worked in detail. For future researchers, I have an index and a guide to save them some of the back-breaking work; even so, it is hard enough.

I had only asked for the bank books from 1740, reckoning on an apprentice period from 1739 onwards, but now I began to think there might be earlier payments, and as the Bank of England was so large, that I might at least find his indenture fees. I could find no evidence of his father being officially discharged of his bankruptcy; I wanted to see if he was being allowed credit by a friend on an inner bank, so I asked if I might go back to 1730 to find how and where John Gainsborough banked, and how substantial his account was. I had found nothing for him on the other banks, but now I started to find payments to a Gainsborough of £300 a year on the account of a man called Samuel Handley. Large capital sums were paid in to Handley's account by a Claude Fonnereau, and some of these monies went to Hayman and to Charles Jervas (an Irish artist), and to a Francis Wynantz. Gainsborough was thought to have been much influenced by the work of Wynantz in all the books I had read. However, they were referring to a man flourishing in the seventeenth century. This one was alive and well and working, it seemed, in Suffolk in 1735. George Vertue tells of Peter Tillman's death in Suffolk in 1735, and as was quite common in those days, this man, perhaps a descendant of the earlier Wynantz, could have been brought over to finish his work. Francis Wynantz also worked for a Dr Macro at Norton, as did Francis Hayman, and for Claude Fonnereau. Going backwards and forwards in the books, it became obvious that the money started to be paid by Fonnereau to Gainsborough in 1736, and continued until 1756. This meant a term of twenty years, as in a trust. It was without interruption, and it was obviously not paid to Gainsborough's father. April 1740 was the year of Fonnereau's death, and from then on the money appeared to have been invested, as interest is paid on the Handley account. John Gainsborough died in 1748, the year, significantly, that Gainsborough was supposed to have returned to Suffolk. It would almost seem that the boy left Suffolk to be away from his father's influence and when his patron (for that is what Fonnereau seemed to be) died. The Andrews family also did business with Fonnereau, and figure largely on his account; they were not simple country people. They may have had houses there, but their natural habitat was London and the City. Mr Robert Andrews lived in Grosvenor Square and, in the main, conducted his business from there; Claude Fonnereau from Scythe Lane in the City, and from a retreat in Richmond, and at Edmonton.

Claude Fonnereau purchased Christchurch Mansion in 1732. He also bought property in Sudbury and Aldeburgh, giving his three sons the right to stand for Parliament, and on his death left funds for this purpose. Therefore, in Whitley's book, the disparaging remarks made by William Wyndham about Gainsborough's ingratitude to Fonnereau over the loan of £300, and the fact that he never even voted for him, refer to Claude's son Thomas (Wyndham's friend) who, from his accounts, seems to have had no dealings with Gainsborough at all.

The land in the country was a necessity for the right to stand for Parliament. The Fonnereau family was only second-generation naturalised Englishmen. Their country connections were the first step to power in government.

It is significant also that William Wyndham chose Hoppner, in later years, to paint his portrait, and that there is an early payment to Gainsborough on Ash Wyndham's account (1748) for £50. On the probate for Claude Fonnereau's account there is a payment for Wynantz of £200.

Fonnereau's personal account is lovely. The old boy obviously enjoyed his money; the steady sums to Gainsborough through Handley are not the only ones – the seasonal payments to Giffard and to Hayman seem to suggest that he also supported the local theatre.

If Gainsborough had been an apprentice at the age of ten his term would have been over when he was thirteen or fourteen, and he would have arrived in London a fully-fledged artist, a young man with a trade. The picture of Gainsborough that emerged from the bank books was that of a working child, a boy educated as an artist but not in 'Latin and Greek', so essential to the well-bred young man of those days. In later life he was said to have never read a book, and although his letters are lively, they are raw. He was reputed to be ill at ease in society, for all his talent, preferring the company of actors and musicians – in other words, people like himself, classless except for their gifts. Although the early trust gave him an income and a profession, it left him unequal in social terms, something, it would seem, a man like William Wyndham would never allow him to forget. So my picture of Thomas Gainsborough was emerging and beginning to make sense at last.

Charles Jervas also died in 1739, after a trip to Italy, so it was reasonable that his name would never have cropped up as Gainsborough's tutor for 'face painting'. It is also significant that the colours Gainsborough used all his life were those of Van Dyck, an artist Jervas admired and spent the last years of his life copying. The death of Jervas may have influenced the young man in another way, too, in that he never ventured abroad. The combination of the death of his teacher after a trip to Italy, and the natural reticence of a shy, untutored country boy, could well have been the reason he never went on the Grand Tour, as did so many of his contemporaries. Even Hayman and Hogarth had tried the continent in the unlikely company of Hudson, but were arrested at Calais for drawing the fortifications there. Poor Hudson, deeply embarrassed, went on alone – perhaps it was just as well for him. They must have made an odd trio.

Therefore, if Gainsborough had been taught by, or been an assistant to, Jervas and Wynantz as a boy, it was not unlikely that at sixteen he could have painted a picture as accomplished as my Garrick; he would have also been well established enough to take his place with Wilson, Hayman and the others in the Foundling Hospital. What *does* seem unlikely is that a young man from the country, with practically no work to his name, should have been asked to contribute. To date, none of the books I have read have questioned the fact that there is so little work to show for the years between 1739 and 1748. This is patently absurd, even supposing he were an apprentice at thirteen; but given the amount of payments on the books for the early years dating from 1736, the idiocy mounts. The lack of work cannot be explained away by bland assumptions. I have never thought myself particularly clever, but at least I now know not to take the word of people who believe themselves without question.

November 10th: To the RSC with Frank Barrie.

My eyes gave out on me today. It was very frightening. I had worked at the books from about 9.30 a.m. straight through until 5.00 p.m., rushed home to change to get out to the theatre, and suddenly the room went misty as though in a sudden fog, or filled with white smoke. I could see, but only through this white haze. I didn't know what to do; I couldn't see to put on make-up or even to find eye drops. I couldn't read the labels on the bottles, and I didn't fancy the idea of putting ear drops in my eyes. I found a bottle of witch-hazel and put two pads soaked in it on my eyes, and lay down for a few minutes. My eyes were hurting like mad. Gradually, the haze cleared and I managed to go out. At the theatre it happened again. I think poor Frank Barrie thought I had gone mad. It was hard to look at the stage, or any light for that matter.

I am obviously just terribly tired; I can't let up now, there is so much to do. Frank had a dreadful evening, a cross between being an escort and a seeing-eye dog. Fortunately, he understood. He and Mary are blind as bats and have had to wear contact lenses for years. I am clearly ready for them any day now.

Reading glasses have been prescribed; only mild, but I do need them. The eye specialist was furious with me and has forbidden me to go on working at the rate of the last few months. I have to disobey him; I must get all the entries I can before 1760. It is terrible not to be able to read a paper without spectacles. I keep losing the blasted things, and they make a mark on my nose, but they do help.

November 25th: Michael Bullock has just phoned from Birmingham with the most dreadful news.

Edmund King has been killed in a car crash. I feel quite sick about it; I had sent him Sir Ellis' last letter and was hoping to have had the article in good shape to show him before Christmas. It is awful that he never had the satisfaction of seeing the whole project through to the finish. He would have been so proud.

I don't think for a moment that Michael or Edmund realised how difficult it has all been; how could they, or anyone know for that matter? The thing was that Edmund at least recognised the importance of the work, and had the imagination to want it to go on, which might not have happened in a lot of provincial towns. I do not know how the new man, or the board, will want to continue with it all, nor what they will want to do with the picture. I feel very depressed. It has been the length of time that has been the real enemy, plus the dilatory attitude of the museums. The very real hostility which the picture has aroused has amazed me. I started out quite humble, ready to be told, but not by fools or superannuated students who haven't done their homework. I have developed a great contempt for this kind of civil servant, for that is what so many people running our museums seem to be. It is because of these people that Edmund never saw the end of the fight. Well, I must continue so that he can have a posthumous victory, if nothing else.

By the end of November, the payments to Gainsborough on the books of the Bank of England read as shown on pages 204–10. With the entries on Drummond's Bank, and the ones on Hoare's, the history of Thomas Gainsborough's life can never be the same again.

December 2nd: Went to see John Hayes again with more evidence, including my entry for Garrick, and a great deal of the new banking notes.

He is still more than sceptical. I met Roy Strong leaving as I went in – what a difference in the two men.

Dr Hayes was interested in my bank lists and photocopied all my notes. The Ash Wyndham payment worried him. 'Not the same family, surely,' he said. I was amazed – he should know. He looked it up there and then and, of course, I was right. I do envy these gentlemen their books; I have to whizz all over London to find my references. If only all I had to do was to turn to the shelves. On the other hand, it does mean I have to work.

The gallery seems so dead and flat now that Roy is no longer in charge. It is self-effacing, diffident to the point of negation. One of my favourite statues of old Lane, the translator of the *Arabian Nights*, has been put out of sight – not in 'good taste', I presume. He is in Arab dress, sitting on a cushion, and it is very funny. One of the attendants was as angry as I when I complained about its absence. 'The first Englishman to speak Arabic, and he's put in the basement!'

When I went to the V & A recently, the air was crackling with excitement and the place was crowded like a station. One of the rooms looked particularly fine and I remarked on it to the Indian attendant, who said, 'This director really works – you should see Room 46, it's like paradise!' I reported this conversation to Roy, who was pleased and vastly amused.

BANK OF ENGLAND
DIRECT ENTRIES TO GAINSBOROUGH

LEDGER *118* G–I	(1736–37)	*SAMUEL HANDLEY'S A/C*	
Folio 2668 Drawn	Aug. 20 1736	120 Gainsborough	£ 150
„ 2675 Drawn	Jan. 27 1737	154 Gainsborough	£ 150
LEDGER *125* G–I	(1737–38)	*SAMUEL HANDLEY'S A/C*	
Folio 2367 Drawn	Sep. 19 1737	3 Gainsborough	£ 125
„ 2368 Drawn	Nov. 11 1737	256 Gainsborough	£ 100
	(1738)		
Folio 2373 Drawn	Oct. 24 1738	274 Gainsborough	£ 100
„ 2373 Drawn	Oct. 26 1738	110 Gainsborough	£ 100
„ 2373 Drawn	Nov. 9 1738	3 Gainsborough	£ 70
„ 2617 Drawn	Dec. 29 1738	105 Gainsborough	£ 50
	(1739)		
Folio 2617 Drawn	Jan. 2 1739	233 Gainsborough	£ 30
LEDGER *132* G–I	(1738–40)	*SAMUEL HANDLEY'S A/C*	
Folio 2334 Drawn	Feb. 27 1739	244 Gainsborough	£ 50
„ 2335 Drawn	May 5 1739	8 Gainsborough	£ 150
LEDGER *134* N–R	(1738–40)	*WILLIAM POYNTZ ESQ.*	
Credit	1739		
Credit bt. up			
Folio 4265	Mar. 12	100 Gainsborough	£ 21
LEDGER *138* D–F	(1740–42)	*FREAME & BARCLAYS*	
Credit	1742		
Folio 1775	Mar. 22	83 Gainsborough	£ 60
LEDGER *145* D–F	(1743)	*GEORGE DENSHIRE ESQ.*	
Credit bt. up		(Lawson	£ 50
Folio 1645	Dec. 5	98(Furber	£ 140
		(Gainsborough	£ 46
LEDGER *149* S–Z	(1742–44)	*WILLIAM SCAWEN*	
Folio 5119	(1744)		
Credit	Jan. 3	142 Gainsborough	£ 50

LEDGER *152* D–F (1744–45)		*GEORGE DENSHIRE ESQ.*	
Credit	1745		
Folio 1210	Feb. 11	154 Gainsborough	£ 100
„ 1211 Credit	May 6	266 Gainsborough	£ 45.15. od.
LEDGER *153* G–I (1744)		*HANDLEY & HOLMES*	
Folio 2265 Drawn	Dec. 20	192 Gainsborough	£ 50.12. od.
	(1744–45)	*BENJAMIN HILL ESQ.*	
Folio 2413 Credit	Feb. 11 1745	154 Gainsborough	£ 100
„ 2414 „	Mar. 29	250 Gainsborough	£ 82. 2. 6d.
LEDGER *159* D–F (1745–46)		*GEORGE DENSHIRE ESQ.*	
Credit	1746		
Folio 1210	Mar. 4	50 Gainsborough	£ 84. 7. 6d.
	(1746)	*ABRAHAM & JACOB FRANCO*	
Folio 1441			
Debit bt. up	Jul. 10	95 Gainsborough	£ 60
LEDGER *160* G–I (1746)		*THOMAS GILES*	
Folio 2070 Credit	Oct. 31	2 Gainsborough	£ 46.15. od.
„ 2078 „	Jun. 12 1747	108 Gainsborough	£ 18.16. od.
	(1746–47)	*BENJAMIN HILL ESQ.*	
Folio 2440 Credit	Feb. 17 1747	137 Gainsborough	£ 98. 2. od.
LEDGER *162* N–R (1746–47)		*JOHN PATTEN*	
Folio 4708 Drawn	Feb. 28 1747	156 Gainsborough	£ 95. 8. od.
LEDGER *164* A–Z Supplement (1747)		*WILLIAM & HENRY SAWBRIDGE*	
Folio 6741 Credit	Aug. 31	176 Gainsborough	£ 86. o. 6d.
LEDGER *167* G–I (1749)		*THOMAS GILES*	
Folio 2674 Credit	Jun. 6	119 Gainsborough	£ 29.11. od.
LEDGER *169* N–R (1747–49)		*REYNOLDS & BRAY*	
Folio 4621 Credit	Feb. 20 1748	33 Gainsborough	£ 28
LEDGER *170* S–Z (1747–49)		*ASH WYNDHAM*	
Folio 5701 Credit	May 3 1748	128 Gainsborough	£ 50

LEDGER *171* A–Z Supplement(1747–49)		*SAMUEL SMITH*	
Credit bt. up	(1748)		
Folio 6557	Jun. 30	271 Gainsborough	£ 73
LEDGER *172* A–C (1749)		*SIR FRANCIS CHARLETON*	
Folio 539 Credit	Nov. 21	104 Gainsborough	£ 47. 2.11d.
Credit bt. up	(1750)		
Folio 544	Mar. 29	167 Gainsborough	£ 43. 4.10d.
Credit bt. up			
Folio 545	May 21	264 Gainsborough	£ 20.12. 7d.
Credit bt. up			
Folio 548	Aug. 20	73 Gainsborough	£ 45. 9.10d.
" 551 Credit	Nov. 27	37 Gainsborough	£ 35.18. 9d.
LEDGER *173* D–F (1749)		*GEORGE DENSHIRE ESQ.*	
Credit bt. up			
Folio 1189	Oct. 31	127 Gainsborough	£ 100
Credit	1750		
Folio 1190	Feb. 7	93 Gainsborough	£ 140
LEDGER *174* G–I (1749–50)		*SAMUEL HANDLEY*	
Folio 2609 Drawn	Nov. 10 1750	194 Gainsborough	£ 50
	(1749)	*THOMAS GILES*	
Folio 2045 Credit	Nov. 7	50 Gainsborough	£ 22.11. 0d.
LEDGER *175* K–M (1749–50)		*HENRY LIEGH*	
Folio 3641 Credit	Aug. 15	222 Gainsborough	£ 11.14. 0d.
LEDGER *177* S–Z (1749)		*WILLETT & WAKEFIELD*	
Folio 5632 Credit	Dec. 4	216 Gainsborough	£ 20
	(1750)	*STORKE & CHAMPION*	
Folio 5802 Drawn	May 8	270 Gainsborough	£1413. 6. 8d.
LEDGER *178* A–Z Supplement(1749–50)		*WILLIAM SAWBRIDGE & CO.*	
Folio 6458 Credit	Apr. 24 1749	174 Gainsborough	£ 94. 6. 5d.
LEDGER *178*		*CHARLES VAVAZOR*	
Folio 6669 Credit	Nov. 15	90 Gainsborough	£ 30

LEDGER *179* A–C (1751)		*SIR FRANCIS CHARLETON*	
Folio 530 Credit	Jun. 25	226 Gainsborough	£ 44. 2. 5d.
〃 536 〃	Dec. 16	38 Gainsborough	£ 22. 1.10d.
	(1752)		
Folio 537 Credit	Jan. 4	178 Gainsborough	£ 20
Credit bt. up			
Folio 539	Mar. 23	258 Gainsborough	£ 46.16. 0d.
Credit bt. up			
Folio 542	Jun. 25	226 Gainsborough	£ 21. 5. 0d.
〃 545 Credit	Sep. 22	155 Gainsborough	£ 44. 2. 4d.
〃 873	Dec. 19	215 Gainsborough	£ 44.10. 8d.
	(1752)	*JOHN CARTWRIGHT & THOS. CLEGG*	
Folio 797 Credit	Mar. 5	217 Gainsborough	£ 25.15. 2d.
LEDGER *180* D–F (1751)		*JOHN DERBIE*	
Folio 1107 Credit	Jun. 8	216 Gainsborough	£ 49.18. 0d.
Credit bt. up	Mar. 9	232 Gainsborough	£ 12.16. 0d.
	(1751–52)	*GEORGE DENSHIRE ESQ.*	
Folio 1194 Credit	May 8 1751	108 Gainsborough	£ 178
Credit bt. up	1752		
Folio 1195	Mar. 20	280 Gainsborough	£ 141. 8. 3d.
〃 1196 Credit	Jun. 5 1752	170 Gainsborough	£ 100
LEDGER *181* G–I (1751)		*SAMUEL HANDLEY ESQ.*	
Folio 2269 Drawn	Apr. 1	81 Gainsborough	£ 50
〃 2271 Drawn	Jul. 13	255 Gainsborough	£ 80
〃 2385 Drawn	Oct. 23	191 Gainsborough	£ 60
〃 2388 Drawn	Mar. 6 1752	249 Gainsborough	£ 80
〃 2634 Drawn	Jul. 13 1752	74 Gainsborough	£ 100
〃 2729 Drawn	Jan. 10 1753	140 Gainsborough	£ 80
	(1752–53)	*BENJAMIN HILL*	
Credit bt. up			
Folio 2330	May 11	177 Gainsborough	£ 60
LEDGER *182* K–M (1751)		*SIR WILLIAM MILNER, BART.*	
Folio 3424 Credit	Jul. 20	267 Gainsborough	£ 37.11. 0d.
LEDGER *184* S–Z (1750–53)		*JOHN VOYCE* (recvr.)	
Folio 5714 Credit	May 17	228 Gainsborough	£ 100
	Cont'd		

		JOHN VOYCE ESQ.		
Folio 5773				
Credit bt. up	May 11 1752	177 Gainsborough	£	200
Folio 5773	Aug. 7 1752	22 Gainsborough	£	200
〃 5774				
Credit bt. up	Jan. 11 1753	50 Gainsborough	£	105
Folio 5774 Credit	Dec. 29 1753	155 Gainsborough	£	105
		HENRY SOUTHWELL ESQ.		
Folio 5769				
Credit bt. up	May 9 1752	127 Gainsborough	£	30
LEDGER *185* A–Z Supplement (1750–54)		*HON. ROGER TOWNSHEND*		
Folio 6584 Credit	Oct. 21 1751	235 Gainsborough	£	82. 4. 3d.
LEDGER *186* A–C (1753)		*SIR FRANCIS CHARLETON*		
Folio 590				
Credit bt. up	Mar. 27	242 Gainsborough	£	6. 11. 0d.
Folio 591 Credit	Apr. 6 1753	239 Gainsborough	£	20
〃 594 〃	Jul. 9	276 Gainsborough	£	32. 9. 9d.
〃 597 〃	Oct. 5	207 Gainsborough	£	40. 15. 3d.
〃 600				
Credit bt. up	Jan. 10 1754	42 Gainsborough	£	42. 13. 9d.
Folio 603				
Credit bt. up	May 2	7 Gainsborough	£	5. 8. 2d.
Folio 605				
Credit bt. up	Jul. 2	216 Gainsborough	£	20. 11. 7d.
Folio 608 Credit	Sep. 20	99 Gainsborough	£	20
〃 〃				
Credit bt. up	Oct. 8	68 Gainsborough	£	25. 19. 9d.
LEDGER *188* G–I (1753)		*SAMUEL HANDLEY ESQ.*		
Folio 2381 Drawn	Aug. 2	236 Gainsborough	£	104. 11. 0d.
〃 2385 Drawn	Jun. 15 1754	50 Gainsborough	£	100
〃 2387 Drawn	Nov. 11 1754	110 Gainsborough	£	70
(Unwin & Burgh on the same account)				
LEDGER *191* S–Z (1753–54)		*JOHN VOYCE ESQ.*		
Folio 5538 Credit	Feb. 26 1753	246 Gainsborough	£	150
〃 〃 〃	May 5	77 Gainsborough	£	200

1981

		THOMAS WEST		
Folio 5583 Credit	Feb. 23 1753	214 Gainsborough	£	96.16. od.
〃 5929	Mar. 19 1754	14 Gainsborough	£	50.16. 6d.
LEDGER *192* A–Z Supplement(1753–54)		*SAMUEL & WILLIAM SMITH*		
Credit bt. up				
Folio 6397	Mar. 12 1753	282 Gainsborough	£	20
〃 6402 Credit	May 24 1753	164 Gainsborough	£	70
〃 6403 〃	Jun. 14 1753	196 Gainsborough	£	36
		WILLIAM SAWBRIDGE & CO.		
Credit bt. up				
Folio 6458	Dec. 22 1753	107 Gainsborough	£	50.12. od.
LEDGER *193* A–C (1754–56)		*SIR FRANCIS CHARLETON*		
	1755			
Folio 525 Credit	Jan. 10	8 Gainsborough	£	25.18. 5d.
〃 527	Mar. 27	94 Gainsborough	£	26. 3. 5d.
〃 530	Jun. 27	279 Gainsborough	£	50
〃 534	Oct. 13	220 Gainsborough	£	40
〃 535	Nov. 29	35 Gainsborough	£	35
LEDGER *195* G–I (1755)		*SAMUEL HANDLEY ESQ.*		
Folio 2370 Drawn	Jun. 7	235 Gainsborough	£	100
〃 2371 Drawn	Oct. 20	214 Gainsborough	£	140
〃 2372	Apr. 22 1756	Probate of Samuel Handley's Will Doctors' Commons		
LEDGER *196* K–M (1754–56)		*SIR WILLIAM MILNER, BART.*		
Credit bt. up				
Folio 3540	Dec. 4	38 Gainsborough	£	50
LEDGER *197* M–R (1754–56)		*OBADIAH RYDER*		
Folio 4462 Credit	Dec. 9 1755	42 Gainsborough	£	10

HOARE'S BANK
PAYMENTS TO THOMAS GAINSBOROUGH ON THE ACCOUNT OF MR. BERTIE BURGH

1748		
February 17th	To Tho. Gainsborough	£145.16. 0d.
1749		
February 16th	To Mr. Gainsborough	£ 20. 0. 0d.
March 19th	To Tho. Gainsborough	£ 20. 0. 0d.
1750		
May 19th	To Tho. Gainsborough	£ 80. 0. 0d.
1751		
December 13th	To Mr. Gainsborough	£100. 0. 0d.
1752		
January 9th	To Tho. Gainsborough's bill	£260. 0. 0d.

PAYMENTS TO THOMAS GAINSBOROUGH ON THE ACCOUNT OF MR. JAMES UNWIN

1755		
February 24th	To Tho. Gainsborough	£140. 0. 0d.
May 22nd	To Tho. Gainsborough	£100. 0. 0d.
May 30th	To Mr. Gainsborough	£ 26. 0. 0d.
November 30th	To Mr. Gainsborough	£ 26.12.10d.
1759		
August 3rd	To Tho. Gainsborough's bill	£ 50. 0. 0d.

Thank God it is a long holiday – I have nearly finished the whole paper. I will be able to get it to Sir Ellis very early in the year. I have to find someone to type it up properly (and who can read my awful writing), then the next step can begin. Sir Ellis is right, I must publish in a really good magazine, the *Burlington* if possible, and then the whole effort will gain full credibility. ACTRESS FINDS GAINSBOROUGH in the *Star* or something just will not do. Sir Ellis' letter has become a crumpled rag, I have read and re-read it so often. I feel so very happy. I have managed, against all the odds, to stick it out, and there is not much further to go. I know the whole subject so well now; I have surprised myself by my tenacity. I never knew I could stick to something so strongly, or feel so deeply about it; not since my early days of wanting to go into the theatre.

December 24th: Christmas on my own.

I did all the shopping, even had my sticky cakes at Fortnum's, and took the banks their presents. (Dropped a bottle of brandy in the doorway at Hoare's – is nothing sacred?) The porters all laughed a great deal; I think it made their Christmas. The weather is cold and horrible, but it doesn't matter. Rushed into Hatchards early, then fell into Fortnum's for coffee and met Terence Stamp. He lives in Albany. Poor devil – he got the Gainsborough Lecture.

I like shopping late like that, the town is so quiet and everyone is good-tempered at the thought of a holiday, and you can park.

Blessed day – NO TURKEY! I went out and got smoked salmon, it was lovely. Then I worked solidly, went next door, then home and more work. The door bell did ring, but I hid. Rang the aunts. I loved every minute, I never want to do the full bit again. I gave all the Christmas decorations to next door as well. They couldn't make the lights work – can anyone ever? I shall never have to think of them again, thank heavens. I promise I shall keep every Christmas like this for the rest of my life, if I can; or not, if I so choose – choice! How wonderful.

Irene has rung up; there is a part in the play she tried out at Watford which she would like me to play. This is the highest compliment I can ever be paid; she is so scrupulous that she would never dream of asking for someone unless she really liked their work. We are going out to have a Chinese meal this weekend; by that time, I shall have read the play and be able to tell her if I think I am right. It is being presented by Bill Kenwright. A friend of the author, a Terence Frisby, is to direct.

I read the play and it was very funny, I thought – nice part for me of a ridiculous doctor's wife. Irene has tried it out already and it filled the theatre at Watford – we both reckon on a year or more, in the West End with luck.

December 30th: I had been working really hard at the books that week and Irene was alarmed by my eyes.

They do look dreadful – it is this wretched trick of block reading, although it means I get through the work with immense thoroughness. I fix-focus for hours at a time and don't blink enough. The end result is that my pupils become pinpoints and the rest of the eye watery and red; *not* a pretty sight. That, combined with the weight of the damned books and my neck and back being constantly strained – I am being wrecked by research. The stage will be a nice rest.

Another Snag. We open at Billingham.

I will have finished what virtually amounts to my thesis by then, and so it will be lovely to get back on a stage. Glynn Houston played the part of the Doctor at Watford, and Irene is praying he will be free to do it when Bill gets it all together. Apparently, he was wonderful. I am very tired, but the end of all this research is in sight, and it will soon be ready to go to be typed up, and then to Waterhouse for approval. Dear God, it has been a stint and, if it succeeds, only a beginning.

1982

January 4th: The year began with foul weather as usual.

The dreadful heavy car, bought from this Irish garage I have fallen in with, is a brute. Every time I turn the wheel I put my back out. I miss my Morris. Things that go bump in the night and Irish garages – the Good Lord protect us. I managed to get to the Bank of England; during the time I was researching the weather froze up and I thought I would never get away. This problem remained all winter, but the findings on the books compensated. I had been cross-referencing the pictures: Admiral Vernon, 1748, payment through Samuel Smith; the Gravenor receipt, 1749, on Benjamin Hill. It was exciting. I will be able to identify most of the early pictures in this way, setting the Garrick in its proper place in Gainsborough's work.

January 7th: More letters from John Hayes.

I begin to wonder if John Hayes really listens or bothers to read a word I write. Certainly this does not seem to be the case here! I really don't want half-digested things published and attributed to me, I must write and correct this little lot. I know I had a cold at our last meeting, but I can't have sounded that muddled! And he *did* photostat everything.

Everything I had read on Gainsborough, I now had reason to doubt. Even the simple list of dates no longer held good for the early years. Even his traditional birthplace, Sudbury, might have to be changed. The accepted version runs as follows:

Born 1726 (?)	Sudbury – precise date unknown.
May 14th, 1727	Baptised at the Independent Meeting House, Friars Street, Sudbury.

Circa 1740	Sent to London to study. Became a pupil of Hubert Gravelot – or Francis Hayman?
Circa 1745	Established his own studio in London.
1746	Married Margaret Burr on July 15th, at Dr Keith's Mayfair Chapel, London.
1748	Returned to Sudbury to practise. Birth of his elder daughter, Mary.
1752	Birth of his younger daughter, Margaret. Moves to Ipswich.
1758	Worked as a travelling painter in the Midlands.
1759	Moved from Ipswich to Bath.

This is the chronology given by Dr Hayes. Sir Ellis gives a minor variation, adding the fact that in 1748, on May 11th, the Governors of the Foundling Hospital accepted the gift of a landscape from Gainsborough; and that his father died on October 29th of that year. He also gives the meeting of Philip Thicknesse *c.* 1753, and the commissioning of the Bedford landscapes in 1755.

So far my researches changed the look of Gainsborough's life to this extent:

1726	Born in Sudbury (?), actual date unknown.
1727	August – baptism.
1736	Is endowed with £300 a year by Claude Fonnereau.
1736–39	Studies and works with Francis Wynantz, Charles Jervas and Hayman.
1739	Death of Jervas in October.
1740	Death of Fonnereau. Goes to London. Still works with Wynantz and Hayman. Meets and works with Gravelot on the Hanmer Shakespeare. (Possibly stays with Mr Robert Andrews?)
1742	Paints the first portrait of David Garrick, March 22nd.
1745	Paints Hill portraits.
1746	Marries Margaret Burr at Dr Keith's Mayfair Chapel, July 15th.

1747	Birth and death of his first daughter, Mary, Holborn, March 1st.
1748	The Foundling Hospital accept the Charterhouse painting, May 11th. October 29th his father dies and he returns for a time to Sudbury where his second daughter, Mary, is born. Paints the Andrews portrait.
1749	Returns and works in London, without his wife. Work done for Sir Francis Charleton among others. Paints Admiral Vernon (?), the Gravenor family, and landscapes for Samuel Smith (?).
1751	Death of Frederick, Prince of Wales.
1752	Returns to Sudbury. Birth of his third daughter, Margaret.
1753	Moves to Ipswich. Meets Philip Thicknesse.
1755	Paints the Bedford landscapes. Spends at least three months of each year in London, notwithstanding the move to Ipswich.
1756	The payments on Samuel Handley's account end, the year of Handley's death.
1757–8	Visits Bath.
1759	Puts his house in Ipswich up for sale. Moves to Bath.
1760	Death of George II.

Compared with the sketchy chronology in all the other books, this makes quite a difference already, and it is now possible that he painted the Garrick at the time I have found the receipt. Even from this, which I consider only a start, his life is very different from the accepted versions. I have written it all up as Sir Ellis has suggested. I haven't fully expanded the origins of his wife, but only taken that as far as the evidence I have uncovered goes. There is much, much more to the whole Scottish connection, and I want to be able to give it my undivided attention for a few months before I write any more.

I sent it all to Sir Ellis for his vetting. As always, he was very encouraging and urged me to get the article into final form.

I have found a splendid lady called Gail who can decipher my writing *and* my rotten typing, so I shall give her my manuscript and the notes when we start rehearsal and it should be finished and with Sir Ellis by the time the tour begins.

January 14th: Rehearsals began and I do not remember ever having been so unhappy.

What I had read as a rather charming little domestic play became befouled with farce; and the two techniques are very different and need quite separate approaches. Even Irene was unhappy – mercifully Bill, as usual, has only given us a short time. Billingham and a live audience seem like the Blue Remembered Hills.

Some of the cast were very good, Christopher Beanie from *Upstairs Downstairs* in particular. I held on to the fact that the audience might have the sense to see what the play was about, and that Frisby would depart and leave us alone.

'Oh Adrienne, dear,' moaned Irene quietly one day, 'how we were looking forward to this!' Whatever Frisby's opinion of me, I cannot forgive him his utter crassness towards Irene. A great comedienne, she deserves better; he should not be in the same room with her.

The tragedy of the theatre is that the actor is an interpreter, an instrument, and if put into the hands of a fool will, of course, sound dreadful, as would a Stradivarius in the hands of an ape – my sympathy is with the violin.

I continued to send Dr Hayes my evidence. The flurry of questions from him at the beginning of the year sprang from the fact that he was correcting the proofs of his book due out later this year, and he wanted to know the sources of some of the information I had sent him. He also asked if he could use the death of the first child, and various other small pieces of research I had sent to him. What bothered me most about his letter was that he seemed to have got so much quite wrong. He had not seen all my research by a long chalk, and out of context it meant nothing but muddle. I was finding out more every day. I had rather hoped to be the first to publish about the child. He offered to give me a credit: 'Miss Adrienne Corrie [even my name wrong] has very kindly communicated the results of her researches in contemporary church registers'; not a mention that the research was about Gainsborough (there's a generous man for you). I had sent him all that I felt I should in order to get agreement of some kind on the Garrick. He still did not agree it, although he agreed with my research.

It was not the first contradiction I had found in Dr Hayes' approach to me. He was wounded at the thought that I should feel he wanted to take my work. He had no need, he said, to use any of the bank entries except for the three payments from Unwin to Gainsborough in 1755 because 'we know they relate to a sum Gainsborough borrowed'; he also wanted to mention that Mrs Gainsborough could be the daughter of Frederick, Prince of Wales – Lord! What would there be left for me?

'I was proposing to say that these entries had been kindly communicated to me by Miss Corrie [again my name wrong].' He wanted to put the first child's death in as a footnote to explain why the Gainsborough marriage had been a clandestine one – and the fact that Mrs Gainsborough had been with child explained why they had not been married in Suffolk and did not have parental approval. Hayes thought the mention of my name in a footnote would be useful to me and whet people's appetite for my publication, rather than the reverse.

I suppose if one has been used to headlines, footnotes hold little attraction; even less when they get your name wrong. Our letters had progressed to the 'Dear Adrienne' stage after our meetings; although he found my work helpful, he was still adamant about David Garrick.

You get a terrible impression at times from the behaviour of the gallery élite that you have fallen into some dreadful girls' school; the same bitching and bickering. Where are the brains of yesteryear? It wasn't always like this.

When I first came down to London, Sir John Rothenstein was at the Tate Gallery. He was splendid. I used to follow him around like a puppy and have wonderful lectures from him, interspersed with jokey gossip. He had stature and wit. I have been spoiled by my past friendships.

It didn't matter to me if John Hayes used my research, with or without credits; I just didn't want him to get it wrong. God knows, the poor students of Gainsborough, as far as I could tell, had been confused enough. I simply reasoned that, out of context, it meant little, and I offered to show him all of it. His wish to use the pregnancy as a reason for the young couple not returning to Sudbury foisted Victorian morals on their behaviour, morals not in keeping with the age in which they lived or with Gainsborough's behaviour later in life, as this letter to his friend, James Unwin, shows:

Bath, October 25th, 1763

My Dear Friend,

Excuse my answering your Letter a little longer, for I am but just able to hold a pen, and not able to know well what I say to you. I have kept my Bed 5 weeks to morrow excepting two hours sitting up for the last three days of a most terrible Fever. It has been all upon my spirits from the first, that is from a single trip I made in London, as you guess'd; and occasioned by the uncertainty which followed the foolish Act. I was safe in the opinion of two of the best of men in their way, but possess'd in my Mind that I was ruin'd.

O my dear Friend nobody can think what I have suffered for a moment's gratification.

My life was despair'd of by Doctor Charleton after he had tried all his skill, and by his own desire Dr Moisey was call'd in when in three days my faintings left me and I got strength. I am now what they call out of Danger; I wish my Dear Friend I could sleep refreshing sleeps, then all would be well again.

You shall hear from me again soon. My Dear Good Wife has set up every night ti'l within a few and has given me all the comfort that was in her power. I shall never be a quarter good enough for her if I mend a hundred degrees.

Keep my secret, but remember us kindly to good Mrs Unwin and believe me

Yrs most affectionately
ti'l Death.

The marriage to Margaret Burr would appear to have been the consequence of him having gone too far with a girl of good background, and whose reputation had to be protected; a shot-gun marriage, for he certainly did not need the money. Once she was safely in the country, he was free to do all the 'chasing' he pleased. As far as I could make out, the young painter found it inconvenient to have a wife who would hamper him by being constantly pregnant.

Once free of his wife, Gainsborough could taste the pleasures of London and gain the experience which led him to give this sober advice to John Henderson in 1773:

> ...and don't run about London streets, fancying you are catching strokes of nature, at the hazard of your constitution. It was my first school, and deeply read in petticoats I am, therefore you must allow me to caution you.

Another letter to the musician, William Jackson, ends:

> ... I could say a deal more but what can a man say pent up in a corner: Thus; if you was a Lady I would say what I have often said in a corner by way of making use of the last Inch.
> Yours up to the hilt
> T.G.

The regrets later voiced to his friend were probably gained in the years between 1748 and 1751. Three years of freedom and success, with infrequent (if any) visits to the country. Mistakes gained in the company of his musician and actor friends, for at what other time did he get to know Giardini and Quin so well? In Bath? In 1760 he was thirty-four; he would have had a hard time attracting respectable young ladies as clients were he to be thought too dissolute. In his letter to Unwin his 'moment of gratification' took place on a visit to London, away from the influence of his family and the more rigorous censure of the small society of Bath.

Why had John Hayes and Mary Woodall not seen all this? Their Gainsborough is belied in Zoffany's portrait of him, which is nearer my idea of the man. It is a wonderful moment, caught by someone who knew his character well, and one of the most vivid oil sketches I know. Unlike his self-portraits, which have a bold, almost challenging quality, this catches him as he turns swiftly to see – what? A new beauty coming into the room? One whom he feels might prove 'frail'? It was not a time for sentiment; people might protest Sterne's sensibility (all that weeping into handkerchiefs), but they did not practise it. Only the naive or the idealistic would ignore the tone of Smollett or Richardson in Gainsborough's letters. The melancholia which frequently afflicted him in later years, and the hypochondria, could spring from his over-indulgence in seeking 'gratification'. Zoffany shows him unguarded and eager, very much a man's view of a man he admires. It is a hungry face, even greedy, with a not unattractive coarseness – the countryman has not been quite banished, the haystack is not too far from the drawing room. Poor, proper Margaret Burr could not hope to satisfy that man.

Those, however, are my personal conclusions, based on my knowledge of the kind of man that picture shows. Perhaps they are biased but (please forgive me, Dr Hayes and Mary Woodall) it takes experience to know experience. Knowledge can only add (if understood) to knowledge; the protected world of curators and colleges may cloud certain perceptions and inhibit others. I do not mean to malign Gainsborough, but if he was such a 'good' man, why did Philip Thicknesse, a boasting, vicious bully, become his friend? Mrs Thicknesse, a lady who was freer than most of her time, flashy and daring and not noted to be over-sensitive, was the subject of one of Gainsborough's most unconventional portraits. Do these people comply with the idea of a man of the spirit? Or a man of flesh and appetite? Why is the simple countryman with these people? Why did he seem to drop them when he returned to London? Had Gainsborough become wiser, in that he saw Thicknesse for the fool he was and not a social asset? Had he realised that the Captain was not wanted in the circles he, Gainsborough, knew and aspired to?

None of these questions are asked nor answered in any of the other books on Gainsborough. Human values and attitudes do not change all that much.

It takes a considerable amount of drive to produce the volume of work attributed to Gainsborough – in time alone they represent too many years to cover the span allotted to them. They become more understandable if they have about ten more years added to the apprentice period; and so does the seemingly erratic style.

January 21st: As Shakespeare, so boringly correct as usual, put it – the troubles came in battalions.

My cumbersome car, the Tank, was smashed into and became a complete write-off, two days before we were due to leave for Billingham.

The only thing that had sustained me during the hideous rehearsals was that my thesis would be in my hands before we left for the tour. I was looking forward so much to seeing it in someone else's neat typing; I felt it would somehow look more real. So, on the day of the crash I tottered home, at least with the cheering thought that it would be waiting for me. It was not there when I got back, so I thought that perhaps it would arrive in the evening. By six o'clock it had still not appeared, so I rang Gail. 'But I left it there,' she said, 'at about four.' She had tried to put it through my letter box but it had been too bulky, so she had left it on the inside of my front doorway, which is quite deep and looked safe enough. She had reckoned without our neighbourhood; nothing is too trivial to attract the attention of petty thieves.

I left her on the phone and went to look in case I had missed it. It was nowhere to be seen. She, poor lady, had by this time an hysterical note in her voice. 'I know it was the right house, the one covered in wisteria!' She offered to come round, and I went to every house in the street to see if it could have been left in some other doorway. The trouble was I had gone, in the first instance, to her home, she had never been to mine; but she knows the area well as her mother lives just around the corner. A cold, numb feeling had settled over me. I knew it had gone and it would not be found. I had a sense of loss, like a death of sorts, and I knew it was not going to go away. By the time Gail arrived, a couple of neighbours had been pressed into service – she was in tears, I was beyond them. I knew, with a horrid clarity, at last what those lines of Løvborg in *Hedda Gabler* meant – I *had* lost a child – I think I could have perhaps borne that with greater equanimity. It was five concentrated years of my life, and in an instant some kids playing around had destroyed them.

Afterwards my next-door neighbour said, 'But you were so calm.' In a real crisis, I generally am. It is only the trivial and irritating things that make me noisy.

The next few days disappeared into nightmare. I felt physically ill, as if I had been crushed by big, flat stones. The really terrible thing was that everything had gone. My notes, my own wretched type-up, and the copy which Gail had included for me to take and revise on the tour. I had to start from scribbled scraps of paper, done during research, and if it was ever to see the light of day, write it all again. During the next two days Gail typed up every fragment we could find. It read like the ravings of a lunatic, or a mad parrot, repetitive beyond belief, but it was something to start with.

January 31st: I bought yet another car from my Irish garage – it was out of a fire, I think, but it went reasonably well and was all I could afford.

I had decided to take my costumes with me to Billingham personally, as we had no wardrobe mistress, but I was still feeling so ill and confused by the horror of the last few days that I left them behind. The start of that year was undergoing its usual bout of train and postal strikes, accompanied by foul weather. Friends in London did their best to try to get the clothes to me before the dress rehearsal; in the end the hotel (I was back in the one I had so liked before) solved my problem. A taxi from the village drove down to London and brought them up for me, so I appeared in the outfits as if nothing had happened. It was expensive, but worth it to avoid scenes.

It was just another part of the dreadful nightmare from which I felt I would never emerge.

The idea of starting all my work on the Garrick provenance from scratch and without my notes was terrible. Combined with the opening of the play, it was almost too much for me to cope with; I knew that if I did not start right away I would never be able to do it at all. I felt so ill that I doubted I could manage it, but I sat down with the garbled remains of my work that I had been able to piece together, using a typewriter of great eccentricity borrowed from the hotel, and began all over again. We had two weeks at Billingham, plus rehearsals every day, which improved the play not at all; the rest of the time I wrote.

Not being in London meant that I could not recheck my original sources, so I had to rely on memory. Fortunately, I was so steeped in the research that a great deal of it came back quite easily; before we left beautiful Billingham I had it in rough shape. Three weeks later I had reconstructed all fifty-two pages again, and had them ready to be typed up. I have never worked so hard. It proved one thing – it was going to take a lot to prevent David Garrick from taking his rightful place in Gainsborough's early work. I took one day off to cheer up Irene; I asked her out to my lovely hotel filled with the locals who, although it is only six miles away, have never heard of Billingham. There are three race tracks nearby, and the hunt leaves from its doors, so they do not lack for entertainment. She was very depressed. The food was good and everyone made such a fuss of her that she revived and got back some of her old spirit.

Before going to the theatre, we decided on a cream tea. Neither of us knew the area; a sign saying SEAL SANDS sounded promising and we had visions of beaches and warm little seaside cafés, so we headed in that direction. It was growing dark at around five o'clock when we found ourselves driving not into lyricism, but a kind of hell. I had taken the one and only road and there seemed to be no way of getting out. In front of us stretched miles and miles of metal towers, large pipes like dinosaurs or huge snakes which writhed alongside us. On top of the towers were great flares of gas like, as Irene said, a woman's hair. As it grew darker, tiny lights appeared, reminiscent of Harrods at Christmas. Nothing around us looked faintly normal; even the ground, sea swamp I think, was an unearthly, violent green. We started to make up a story, and the whole place became a science-fiction city – not a living soul could be seen. 'It's the child's nightmare in my book,' said Irene. It was. The night sky, in particular, grew strangely beautiful, purples and reds, and 'The City' entangled us for four miles, like a great retort. Irene clutched Beulah and the whole adventure ended when I drove down a very long pier, black sea on either side, with Irene screaming faintly that she couldn't swim, on to the deck of an oil platform. There, security police caught up with us and we were politely but firmly asked to leave. The place was Top Secret. Had we been saboteurs, we could have blown up the largest petro-chemical plant in Britain.

The whole episode quite exhilarated Irene, and she could talk of nothing else all evening. We had spent the afternoon in a terrible future that even Stanley Kubrick could not have dreamed up. We had found out the reason for Billingham – the workers in that plant lived there, it had been built for them. One hell for another. It was not like the Sargent exhibition, more Gustave Doré – we enjoyed it almost as much.

February 22nd: I received a kind of summons from the new chairman of the Alexandra Theatre, the ex-secretary, Bob Oulsnam.

Dear Adrienne,
As you may know, I have taken over the chairmanship of the theatre following the very sad death of dear Edmund.

I am having a meeting of my Finance & General Purposes Committee on Wednesday 17th March, and I see that this coincides with your visit to the theatre in *Local Affairs*.

I would like to take this opportunity of getting you to report direct to my fellow directors on the current position regarding the picture, and I hope this will be convenient to you.

We will commence our meeting at 12 noon and if you could come along at say 12.45 that would be very helpful. We meet in the theatre, in the Leon Bar, and we usually have a drink and a snack after the meeting. You should be in ample time for the matinée as the dressing rooms are only down the stairs.

Perhaps you could kindly confirm that these arrangements are convenient to you, so that I can have you put on the agenda!

With kind regards,
Yours sincerely,
Robert M. Oulsnam

The last week with the play was to end in Birmingham, before (if) we go to London.

March 8th: Norwich. Found another bank.

The Barclays was originally a Gurney branch before it collapsed; quite interesting stuff.

The museum is in the castle, up far too many stairs for Irene to see it with me. Interesting – two very early little landscapes by Gainsborough, unusual style, not Dutch; very light and feathery. The dreaded William Wyndham's grand portrait by Hoppner, much in the style of Mr Gainsborough – supercilious face. Don't like him; I must admit I am biased.

Next week we finish in Birmingham at the Alexandra.

March 15th: Miserable week with this new man in the chair of the theatre board.

One of the staff confessed that he had intended to cut the head out of the Garrick if it had deteriorated any further, and would have taken it home. It seems I arrived just in time. I am very tired. When not on stage I have been writing or making photostats or seeing the board – so depressing. I am sorry the play is over, it could have been a great success.

Irene was shocked beyond words at the lack of interest from the theatre board. I tried to photostat the thesis in the theatre office, but the machine wasn't good, the paper bad. At least I got a few usable copies for them to read.

That was at the beginning of the week, and I haven't heard anything more. I left without another word from them all.

Irene gave the cast a farewell dinner in the one good restaurant. It was a bit fraught; so many intrigues, very like those in Michael Frayn's farce *Noises Off*. Each play has its own off-stage life for the time it runs – it is amazing how much can happen in so short a time. So many loves, hates, and friendships for life. It is always different. Irene and I will continue our little meals in London.

March 29th: Home again.

Rang all the banks to warn them that I was back in town. The paper may be written, but I have not finished with Gainsborough nor the bank books. One of the letters waiting for me was from Hugh Casson, and a note from his wife, enthusiastic and encouraging. It is good to be back.

The thesis was, in many ways, improved although I was still feeling fairly shattered. I rechecked a few minor points, and then it was ready to be sent to Sir Ellis for his approval.

April 1st: Letter from Sir Ellis.

Dear Miss Corri,
I think that, in the main, this now reads very well. A difficulty is that it is too long for a normal *Burlington* article – unless it is divided into two or more bits. I have written to the editor of the *Burlington* and encouraged him to consider it seriously, but we had better wait and see what happens.
Yours sincerely,
Ellis Waterhouse

Hugh Casson introduced me to his very nice literary agent, Andrew Hewson, who sent my thesis to the *Burlington*, as Sir Ellis had suggested. I was particularly happy to see, in their reply, how much Sir Ellis had committed himself about the authenticity of the Garrick portrait – another letter I learned by heart.

The *Burlington* has too good a reputation to allow mistakes; contributions are vetted mercilessly. You achieve publication only after they are satisfied you are correct and have consulted as many eminent authorities as they can to make sure. Their acceptance sets the seal of approval on your work, and as it is mainly a magazine which goes to all major museums and universities, it is regarded as a kind of bible and used by students in the future for research. It is daunting to submit research to their scrutiny but, if accepted, the satisfaction of the confirmation is worth all the time it may have cost.

In fear and trepidation I sent my original, full thesis. Their reply was beyond my wildest hopes. The six years seemed to be completely justified in every way.

Dear Mr Hewson,
Thank you for your letter of 2nd April and for enclosing the article on the 'Garrick Portrait by Thomas Gainsborough' by Adrienne Corri.

I read this with great interest and admiration. The argument on the Garrick portrait is certainly convincing, indeed Sir Ellis Waterhouse had already written to me to say that I should find it so. The bank documents and all the other supporting evidence are valuable archival gain and I feel that both these and the 'Garrick' portrait should be published.

As the article stands, however, it is much too long for us to publish. In effect it contains at least two separate pieces: the 'Garrick' portrait and the new documents, which could be tackled separately. Our standard article length is around 3,000 words. Would it be possible for Miss Corri to reduce her text to this amount? I realise this would be hard work, but I feel that the essence of Miss Corri's findings would become more accessible as a result. Much of the more general information would be already familiar to our readers so could be abridged or relegated to foot-notes.

I look forward to hearing Miss Corri's decision.

Yours sincerely,
Neil MacGregor
Editor

May 1st: Another letter from Sir Ellis.

Dear Miss Corri,

I am very sorry not to have sent these back before. They got buried under a mass of papers on top of the piano.

I am delighted to hear the *Burlington* will publish a version of the article. I think the Burr and Frederick collection would be much better in another article to themselves.

It looks as if you may be able to get at the Kent records before too long!

Mary Woodall has a nice, but not very enquiring mind. I found by accident in the Denizations lists the other day: 24 April 1718 Elizabeth Burr, wife of Daniel Burr, late of Amsterdam, and now of the city of London, merchant, and daughters Sophia and Rebecca and sons Frederick and Daniel. They were naturalized 22nd March 1722/3, when Frederick was aged about 14. Are these the same family?

Yours sincerely,
Ellis Waterhouse

As usual, Sir Ellis had looked up my sources; he never missed one reference or let me get away with one fudging of my facts. He had found the correct Burr family, but not all of it, which I will publish at a later date.

I had also put my questions about Gainsborough's character to him, hence the reference to Mary Woodall. I may not be so 'nice', but at least I seem to amuse him at times.

May 1st: Another wedding, a little different from the last two. John Wedgwood has decided to take the plunge again. It is to be at Westminster Abbey.

I was late, of course; the bride was waiting in the porch – eight bridesmaids! It was such a high Anglican ceremony that I got confused and wondered when John had become a Catholic. One side of the church was filled with several generations of Darwins, Huxleys and Wedgwoods. They made a pretty funny congregation. Considering that John's children and grandchildren were there, a large one too. Afterwards a reception at the Society of Architects nearby. The bride had made the cake – it was in the shape of a parish church.

She restores and lectures on early Gothic, I think. Quite a few historians were there; the introductions went rather on these lines. 'I am fifteenth-century, what are you?' I found myself quite naturally replying, 'I am eighteenth-century.' 'Oh, he's eighteenth-century over there,' came the helpful answers. It was very funny, very Alice in Wonderland. Many of the family had not seen each other for some time, if at all. 'There's a Darwin head, go and see if he's your cousin,' I heard.

The bride's going-away dress was knickerbockers. They were having a honeymoon walking tour. I complained gently that I now expected my twice-monthly postcards would stop. John has sent them to me from all over the world for over twenty years, and they are very popular with the small stamp collectors in my district. 'Not at all,' he said – nor have they.

May 12th: Hanging day at the Academy.

I love it. There is a great table of food and drink, and artists go around with much the same spirit as in Turner's time; as the day wears on some tempers wear out and an old contretemps is generally aired. I have seen it go further, when 'friendly criticism' bordered on something stronger, but then a first night always has its nerves, and this one does have the whole year to build up.

This year the photographer snapping away for the *Sunday Times* was my old friend, Michael Ward. He had been a rather good actor, but too unambitious to make his career really work. The ladies (he has married six times) and a sense of humour were also slight impediments. Hans Fletcher was walking around with me. I had just taken a copy of my revised article in for him. Michael, ever curious, started to look at it and Hans gave a little lecture on how much work I had done. Michael sensed that there might be a story there, and asked if he could read it. I told him that it was the *Burlington*'s piece and that, if taken by another paper, it would kill my chances with them. Publication in the *Sunday Times* did not carry the same weight as the *Burlington* for me. The Garrick needed academic standing rather than a quick, soon-to-be-forgotten bit of newsprint. Michael swore that this would not happen. We are old friends and I knew he would keep his word.

Approval came from Sir Ellis, but also a rap on the knuckles for a petty dig at the NPG, which I removed. Quite right, too, in the context of the *Burlington*, but I was so fed up by the silly niggling I had gone through, and it showed:

Dear Miss Corri,
This is full of fascinating matter – with all kinds of open ends! I think it makes a very manageable article. Perhaps it really ought to be published in *The Economist* or some such paper.

A difficulty about the *Burlington* is that you never know how long it will be before they publish an article as so much seems to depend on adjusting lengths of articles.

I am afraid I still don't understand the banking system – but I don't understand merchant banks.

I don't think there is any harm in quoting anything rash I may have written. I wonder, however if it is altogether judicious to give the reason you give (which may well be true, but looks silly) for the NPG's scepticism. It isn't really necessary to suggest any reason.

Yours sincerely,
Ellis Waterhouse

The upshot was that I agreed to let the *Sunday Times* know when it was to be printed and, together with the editor of the

Burlington, they would sort out complementary dates. Publication day seemed a very long way off, and there were times when I became so tired of all the waiting, the temptation to have it published elsewhere almost got the better of my judgement, but I had waited so long, a little longer would not harm me; among other things, Garrick had taught me patience.

May 20th: A lone Labour voice in a Tory neighbourhood.

I have long ago agreed to differ with my friends here when it comes to politics; the Falklands have put a strain on me and my neighbours. I will keep my head down and not listen to the radio until it is over. The machinations of William Pitt on the bank books will keep me occupied.

June 1st: Reception at Apsley House.

It has been re-done by the V & A, and is back as the old Iron Duke knew it. Well, I am not so sure this is the best idea in the world. Win battles he could, but his taste in hanging his pictures was not all it should be. My favourite picture in London, that fantastic equestrian Goya, is tucked behind the door in the main room. Wellington may not have wanted to see himself so prominently displayed, but I do – Goya at any rate.

I have always laughed at the nude Canova of Napoleon in the stairwell – it must have been a great joke to bring that back as spoils of war.

Tim Clifford from Manchester was there. At first I didn't recognise him out of context, so to speak, then I realised he has changed. He looks a bit less crisp than he did at first in Manchester; he has taken on local colouring. What a pity. I thought Manchester might erode him. Dr Johnson, bless him, was right about London, its character does rub off on you; you have to live up to London.

I complained to him about the position of the Goya. 'Terrible painting,' he said. Where have his eyes gone? There sits Wellington, a toy soldier on a horse like a little black Murillo bull. The blankness on Wellington's face is that of the true professional soldier; criminals often have the same glassy, impenetrable eyes. It *is* a terrible painting, but not in the way Tim Clifford means.

June 7th for two weeks: Coral and Vincent Price here again.

He is doing *Ruddigore*. He wandered in with the script and asked me to hear some of it to the music (on tape) with him. Very complicated stuff, all that Gilbert and Sullivan patter. Moans from Vinnie: 'I'll never learn it', etc. Next night on Terry Wogan's show he knew the lot. He is unbelievable. Both Coral and he read my thesis, and the shortened version, and were so nice about it. I know if they had not liked it they would have said so and been constructive.

Coral put her back out and spent most of the time in the Nuffield Clinic in great pain. The trouble is she is so funny that you forget to have sufficient sympathy. I had to find a bit of hardboard to put in her case so she could take it on the trip they are both about to embark on. It's a cruise around the fjords, and Vinnie does the occasional lecture on art and is the host, in a way. It all sounds a bit too social for my liking, but he loves it. As far as I can see, Coral will be flat out in her state cabin for most of the time. 'The doctors say I shall never be able to bend again,' she announced with great satisfaction on my last visit to the clinic.

Her departure was wonderful. I picked her up in my tatty car, Vinnie carrying all the accumulated gear. She was very stately, wearing a corset under a rather sheer nightgown, a sable coat, pink satin mules and nothing else. When we got to the Grosvenor House we couldn't get Vincent out of the back of my car – his legs are too long and they had locked; for a dreadful moment I thought I had disabled him as well. It didn't look too good for that cruise.

After I had left my work of the last five years with the theatre board, I waited for their reaction. I suppose at the end of it all I expected something encouraging; at least a 'well done', or perhaps a 'thank you' – a pat on the back for all my effort would have been nice. I heard precisely nothing – nothing at all. After all, now they could sell the picture and save the theatre.

After six weeks I could not believe it. All I could think was that a letter must have gone astray, so I telephoned the 'head' of the

Theatre board. He seemed surprised to hear me. 'I just wanted to know what you and your board thought about it all,' I said, 'what your reaction was.'

'What reaction did you expect?' was his reply. I couldn't believe I had heard him properly. I just put the phone down. Was this the kind of crass idiot I had done all this work for? Then, that wasn't true. I had worked for myself and David Garrick and Thomas Gainsborough. I couldn't put the theatre in their class.

I accepted another tour in the company of an old friend, Dermot Walsh, and his wife Elizabeth Scott – *Blithe Spirit*. Getting out of London for a time would give me a chance to reduce my unwieldy thesis to the length required for the *Burlington* article.

Jonathan Miller was working in the same rehearsal building. I used to creep down and sit in a corner, listening to the Kent Opera Company with great pleasure. It was good to see Jonathan again; he was interested in my work on the banks, and I was able to indulge myself in talking obscure rubbish about the eighteenth century, as well as opera, to someone who understood.

Jonathan is contemplating a work on some very quirky individuals at the end of the eighteenth century, including Gainsborough's friend De Loutherbourg. That reference gave me a chance to deliver the full Lecture, which he took with grace! It must be a great change for him to have someone lecture him; it is, after all, generally the other way around.

I like Jonathan, even though he does rather behave as if he has discovered whatever he is working on, as if no one else had ever heard of it. This week it is Beethoven. Apropos of De Loutherbourg we discussed Freemasons and Mozart. I have always thought that *The Magic Flute* should be done as a psychoanalysis, Jungian in character. It would blend well with the mixture of pantomime and mysticism coupled to Mozart's initiation to the Masons. Frederick, Prince of Wales, was the first Royal Freemason. I was surprised that Gainsborough had not been one; perhaps another example of his not being accepted. I have promised to make notes on De Loutherbourg if he comes up on my bank books, and hand them over to Jonathan. I was going through one of my bouts of impatience at the time it took to get anything into the *Burlington*, but Jonathan persuaded me that it would be best to wait. It just seems so long before I shall see any result from all this work.

The business of condensing the material into twelve pages was almost more difficult than writing the original. This, plus the fact that it was now the third time I had to go through the work, gave me an almost permanent feeling of *déjà vu*. I also worked at the ledgers during the day, and more and more payments were turning up in the so-called Suffolk period. I desperately wanted to get entries for the appendix to the *Burlington* article, and as many as possible before 1760, when he was established in Bath. I was glad to leave out the Margaret Burr material, as there was so much there and it was a digression from the original aim of proving the Garrick. Also, now I knew that Gainsborough was an undiscovered man; an interesting, moody, selfish, son-of-a-bitch probably, not the idyllic idiot of the other books I had read. I wanted to put the record straight, and one article was not going to do it. What I wanted was to write the definitive Gainsborough book, and *that* is the place for the other research.

June 8th: My eyes again.

Frank Barrie and I were supposed to do a very grand evening at Apsley House for the V & A. I have been taking great care and not working so long at the books, and I had asked for the lighting to be angled so as not to be in my eyes; of course they got it wrong. It was a lousy evening. Frank realised as soon as we got on to the stage that I would have problems, and was a great help. It really is no good – I will have to stop doing the shows, or get contact lenses. The trouble with these is that the bank books are very dusty and that can cause irritation to the eyes. It looks like no more readings; a pity, I used to enjoy them.

June 9th: The revised article accepted!

With a few minor changes. The *Burlington* is great for qualification and tried to put in 'small-scale' before my Rosetta Stone bit, but I corrected that!

My eyes are starting to worry me so much, I can't do readings any more. I did one at St Paul's in Covent Garden for the Actors'

Benevolent Fund, and half-way through the whole page just blurred. I couldn't see anything. I couldn't explain, it sounds like making excuses; Moray Watson was very cross. I thought it was just the lighting at first – it was bad, but even when I compensated for that by taking care not to look into the spots, I still couldn't see very well. Sheridan Morley was doing the narration. I felt I had let them all down terribly.

July 26th: My agent is at last forced to admit he is ill.

He is in a hospital at Kingston. I go to visit him every day when I finish at the record offices. He is dying and he worries about me or others being in silly plays. That is not what reality is about. Some people have been ringing the hospital to ask about jobs, or if he has put them up for certain parts.

Many of his friends are looking after him, and we have established an unspoken rota of visits so as not to tire him with too many people at the same time. There is little else we can do. I realise that I do not care about the theatre as I did any more. I care about the research, the paintings and Tim getting better, if only that could happen. He read some of my work before he went into hospital, and he was very proud of me. I just wish it were in print. I try not to admit it, but he is so very ill, I can only hope for a miracle.

August 4th: Tim died today.

I had not the heart to find someone to take his place so, for a time, dropped out of the theatre altogether.

August 7th: I couldn't stay in the house. Tim's death on Wednesday had been so dreadful, I could think of nothing else. It all seemed such a waste. I had been trying out a 'sample' chapter on Gainsborough, but I couldn't get it to work.

I thought a walk at Kenwood might clear my depression – it was a beautiful day and the sight of that house always cheers me, and perhaps a quick look at Lady Mary Howe would give me back some sort of faith. I found that the Batoni, which was the special summer exhibition, was still on. It was a great comfort, there were all the people I had been working on: Matthew Fetherstonehaugh and his wife, so English even through Batoni's eyes. She, a self-conscious Diana with a very discreet curve of diamonds in her hair; he, holding a sort of hoe, as if he denied all knowledge of the implement. I lost myself in it for two hours. Some of them were unintentionally very amusing; all those English gentlemen in Italy pointing at various bits of classical sculpture or buildings, just to make sure you knew they had really made the journey.

The drawings were nice, rather scholastic and dead, those young Scotsmen! What happened to their descendants? I don't remember seeing their like – well, maybe one or two. No one as pretty as the Earl of Dunraven; how beautifully Batoni painted fur and velvets. The portrait of Lady Fox looked almost Victorian and was a good example of how individual taste in dress jumps all fashions and styles. I presume it was a sort of travelling outfit.

I paid my visit to Lady Mary afterwards, but my heart was not really in it. The Batoni had been unfamiliar, so I had forgotten myself for a while. Gainsborough was back to normal, in my terms that is. All that classical pretence had cheered me up, a bit like Americans coming to Europe in the nineteenth century – all those Henry James ladies. The Italians surely invented the tourist trade.

August 20th: Vincent Price is in town again, this time by himself.

He is making a film with Peter Cushing and Christopher Lee. It is lovely to see him and get a chance to talk to him. We were supposed to go to a party – some sort of promotion thing – we decided to have dinner first and were still talking at one in the morning! Neither of us really likes parties. He told me that one of the things that had made the greatest impression on him when he was young was the Dürer bird wing – strangely, a version of it is to be auctioned next week.

Mine, of course, was the Hon. Mrs Graham – his taste is more sombre. I have promised to find him a Rembrandt! He told me that he had won the 64,000 dollar question on television, taking Rembrandt as his subject! I have never been so impressed in my life. To have the nerve to do that! I know that everything I had ever learned would desert me under those conditions. He'd never mentioned it before, he just dropped it as a casual remark.

He once had over $50,000,000 to spend on pictures; not for himself. He had persuaded Sears Roebuck to sell them by mail order catalogue. He just came to Europe and bought up whole salerooms. What a marvellous job – that would suit me very well. He said it was a great feeling. It was just after the war ended and some wonderful stuff was on the market at bargain basement prices. The trick was to go for the unfashionable; at that time that would include a lot from the seventeenth century, certainly eighteenth and nineteenth. I wonder how many early Gainsboroughs were among them? Where are they now – Omaha?

I had told him over dinner of a film I would like to write, when all this is over; he wants to play the part that I have based on Arthur Lucas! I had better introduce them.

Sir Ellis had sent a researcher, Malcolm Brown, to see me. He is doing work on the Jewish banking families and wants to look at my notes. Ellis has told him about the Abraham and Jacob Franco payment in 1746. My notes seemed to alarm him considerably – he is an economist. I have been only too aware how different the eighteenth century appears from everything I have read before, compared with the statistics I am getting from the books. He is a little shaken. 'Why do you keep calling them bankers?' he said at first, but when he saw the enormous sums passing through the ledgers each week, trading amounts, he understood. He has asked me to dinner, and some other historians will be there too.

August 26th: I went to dinner and took a few of my notebooks.

I had always thought the stuff I was getting remarkable, only I have never had anyone to share my enthusiasm for them. Sir Ellis says he doesn't understand figures, and no one at the bank seems to know much about the eighteenth century.

The notes had an extraordinary effect. Malcolm Brown's wife had cooked a beautiful dinner; we all talked far too much to appreciate it. At least, I did. The relief of being with people who actually knew what my work was bringing to light was too much. To an outsider, it would all have seemed like gibberish. The problem has been that no one has worked, as I have, with ten ledgers at a time; the banks have not allowed it. Therefore, not much information has been obtained. Ideally, all the interior bankers' accounts should be broken down and indexed in the way the banks' own books are, and then cross-referenced; any researcher would be able to use them with comparative speed. At the moment, it takes about two days to work through a payment on my own. They seemed a bit stunned but very impressed by my work. I hadn't realised it was quite such a breakthrough as they seemed to think. It was so nice to meet with such enthusiasm.

Later I got a letter from one of them, Dr Aubrey Newman, of the Department of History, University of Leicester:

> Dear Miss Corri,
>
> I had not forgotten that I was to write to you and that I have a number of queries to answer on your behalf. When I can decipher my notes I will be in a better position to discuss them with you. In the meantime, may I say how fascinating I found the way in which you have 'broken' the Bank of England code. I really do think that you have got on to a new insight into eighteenth-century banking and it is indeed very exciting to contemplate what might come out of it... When you have a little more time, I would really welcome the opportunity of a full discussion with you, either in London or in Leicester. Nor was I being facetious in my suggestion of doing some formal research; I can just imagine the reactions of my colleagues if I were able to include amongst my research students Miss Adrienne Corri . . .

Very flattering, but no time to spare at present. Gainsborough is consuming all my time.

An ignoble streak is sometimes a help. At Christmas, feeling pleased with myself, I rang the National Gallery to tell them that I had proved my point and was to be published in the *Burlington*. All those cracks at my expense that I had put up with – 'This was painted by Titian when he was five!' and so on. I did not manage to get Martin Wylde, now head of the department after Arthur Lucas, but I got Ken Malcolm, who congratulated me, and when

I told him I could prove Gainsborough was working at the age of ten there was a silence. 'Oh, dear,' he said at last. 'That man's picture could have been right.' It transpired that fifteen years before, a small oils on paper had been brought in to be rebacked. It was on a wooden panel which was cracking; a portrait of a small boy which was said to be a self-portrait of Gainsborough as a child. Of course, in the absence of the dreaded 'documentation', after being shown to the NPG next door, in spite of the fact it was an attractive little picture of the correct date, the poor man had been sent away. Ken remembered his name and where he lived but not the phone number. I got hold of the telephone operator and managed to obtain the numbers of everyone of that name in the county – fortunately there were not many. At the seventh try, I found the right man. He still had the picture and said I was welcome to come and see it whenever I liked, but 'I haven't been able to prove it. I don't think you will have much more luck.' He did not know of the past five years, and what they had done to my spirit of perseverance.

As I drove the fifty or so miles to where he lived I had no great hopes, rather the reverse. It was cold and damp, typical pre-Christmas weather. 'I must be mad,' I thought; if it was like the preceding five years it was a fine madness. The village was pretty, until now simply a motorway stop to me. The shop (he was a dealer) was in an Elizabethan cottage.

One look at the little picture was enough. It was right. A small boy determinedly holding his palette looked at me. Fifteen years of smoke since he had been cleaned at the National could not obscure the determination on that small face. Gainsborough – a boy with the eyes of a man, the eyes of all the subsequent self-portraits until the last, cynical one in the Academy. The wheel had come full circle; on the palette he had laid out his colours carefully, a sombre range, but in the centre a blue and a green – the blue of Mrs Andrews' dress, the green he was to use in his white all his life, Van Dyck colours. I looked at him for a long time. I knew the man, I had now found the child.

His owner was amused by my reaction. I explained the quest for Garrick and showed him the banking figures. He was very interested, a man who had a good eye but was tired of beating his head against the closed doors and closed minds of the 'experts'. 'It's all very well for you,' he said, 'you get in to see them. I am only a provincial dealer, they can't be bothered with me.' I knew what he meant, but I had to remind him that, once in the door, I had to overcome the prejudice of 'actress = idiot'. I asked eventually if I might bring someone out to take photographs. I thought I might drag poor Sally from the V & A out on her free day. His reply astounded me. 'Take it,' he said, 'even with all your research I doubt if you will do any better than I did.' I could not believe it, he was willing to let a stranger, someone he had only met a couple of hours previously, walk out of the door clutching one of the most important 'finds' in art history; however, he trusted me. I cannot remember feeling happier than I did on that drive back. The little picture, wrapped in tissue, lay on the seat beside me; every now and then I patted it to make sure it was really there.

I knew without doubt what love, passion, addiction, you name it, any obsessive emotion, meant to me. Everything else in my life up to then had led to that moment. All the mistakes, the stupidities, the failures that any person goes through – had they been in one event different, I would not have been in that car with that picture. I could never say again, 'I wish I had not done that.' To have all regrets swept away in one afternoon, all reservations and doubts wiped out, all mistakes vindicated, is an extraordinary feeling, but that is what the discovery of young Thomas Gainsborough had done for me. One perfect achievement had made sense of it all – and if nothing else ever happened, it was enough.

I took the young Gainsborough self-portrait to the V & A for Sally to photograph. I gave him a very quick wipe over just to take the cigarette smoke off and he looked lovely. Under the lights the quality was unbelievably fine. Sally, who is used to photographing the beautiful and the rare (a trolley arrived while she was working on Gainsborough – fifty masterpieces for tomorrow afternoon), thought he was very special. After the session, I took him upstairs to show him to Dr Strong. He looked at him for a long time; his reaction was the same as mine had been. No doubt. 'I would never have questioned this, even without your research, if I had seen it,' he said. The picture had not got as far as his office at the NPG, someone far down the line had passed judgement, so it might have been lost for good – how many others go that way? When I got home, I telephoned Sir

Ellis. He said it was fine to take the picture to him the next day. That was on December 20th, 1982.

I always seemed fated to see him in bad weather. He was upstairs in a small room with an open fire, reading. The book, which he was slightly self-conscious about, was a romantic novel called *The Princess and the Parvenu*, written by my friend Julian Fellowes! His pen name is Alexander Morant (the persona he chooses as a writer is an accountant with six children). 'Why doesn't he *say* he's an actor,' said Sir Ellis crossly. He was appalled by the portrait's hardboard backing. 'It makes it look so very fake,' he said, but his opinion was the same as Dr Strong's; it is the eyes of the little picture which are so compelling. Sir Ellis agreed there was no question as to its authenticity. Two Gainsboroughs in one lifetime – rather more than anyone could hope for. When I left later, I felt rather guilty. I have had more luck in my six years than could be expected in a lifetime of study. I had begun at the top, where was there left to go? One thing was certain – my article for the *Burlington* had to be entirely rewritten as soon as possible to include the small picture. The article would now have to be about the first grand portrait – Garrick 1742 – and the first self-portrait, 1736–38. I, personally, was in favour of the earlier date, considering the £300 a year from the Fonnereau account. It rather tended to overshadow Davy, but it was more than satisfying to know that my work of the last five years had allowed the small picture of that working child to be recognised. The timing was superb – a Christmas card two hundred and fifty years or so old. The most unique one I would ever know.

I had made my appointment to meet Neil MacGregor, editor of the *Burlington*. Until now we had only chatted on the phone. I was to take in the folder so that he could select whatever he felt was relevant, and as a great treat I thought he ought to see the original little Gainsborough in all his glory. The *Burlington* is not given to wild displays of enthusiasm, but even they raised a faint appreciative sound at the sight of the small fellow. 'Very exciting,' murmured Robert Torday.

Margaret Burr is going into another article as soon as I can finish the full research on her. There is still plenty left for the 'Definitive'. The owner of the small portrait was delighted, although a little perturbed at the idea of owning such a valuable picture. They were worried by the hardboard backing at the V & A, because hardboard contains chemical. The National are rather red-faced and are going to reback it. Judging from the amount of payments on the books, there should be more of this period around; the two small landscapes in Norwich Castle Museum fit into this category, I think – they have a feathery, lighter quality than his known later work. More is bound to surface, although I think there is a great deal around just misdated. As far as I can tell, the 'Suffolk' period hardly exists, or at any rate is a great deal shorter than has been supposed up to now. I daresay after I get the article published, more will emerge.

Another exhibition, at the NPG, this time of Van Dyck. Too many pictures in a confined space, the light carefully placed to bounce off the canvas – people were backing into each other in an attempt to get the pictures at a distance. It was also very hot, stifling in such a small area. I met Joan Bakewell as I was leaving – we both looked as if we had been in a Turkish bath. The attendants were very sensibly allowing people to go out for air and come back in again without charging a second time, otherwise they would have needed nurses in attendance. I begin to wonder if some of these big retrospectives don't do more harm than good, especially when badly displayed. I can't take too many pictures in one go any more; I don't think you are meant to look at them that way. I do like to see the sequence of work from early to late but, in some ways, looking requires as much energy as the painter put into the picture and you get drained by too many in a great lump.

It also manages, if badly chosen, to show off an artist's weaknesses as much as his merits. I am glad I did not see the Sargent in London – the rooms in Carlton House were so ugly for the 1979 Lawrence. To look at pictures against a background of aggressive pea green was in defiance of the work displayed – but I did love the Duke of Aberdeen! Another beauty for my gallery; pictures, like people, must be loved. Perhaps that is why too many are bad in an exhibition – you can't love a crowd.

23rd December: Last-minute ritual of shopping at Hatchards.

Very social – Ken MacMillan and Sidney Nolan amongst

others. They both got the Gainsborough Lecture, especially now I have found the young Thomas. Ken is directing plays. I can't think why he should want to, except the idea of staying stuck may have been frightening him as much as it frightened me before I found Thomas Gainsborough and Garrick.

Sidney Nolan says, when I tell him about the little picture and how old and grown-up the eyes are, 'No artist has young eyes – put that in, it is one of the most important things about a painter.'

Christmas greetings at the Academy – everyone very jolly in Fortnum's – I enjoy this bit of Christmas most.

I bought myself Sir Ellis' new book for Christmas, his *Dictionary of British Artists in the 18th Century*. It is so good, I don't know how I had the nerve to tangle with him, or to argue on the same ground. It is invaluable. I went through all the artists in the early dates when I did my first research. I only wish his book had been around then. I had to wade through everything I could find at the Witt and other places. It would have been a tremendous help, and saved me a lot of time, as it will other people in the future. I am pleased to see, however, that I was so thorough.

New Year at Frank and Mary Barrie's. I have taken the little picture, mainly so that he will be safe, and because I want Frank to see him – also because I can't bear to be parted from him for a moment.

Frank is going to do *The Entertainer* for Arnold Wesker, who saw his *Macready* at the Arts and thought it marvellous. Arnold is a great enthusiast and he fell in love with the story of the paintings. He loved the little picture, so I end the old year among friends and see the new one in, quite properly, with Thomas Gainsborough.

1983

Nineteen eighty-three began, as usual, with pictures. I had gone for a walk on the Heath when the realisation that I had almost missed the Richard Wilson exhibition hit me. I was trying to give myself some exercise as I felt very unhealthy with so much writing and research, but the open air is not, strictly, for me. I had worked myself into the conviction that I was about to get flu from the cold, damp air when the thought of all those landscapes of Italy came to mind, and I was off down to the Embankment and my usual form of escape.

January 2nd: The Tate again – the Wilson exhibition. Lovely, what a contrast to the Gainsborough.

Beautifully lit, perfect progression from a Tillman to Wilson's contribution to the Foundling Hospital, then the drawings and those glowing Italian landscapes; finally (very funny) the one of Niagara rescued from the Wolverhampton coalhouse! The catalogue, by an American, David Solkin, says, 'There is no way of telling who Wilson's first patrons were, or who bought his first pictures.' Well, of course, there is now. I shall look up my notes. I know I have early Wilson payments. Solkin has also taken very fiercely against the eighteenth century. Diatribes against the landowners, etc. All a bit wrong, but in the right direction. How he would go mad about the bank books – even more justification for all my work and my lost eyesight.

January 8th: Looked through my bundles of letters, collected in my attempts to confirm the Garrick.

I am so struck by the kindness and generosity of Hugh Casson, and I realise that he has not seen the small portrait. I rang him up and, as it was a good time for him and his wife, I took it round at once.

It is the first time I have seen his new flat – they both work in a lovely studio room on the first floor. Young Thomas is set up under a strong working light, and he looks lovely. At least he gets on with this president of the Royal Academy. As an artist, Hugh recognises the worth of the small picture at once – he also recognises the look in the eye, I think. Both he and his wife find it enchanting. It has been a long haul – I could never have done it without his help. We talk about the past five and a half years. Of our first meeting about the Garrick, Lady Casson says, 'You were beside yourself with desperation then.' (I think she also used the word 'demented'.) She is right, I was; I didn't realise it had been so obvious! Now I am tired but very happy. The New Year could not have had a better start, nor could I wish for better friends.

January 10th: Drummond's had a splendid party to open the newly re-furbished bank, and very grand it is.

I had young Thomas Gainsborough with me, as I had been to the Academy with him – the bank loved him. I was down on the guest list as actress/historian!

Lovely party – I left late. There is a new manager taking over.

'Why don't you bank here?' they said as I left. 'We will give you all the credit you like.'

Witnesses. Witnesses.

January 19th: Carl Toms has designed the sets and costumes for The Rehearsal *by Anouilh.*

I did it with Coral Browne years ago in New York. Leslie Caron is playing the wife (Coral's part), Kate O'Mara the part of the mistress (my old role). I never play wives. I like the sound of the whole thing, and it will be interesting to see another cast in it. Carl asked me about it, but I had forgotten it almost entirely. I only know our production wasn't sharp or modern enough, even then. This dreadful long winter and not getting out – I have a lousy cold, so my handbag is stuffed with cough mixture. There is nothing worse than people coughing in an audience. I shall go straight to Guildford for the first night from the bank at Roehampton.

I had absolutely no recollection of the play at all, except that the wife went on a bit too long in the beginning – even Coral had been stumped by that scene. In our version, we had both cut our dresses down as low as they could go, thinking it might be the only way to keep the gents in the audience awake, and one night Coral began coughing during one of the mistress's scenes with the ingénue, and beating her bosom. I couldn't think what was going on, until I noticed that I had completely come out of the top of my little number. I had to shove my nipples back with my fan.

Nothing as jolly happened to this cast, but the theatre was packed and Leslie was obviously going to pull them in.

The press was there in force. 'Hello,' said a lady journalist, 'what are you doing?' Now, if you are an actress by profession, this is to be interpreted as 'What play/film/television programme, etc., are you in?' 'Nothing,' I replied. After a few more gambits, each drawing a blank, she reverted to the last resort of the gossip columnist: 'How's your love life? Any nice man around?' 'No one,' I said cheerfully (as if I would say anyway!). 'Oh well, tell me if anything should happen.' And that was the end of that conversation.

As usual I had sent all the revisions of my article to Sir Ellis. Now he has started to address me as Ms – I wonder if that is good or bad? I do hate that prefix so much. I must get back to Miss.

January 23rd: Letter from Sir Ellis.

Dear Ms Corri,

I am just back from ten days, mainly in Texas, which were instructive but exhausting, so I have only just read your article. It is full of meat, but I confess that there is a good deal that I don't understand, owing to my ignorance of banking! The references to the Charleton a/c are rather puzzling and why people paid for portraits through other people's accounts is to me a mystery.

I have seen Van Dyck. The rooms seem to me horrible and one can't get far enough from the full lengths. The only thing that lighting really shows up is the grain of the canvases. They would be much better shown at the RA.

Yours sincerely,
Ellis Waterhouse

January 28th: Turned on the television; there was Jonathan Miller being interviewed.

He is, as usual, enthusiastic. This time it is about *The Magic Flute*, which he is doing with the Scottish Opera. He has always thought it should be done in psychoanalytical terms. He is most definite! As Freud says, mnemnosis, I suppose.

February 14th: A very important event on the calendar.

One of Jean Muir's rare sales for friends. Social event, too – every lady in the public eye desperate to stock up wardrobes at bargain prices. Joanna Lumley, Joan Bakewell, Sian Phillips, looking wild in various states of undress. No holds barred, but friendly; if you try on something which might be good for someone else, you hand it over. Judy Parfitt and Sian are roughly the same size and can choose for each other. Joanna is skinnier than I am and I always seem to grab things that are good for her. She looks pretty good in anything (and she writes well – I look forward every week to her column in *The Times*). Joan Bakewell is inclined to hoard things in a corner and not make up her mind; she asks us all in on the decision. It is a bit funny to see her on *Newsnight* looking calm and intelligent, wearing a top she couldn't decide on that morning. We stock up for the year at that sale; the invitation is worth more than gold.

February 15th: Working with John Copley on A Midsummer Marriage *by Michael Tippett for the San Francisco Opera.*

Years ago I tried to persuade John Copley that *The Magic Flute* was really a psychoanalysis based on Jung. That will teach me to open my big mouth. John remembered all my chat. We once saw a very bad production of the Tippett together, and giggled all the way through it – now the laugh is on us.

I missed his production of Handel's *Semele*. I was meant to go with David Walker, who designed ravishing costumes, but I got the nights mixed up. The *Burlington* is a Walker-Copley fan club, I daren't admit I missed it through absent-mindedness. John has got a wonderful set designer for this, but the technical difficulties are enormous. I haven't made things easier by saying that everyone who sees it in San Francisco will know about analysis because most of them have had a session or two with analysts.

It is John's first modern opera production. He doesn't really need me, but it may help to have someone to kick around the ideas with. Also, the acting style is going to be hard, and I can help there. He is a brilliant director of eighteenth- and nineteenth-century opera, but he is not terribly in sympathy with this century. Nevertheless, the hero and heroine, a modern young man and woman, must also be archetypal images come hell or high water. Neither of us has had personal experience of analysis, but I had a lot second-hand when my ex-husband was going through it all (he loved it; talking about himself for hours).

For his sake, I ploughed my way through Jung and Freud, so I am now quite useful to John, who hasn't got the time to read up all the references. It's quite good to get away from research for a bit, and it is an interesting problem to help to solve. I have missed the opera and music.

John is very generous and I got my first credits on an opera programme as 'Adviser' – it looked good.

Easter: Laurence Olivier as King Lear.

A beautiful performance – no, that's not right. For me he *was* Lear, no tricks, quite simple – 'every inch a King'. Flaws in the production but it didn't matter, at least his Lear is recorded for ever. His death scene was extraordinary – he did nothing at all, life simply left him. One moment, and then it was over – being, not acting. How terrible not to have that *Macbeth*.

All the parts he has been best in have been the Garrick roles. Who will carry on this tradition? The links are broken – there will be 'nothing left remarkable'.

I had investigated the little picture's background – happily, it turned out to be impeccable. It had been owned by a family called Butcher, direct descendants of the Stewards of the Duke of Bedford, and friends of the Gainsborough family from his childhood.

I had been on my best behaviour as far as Dr Hayes was concerned, and had scrupulously sent him all my evidence as I collected it. I offered to show him the small self-portrait but he was going away and didn't seem wildly interested.

To keep the record straight I also sent the proofs of my article and a transparency of young Thomas, so that he had a chance to see him before publication. Apart from a letter of acknowledgement, I heard no more at that time.

When the proofs came through they looked lovely – my first 'galleys'! I did a few corrections – they had taken out my notes on Wynantz, but I had to ask for them to be put back as they affected the early datings so much.

The photographs of Garrick didn't do him justice – too dark and brought out all the 'stiff' quality. I could only hope the actual magazine would be better when printed; so difficult to tell from photostats.

At last the duly altered article was finished, and the *Burlington*, with a few minor changes, set it up to be published in the April edition. Just a week or so before it was due to appear, I got the final accolade from Sir Ellis through a letter from Henry Wyndham, of Christie's:

> Dear Miss Corri,
> Sir Ellis Waterhouse recommended that I drop you a line regarding a very interesting painting, most likely by Thomas Gainsborough. It is an early portrait and we have reason to believe that the sitters are Mr and Mrs Carter, who were the parents of Mrs Andrews.
>
> According to John Hayes' book, there is a missing portrait of the Carters. I would be very grateful if you could give me any information that may be relevant to this problem, and look forward to hearing from you soon.
>
> Yours sincerely,
> Henry Wyndham

This picture might fit into the early category. Where I had

previously feared to tread I was being asked for an opinion.

After my visit, I could not understand why they had bothered. I was met, after being kept waiting a little, by a tall, rather vague young man, and led through stacked treasures, muddled in heaps in a way that reminded me of a very grand property room in a film studio, to the holy of holies, a locked room with some rather fine pictures – Constable, Hogarth, Reynolds and a very peculiar Turner. Ruskin told Frank Harris that he had burned all Turner's figure studies to 'protect the reputation of a great artist'. Harris had taken this to mean that prudishness had been the cause of this vandalism, but having seen some of the pictures that had escaped Ruskin's fire I began to think he must have meant because they were so bad. This Turner would not have survived, I fear; very odd figures with cherubs like rambler roses all over the place. God bless Ruskin.

I glanced at a pleasant Hogarth; before I could open my mouth (to stop me from being foolish, I suppose), the young man said 'Hogarth' rather quickly. The Gainsborough was at the end of the room – it was lovely. Very early, I thought. 'That is the Gainsborough,' said the young man. Bless him, if they thought I was a congenital idiot what was I doing there? 'We date it around the Andrews picture,' he informed me (1747/48). I thought it much earlier. 'Well, it *could* be earlier,' he conceded. 'It is of the Carters.' This was to my mind plainly not so. The man was of a generation before, a contemporary of Admiral Vernon. Unless Carter was as mad as a hatter, he would not be wearing those clothes. The picture was very curious indeed. The man was beautifully painted, with great care, and was a completely successful portrait – the woman was another matter. Very small in comparison to the male figure, and rather plain, she was not painted with quite so much love, although very painstakingly. The background was completely assured, but the people lacked the ease of the Andrews or even of the Kirbys (in the Tate Gallery – a picture I would place around 1745). The person who sprang first to my mind was old Claude Fonnereau. This man was about the right age and was looking at the painter with great amusement. It was a very personal picture indeed; one also felt the boy (I was now convinced it was very early) liked the old man a great deal and that the feeling was reciprocated. In the background was a classical statue. In plain terms, the picture was that of a country squire of the old school, who had a comfortable house, a good library and had gone on the Grand Tour and brought back some 'antiquities' to prove it. The woman could have been his daughter. If she were Mrs Carter, and the picture 1748, she would be too young to have a daughter of the age of Mrs Andrews; if it were earlier, the man could not be Carter – the picture was a puzzle. It was without doubt by Gainsborough, but when? My guess was before he had gone to London, 1739/40. This would be at the end of his apprentice period and what would be more fitting than a picture of his first patron and his daughter? I ventured this opinion. I might just as well have shot the young man. He would in no way contemplate such an early dating. He pointed out how good the landscape was, it was very like the ones in Norwich. The dress, he said, was painted in the same way as the Andrews, and was the same style. The dress was, indeed, much the same style – it was a morning dress and came into fashion around 1735 and continued much the same, with small variations, late into the century. The colour was the same as that on the palette of my young Gainsborough. I had a colour slide of him with me and I showed it to the young man. He was not unduly impressed. 'Very interesting,' he said, which translated meant, 'I don't know much about this and I am not committing myself.' I left, saying that I would do a little work on the picture and let him know what I came up with. I went home enchanted – the first self-portrait, the first grand portrait and now the first conversation piece. It was all too good to be true. It was really early Gainsborough year. I had taken a photograph of the picture with me, and a family tree in which the owners claimed descent from the female side of the Andrews family. Next day I went to the Society of Genealogists to check it out.

The lady, they claimed, had died unmarried and was buried at Great Cornard; that settled that bit of evidence. I phoned Christie's with this information. I was thanked but told not to trouble myself further – the picture, it seemed, had been bought in a sale in 1920 on the death of a J. B. Andrews. The family tree no longer mattered. This was in spite of the fact it had been given to me as 'evidence' the day before. It was the Carters, it had always been known as the Carters, it was going into the catalogue as the Carters, and no two ways about it.

Poor young man! He actually thought that was that! By this time I was not to be put off. That weekend I drove to Ipswich to have a look at the Fonnereau house, Christchurch Mansion. I arrived late, with just enough time to have a quick look round. The pictures looked promising, but I was not able to see them all. I *did* walk round the park looking for a likely spot which might correspond with the picture. The easiest thing to do was to look for the oldest patch of trees, always supposing (and I have a very literal turn of mind) that the picture had been painted, as it seemed to be, in the park. There were no statues; however, a park attendant told me there had been some. They had been sold in 1892, by one of the last Fonnereaus to own the house. A beautiful old place, destined for redevelopment, it had been saved by the Cobbold family and preserved as a museum. Quite casually he mentioned that the river had been covered in to make the road. The site I had found could have been right – the river would have been where Gainsborough had painted it. So at least I managed to establish a couple of facts. Fonnereau had been the kind of man I had supposed – solid country squire, although only second-generation Huguenot. Until now I had only known him from his bank balance. That night I talked to Sir Ellis. He thought the background need not be as realistic as I supposed, and found it hard to believe the picture had been painted before Gainsborough went to London and was influenced by Hayman. Fonnereau had paid Hayman £500 in 1737; it was quite possible, therefore, for young Gainsborough to have seen his work in Ipswich *before* London. The next day I went to the PRO to look at the wills of Fonnereau and Handley, his banker. No mention of Gainsborough by name, although 'the several trusts and bequests to be continued'; he also divides his property very fairly between his sons and daughters, leaves handsome bequests to churches and hospitals in London, and Christchurch to his son, Thomas. His London house he divides between the family, leaving his wife the larger rooms and the kitchens, and his daughters by his first marriage their apartments; that must have made for peace. 'For the rest, it shall be share and share alike.'

I went to Ipswich again. The curator was young and harassed, nevertheless helpful and enthusiastic.

The family pictures had been muddled and some of the labels

had been mixed up, but the family face was a very strong one. Generation after generation of Fonnereaus looked very like the old man in the picture at Christie's. One was of Fonnereau himself, twenty years younger and by an indifferent artist, it resembled the conversation piece strongly. A portrait by Smart of Norwich of Fonnereau's daughter in her sixties was the image of the old boy in the picture. The likeness was more strongly stressed because of the naive quality of Smart's work, which has a primitive look. The childlike, undeveloped work of the young Gainsborough was as literal at this stage, and as awkward.

Another fact emerged at Christchurch. It had seemed strange to me that the picture should have surfaced in New Zealand without any previous background or knowledge of its existence. I asked the curator if any of the Fonnereau family had died recently. She seemed surprised. 'Yes.' A Noel Fonnereau had died a month earlier; they had managed to buy some of the original furniture from his sale.

In London I managed to get in touch with some of the family; as all families, it had its share of small scandals. One of the Fonnereaus, it seemed, had gone to America in the 'thirties with a few goodies from the estate. He had subsequently gone to Australia and then, family rumour had it, to New Zealand. Noel Fonnereau would have been the only one left in the Fonnereau family who could have identified this picture if it had come on to the market, and it was 'discovered' one week after his death. It did seem an interesting coincidence.

The most important fact was that Fonnereau had remarried at the age of sixty. So the lady in the picture was the new wife, which explained his look of self-satisfaction (male chauvinism, according to Sir Ellis). Anne Boehm, his bride, was the daughter of a banker and had been on the shelf some time, poor lady. Actually, she was far from poor in her own right, which explained why she appeared to have been left so little in the will. The Fonnereau pictures (an early one of him, later one of her) compared well with the conversation piece, so I came back quite happy that my original thought was probably correct. The young man at Christie's prevaricated; it seemed to me pointless to have gone to so much trouble to be argued with, without any work having been done on his part, so I left the whole question. I did do one further bit of work for my own satisfaction. I went to

Somerset House and looked up the Andrews will, from where I was now assured the picture had originated. There was a two-year gap between the death of Canon Andrews and the sale – that meant there was an inventory somewhere, or other papers. In my own good time, I would find out more about the picture.

March 29th: A letter from Sir Ellis.

Dear Ms Corri,
I am more and more puzzled about the conversation piece. The old man is reasonably like the portrait called Claude Fonnereau – but why is he wearing a much more old-fashioned wig? I wonder if the male figure isn't posthumous. I don't think the conversation piece can possibly be eight years earlier than Mr and Mrs Andrews: and I doubt if the lady's frock, with those very modish hoops can be as early as 1738. I think you want a costume expert on this. (I think there are some datable figures by Sandby with almost identical frocks, but I haven't photos here.)
Yours sincerely,
Ellis Waterhouse.

Everyone is still getting the Gainsborough Lecture; I am quite impartial. There is not a friend, passing tradesman, telephone, gas, electric-meter man who does not get a quick run-down on the latest developments. 'I prefer Turner myself,' said the telephone engineer putting together the wire that my squirrel had gnawed through. He got the Fonnereau pictures to look at. 'Well,' he said, looking at the comparison between father and daughter (which I think is the best piece of evidence in the portraits), 'he couldn't say it was the milkman!'

Would that Christie's used such a direct approach.

April 2nd: Letter from Sir Ellis.

Dear Miss Corri,
There is something very funny about the conversation piece at Christie's ('comical' too: but it must have been commissioned to look like that). I don't believe TG can have painted it

before he had some experience of London and Hayman – and I still think 1738 *very* early for the lady's frock. I don't know anything quite like it in Devis. Also, she obviously wasn't dressy!

The statue in the engraving of the house, which gets mixed up with the pine tree, is very odd. It had never occurred to me that the landscape was taken from nature and I suspect it rather to be stage scenery of the type of the Louvre or the Fitzwilliam pictures. The old gentleman's waistcoat also needs a good deal of explaining.

It was very careless of the NPG to get the blocks mixed in their Beningborough catalogue.

I laughed a good deal at your account of your visit here – but didn't really recognise the scene!

I don't see that Christie's can do anything but catalogue the picture as they have – and, in any case, I doubt if it would make any difference to the price if the sitters are rightly or wrongly identified.

Yours sincerely,
Ellis Waterhouse

Elderly Carters (ninety, one of them) were trundled in to confirm the identification of the sitters, and the picture was duly sold at a rather low price because buyers found it, not unnaturally, difficult to reconcile the difference between the ease of the young Mr and Mrs Andrews and this particular work. Perhaps they would have had a higher regard had they been told what it really was, Gainsborough's Master-Piece.

The article was published a little late – the *Burlington*, like a lady (as I was told at school), never hurries. Inside facing the index, and rather a long way from my article, was young Thomas Gainsborough, looking splendid in full colour. Garrick still looked dark and not as fine as he really is, but then photographs are no real guide. I was not unhappy; it left me a great deal still to keep in reserve for when I could arrange to have him exhibited. At least his existence was now an established fact, and in spite of all my letters from Dr Hayes, he did not raise his voice publicly against the two pictures, nor did I hear from him for a time. I did think if he had any objections to the pictures, now was the time to voice them or to 'for ever hold his peace'.

I have never spent a happier week. I felt as if I had achieved something for the first time in my life – it was a very good feeling. In the theatre, everything passes and whatever work you do is always subject to so many outside influences, but this was all my own. The tone of surprise used to me by interviewers was not always particularly flattering, '*You* wrote this?' said a young man at the BBC. The temptation to ask if he had *understood* it was almost irresistible. All in all, it was a great success, and Sir Robin Day saw fit to put it on the news. The *Daily Telegraph* ran a short item, which meant the *Sunday Times* dropped its interview as it was no longer a 'scoop'. They had missed putting it out to coincide with the week of publication, as had been planned, and run another story. The editor had thought speed unimportant because 'nobody reads the *Burlington*'. The magazine sold out for the first time in its publishing life. 'Unprecedented!' said Sir Ellis. He was delighted for me, yet pointed out (after I had gone on far too long about myself) that he, too, had a piece in the same issue about an exhibition of Ribera at Fort Worth, Texas.

There was also a very long review of John Hayes' new book *The Landscape Paintings of Thomas Gainsborough: A Critical Text and Catalogue Raisonné*, by the Tate Gallery's Martin Butlin. In a note on the text he said:

> Another work regarded as a genuine repetition of a larger canvas, but looking unsatisfactorily weak in reproduction. It is said to have 'an excellent early pedigree', but its ownership by George Gostling cannot be traced earlier than 1814 and the connection with Gainsborough is pretty indirect, Gostling being 'perhaps... a colleague of Gainsborough's friend William Pearce'. The other picture from the Gostling Collection, No. 168, is uncharacteristic with its quaint oval composition and apparently clumsy treatment. On the other hand it has to be said that both works were accepted as genuine when exhibited at the British Institution in 1814.

The Gostling connection would not, I think, seem quite so indirect in the light of my research, George Gostling being the eminent lawyer I discovered him to be (and had told Hayes of him) and the executor of my Giffard wills. I was right after all.

John Hayes did *not* read all the evidence that I sent to him.

Anthony Blunt's last critique was in the book section, a very bad-tempered one of the re-issue of a book on Pietro da Cortona.

'Quite right, it is dreadful,' said Sir Ellis.

Weeks after my article was published, I at last heard from John Hayes. A rather silly letter, I thought, to the effect that he was not convinced that the small picture was a Gainsborough self-portrait, but could have been painted by *any* artist of that period. I replied, 'I am writing a book based on the last six years. Sir Ellis has said I may publish anything "rash" he may have written to me; may I take it that you will also allow me to publish your letters?' Dr Hayes declined the honour rather hastily, by return of post, unlike the usual delay in his answers.

Sir Ellis says that, to the best of his knowledge, there is not another picture like the small self-portrait, and Dr Hayes has been unable to produce any others of a similar nature. I have never seen one to compare; to my mind the pigments on the palette are as good as a signature. Even though Dr Hayes has examined the small picture under an electro-microscope (a test it passed with flying colours) he does not agree. He made a careful note of all the tests and still stuck to his turn-down. He also pointed out, in a somewhat contradictory manner, that they already had a self-portrait of Gainsborough. At ten years old? Really, Dr Hayes.

Hayes' rejection of the small self-portrait seemed so perverse. Sir Hugh Casson said to me, gently, as I voiced my bewilderment about the entrenched attitudes I had encountered, 'But Adrienne, why do you expect them to be pleased? Nothing like this has ever happened to *them* in their lives.'

I now know that Hayes' 'caution' errs on the side of self-denial. To begrudge a new piece of information, which could help greatly in the future, or only to admit to an event if it is of your own making, is like believing the earth is flat. Young Thomas exists, so does the Garrick. So do the bank books and the evidence on their pages, and without John Hayes' intransigence I should never have had to go to the lengths I have described to find them; for that I shall always be grateful.

Now I am certain I know what I am looking at and I can back it up with facts. I also know that the life of Thomas Gainsborough has to be rewritten, based on these facts. Hopefully, I shall do that, after more research, in the next four years before his bicentenary. What I have discovered does not invalidate what Dr Hayes has written – it could give it a new dimension. My discoveries, happily, will not go away. Nor will I. It is wonderful that there is so much more to find. I am grateful to those who helped me – to Sir Ellis, to Sir Hugh Casson, whose letters speak for them and reflect their generosity of mind.

One great difference in Sir Ellis' turn-down letters was that they always ended in something which kept me working to prove my belief in the picture. They could not have been more abrupt or definite, but when I did come up with an answer, he always replied at once, sometimes demolishing me or adding a new objective. To convince *him* became the focus of my search, as much as proving the picture, for I knew that his word counted most. Plenty of people asked me what Hayes thought, but it was always *after* they had asked about Sir Ellis. Even if I did manage to get Hayes to agree, I still had to get Sir Ellis' approval, as the most senior and respected.

In spite of the six years' work, certain ranks remained unbroken; the Tate Gallery, firm friends of Dr Hayes, were unconvinced. They did not even need to see the pictures. Miss Einberg and Dr Hayes' word was enough. Miss Einberg also wished me not to publish her letters in full, although they were quite pleasant and unexceptional, with a kind of lumbering archness about them, reminiscent of our meeting.

I was no longer dashed by their refusals. After all, I knew now, eminent though they had managed to become, their work had been inadequate. It had been based on an accumulation (in Gainsborough's case) of inaccurate rehashing of earlier writers, and their own opinions in an airless world that admitted no others. They were extremely good on minor painters, but then it is easy to be so. It is recognising the great that is difficult. Minor painters have lovable flaws, which is why they are minor in the first place. It was also annoying that an outsider should manage to come up with new and exciting research. I was a fool to think the picture, and ultimately the small self-portrait, would be welcomed.

The first advice I had been given was correct – to search for documentation. Instinct is not enough, nor is informed opinion; it must be backed up by facts, and in the end those are the only things you can rely on to convince the doubtful. So many acres of bad canvases have been painted, and still remain, that in some ways one can understand the reason for the resistance on the side of the auction houses or the galleries. What I cannot forgive is that they do not do their homework. If they had done so, it would not have been left to an 'outsider' like me to have traced and appreciated the value of the bank books. Equally, so much in the way of documentation would not have disappeared. All one can hope for is that whatever lesson there is in this quest of mine may be learned, and that the stages of my research may prove of value to others.

The Garrick portrait had doors closed upon it by closed minds, and minds are generally closed through fear. To make an honest mistake is not the end of the world, but to have lost the wish to find the truth, or to deny it because it is not *your* truth, is bigotry.

Knowledge should not reduce, but enlarge; a little knowledge nurtured tends to shrivel and to warp all it touches – therefore, it is a very dangerous thing indeed.

Ultimately my battle with the doyens of the art world was more than just the need to prove the Garrick and to win. It was an expression of all I had really cared about for years, and the events of the search had allowed them to surface.

We judge preceding ages, devastated time after time, by the objects they leave behind. Museums in all countries are filled by art that has survived small holocausts; is it so silly, then, to see hope in art? One thing I discovered was that each museum has, in its back yard, lead-lined vans to take the finest treasures to secret shelters should a nuclear war take place. They have been chosen to represent the best and most beautiful achievements of our civilisation, and will be sealed into their shelters for future (if there should be any) people to see how great we were – tombs of collective Pharaohs, so to speak. I have a mad vision of them being picked to pieces by mutants thousands of years from whatever war engulfs us. What will they make of Titian's *Bacchus and Ariadne*, one of the chief treasures on the list?

When I see those vans leaving their institutions, I shall know all hope is gone. It was on the day that the Poussin was slashed that I found out about this emergency plan and saw these ominous-looking vans standing, waiting, at the back of the

National Gallery. Perhaps the madman who slashed the picture knew a thing or two – God and Mammon cannot function together or the ultimate result is the use of those vans. Sanity, I now know, has always been to me those moments captured in canvas, sound or stone; the immediate transmissions of the individual vision to those about them. There has not been much more to the artist's endeavour, perhaps, than the solving of a particular problem of light or perspective, or a point of view, but the sum total has a common theme – the giving to the future of a piece of one man's world.

I want those two pictures, those portraits of young Garrick and young Gainsborough, to be there; to show future generations Gainsborough's world and his progression through it, so that they can learn, as I did – and I am trying now to tell, however imperfectly, what it means to me. I am not talking of an ideal man, but one who, two hundred years after his death, still has the power to move or give pleasure with his works. A talent which, like Mozart, he displayed at such an early age; and, like Mozart's, it had to be used to serve those who did not, on the whole, understand. Art is not outside living and is often a by-product of earning enough to eat, like most other occupations. Yet, unlike other, more mundane work, it has the chance to live on and to grow after the death of the man who conceived it, and can often teach a lesson he never dreamed of at the time.

If my original search became a kind of 'pilgrim's progress', I am the richer for it. If I can hand on the lessons it taught me, not just in practical terms, I have been given another dimension for my work and an explanation as to why it became so vital for me, against all odds, to complete it. One thing is certain – once begun it would admit no denial. 'Are you looking for Thomas Gainsborough, or is he looking for you?' I was asked once at the Royal Academy. I could not answer then, and I do not think I shall ever be able to. Perhaps I shall learn in time.

Meanwhile he is still with me, and my life can never be quite the same again.

Sources

I wish to thank the staff and members of all the Institutions listed for their help, patience and forbearance. I would like to mention everyone by name but the list would be too long, so I hope they will understand.

Research sources

The Victoria and Albert Museum
The Duchy of Cornwall, accounts (Household of Frederick, Prince of Wales)
The Bedford Estate Archives (Archivist: Marie Draper)
The Public Record Office
The General Register Office
The Law Society Library (Mr Richardson)
The British Museum (John Barr)
The Royal Academy Library
The Ormonde, Ossory and Butler papers
The Society of Genealogists
Somerset House
St Catherine's House
The Taunton Records
Buckingham Palace Road Library, London Churches
St George's, Hanover Square
The College of Arms (Mr Dennys)
The Harleian Register
The Huguenot Society, Registers
The Witt Library, Courtauld Institute
The London Library, St James's Square
Mander and Mitchenson Theatre Collection

Bank archives

Hoare's Bank (Archivist: Maurice Lloyd)
Barclays Bank, Gosling Branch, Fleet Street (Mr Rogers)
Drummond's Bank (Brian Cooper)
The Royal Bank of Scotland (Archivist: Christine Robertson)
The Bank of England (John Keyworth)

Select Bibliography

For Thomas Gainsborough

Armstrong, Sir Walter, *Gainsborough and his place in English Art*, 1898.

Cunningham, Allan, *The Lives of the Most Eminent British Painters*, 1829.

Edwards, Edward, *Anecdotes of painters...*, 1808.

Fulcher, George William, *Life of Thomas Gainsborough*, edited by E. S. Fulcher, 1856.

Gainsborough, Thomas, *Drawings*, edited by John Hayes, Zwemmer, 1971.

Gower, Lord Ronald Sutherland, *Thomas Gainsborough*, 1903.

Hayes, John, *Gainsborough: Paintings and Drawings*, Phaidon Press, 1975.

Jackson, William, *The Four Ages, together with essays on various subjects*, 1798.

Leonard, Jonathan Norton, *The World of Gainsborough 1727–88*, Time-Life International, 1970.

Proctor, Ida, *Masters of British Painting*, 1955.

Reynolds, Sir Joshua, *Discourses*, 1788.

Sitwell, Sir Sacheverell, *Conversation Pieces*, B. T. Batsford, 1936.

Smith, John Thomas, *Nollekens and his times*, 2 vols, 1828.

Smith, John Thomas, *A Book for a Rainy Day*, 1845.

Thicknesse, Philip, *A Sketch of the Life and Paintings of Thomas Gainsborough Esq.*, 1788.

Vertue, George, *The Walpole Society*, from the *Notebooks* series, Oxford University Press, 1933–34.

Waterhouse, Ellis, *Gainsborough*, Edward Hulton, 1958.

Whitley, William Thomas, *Thomas Gainsborough*, 1915.

Whitley, William Thomas, *Artists and their friends in England (1700–1799)*, 2 vols, 1928.
Williamson, Geoffrey, *The Ingenious Mr Gainsborough*, Hale, 1972.
Woodall, Mary, *Gainsborough's Landscape Drawings*, Faber & Faber, 1939.
Woodall, Mary, *Thomas Gainsborough: his life and work*, Phoenix House, 1949.
Woodall, Mary, *The Letters of Thomas Gainsborough*, 1963.

For David Garrick

Angelo, Henry, *Reminiscences*, 1828.
Angelo, Henry, *Picnic*, 1834.
Baker, G. P. (ed.), *Some Unpublished Correspondence of David Garrick*, 1907.
Barrett, Charlotte (ed.), *Diary and Letters of Madame D'Arblay* (Fanny Burney), 7 vols, 1842–46.
Cibber, Theophilus, *Theophilus Cibber, to David Garrick, Esq. with Dissertations on Theatrical subjects*, three parts, 1759.
Collier, *English Dramatic Poetry and Annals of the Stage*, 3 vols, 1831.
Fitzgerald, Percy, *The Life of David Garrick*, 2 vols, 1868.
Fitzpatrick, T., *Inquiry into the merits of a certain Popular Performer*, 1760.
Genest, J., *Some accounts of the English Stage, from the Restoration in 1660–1830*, 1832.
The Gentleman's Magazine, 1742 editions.
Hedgcock, Frank A., *David Garrick and his French Friends*, 1912.
Hill, George Birbeck, *Boswell's Life of Johnson*, 1887.
Kirkman, J. T., *Memoirs of the life of Charles Macklin*, 1799.
Knight, Joseph, *David Garrick*, 1894.
Lewes, C. L., *Memoirs ... of the English and Scottish stages ...*, edited by J. L. Lewes, 4 vols, 1894.
Malone, Edmond, *Historical Account of the English Stage*, 1790.
Mantzius, Karl, *A History of Theatrical Art in ancient and*

modern times..., translated by Louise von Cossel, vols 1–5, 1903–21.
Murphy, Arthur, *The Life of David Garrick*, 2 vols, 1801.
Northcote, James, *Memoirs of Sir Joshua Reynolds*, 1813–15.
Noverre, C. E. (ed.), *The Life and Works of the Chevalier Noverre*, 1882.
O'Keefe, *Recollections*, 1826.
Oman, Carola, *David Garrick*, Hodder & Stoughton, 1958.
Parsons, Florence Mary (Mrs Clement Parsons), *Garrick and his Circle*, 1906.
Rae, John, *Life of Adam Smith*, 1895.
Smith, Adam, *The Theory of Moral Sentiments*, 1790.
Sterne, Laurence, *Letters of the late Rev. Mr. Laurence Sterne*, 1775.
Walpole, Horace, *The Letters of Horace Walpole*, edited by P. Cunningham, 9 vols, 1857–59.

Dramatis Personae

Sir Hugh Casson, President of the Royal Academy of Arts

Sir Ellis Waterhouse, formerly Barber Professor of Fine Arts and Director of the Barber Institute, Birmingham University, and Director of Studies, Paul Mellon Centre for Studies in British Art

Sir Roy Strong, Director of the Victoria and Albert Museum

Mary Woodall, British Museum Department of Prints and Drawings

John Hayes, Director of the National Portrait Gallery

Sir Oliver Millar, Surveyor of the Queen's Pictures

Elizabeth Einberg, Assistant Keeper, British Collection, Tate Gallery

Martin Butlin, Keeper of Historic British Section, Tate Gallery

Stephen Jones, formerly Curator of Gainsborough's House, Sudbury

Index

Abbreviations: in the index, AC stands for Adrienne Corri; DG for David Garrick; TG for Thomas Gainsborough

Freame & Barclay Cr

599

Date	Fo.		Name		£	s	d
1741		To their Acc.t fo.		1774	221065	7	3
Mar 22	78	To Cash	Stallard		1320	3	4
			King		1375	8	11
23	266		Cowthrop		2354	3	4
	127		King		1139	6	2
1742 27	42		Smith		3000		
	45		Cowthrop		1960		
		To their Acc.t fo.		1776 / 72	232214	9	

Date	Fo.		Name		£	s	d
1742					239303	1	7
Mar 26	90	By Cash	Andrews		821	8	7
			Daking		80		
			Middleton		50		
			Davis		25		
			Lee		120		
			Baker		150		
			Goddard		135	2	8
	92		Dorice		62		
	93		Minors		100		
			D.o		91	19	
				F.L	240938	11	10
27	130		Pomfret		30		
			Doneufvile		600		
			Hatton		70		
			Combrald		125	7	9
			Salomons		100		
			Attil		30		
			Wilkinson		150		
			Mailman		200		
			Flower		271	7	1
			Eyre		271	7	1
	136		Moses		50		
			Jansen		155	2	9
			Hill		50		
			Hodshall		20		
		By their Acc.t [illegible]			[illegible]206	16	6

Date	Fo.		Name		£	s	d
1741		By their Acc.t fo.		77	234792	7	
Mar 19	120	By Cash	Page		80		
	125		Salomons		180		
			Adair		180		
			Guerin		275	10	
			Child		30		
			D.o		1020		
			Hoare		200		
			D.o		300		
			Astell		290		
			Johnson		59	14	
			Knight		42		
			Kraguelius		100		
				F.L	237549	11	
22	77		Fitzgerald		100		
			Dufresnay		50		
			Loubier		50		
			Kingsley		13	12	
			Dover		52	11	
			Thursloneau		60		
			D.o		100		
			Barbut		200		
			D.o		50		
	78		Harding		222		
	83		Frokock		100		
			Hog		50		
			D.o		51	8	
			Child		42		
			Adair		40		
			Middleton		111	4	6
			Petre		75		
			Johnson		20		
			Fromantle		50		
			Gainsborough		60		
			Buran		50		
23	36		Hill		50		
1742 26	9		Edwards		75		
	87		Bullock		80	13	
		Carried up		F.L	239303	1	7